Advance Praise for

GATEWAYS *to* SPIRITUALITY

"Anyone interested in the role and the teaching of religion(s) in our schools will find *Gateways to Spirituality* an exceedingly rich and indispensable companion. Edited by veteran headmaster Peter W. Cobb, and written by seasoned and creative teachers, this volume illumines the range of issues and approaches that arise in giving responsible attention to religion, and the religions, in K–12 educational contexts. These informed, practical essays are packed with insights and experiences useful for current and future approaches to the teaching of religion. An extensive bibliography of resources and curricula make this collection invaluable. There is nothing else like it!"

James W. Fowler, C.H. Candler Professor of Theology and Human Development,
Emory University; Author, Stages of Faith

"*Gateways to Spirituality* is a provocative, lively, and insightful collection of essays about the role of spirituality and religion in K–12 schools. Anyone who cares about what kinds of human beings we are graduating from our schools (and that should be everyone) is encouraged to read this book. Any system of education, public or private, that ignores questions of meaning and transcendence is not only impoverished, it is dangerous."

Charles C. Haynes, Senior Scholar, First Amendment Center

"This diverse collection of essays represents a range of perspectives in the conversations regarding religion, spirituality, and education. Most of the contributors are teachers or educational practitioners and it is refreshing to hear these experienced voices. This is a helpful and important addition to the growing literature in the field."

Diane L. Moore, Member, Faculty of Divinity;
Director, Program in Religion and Secondary Education, Harvard Divinity School

GATEWAYS *to* SPIRITUALITY

STUDIES IN
EDUCATION
& SPIRITUALITY

Peter Laurence and Victor Kazanjian
General Editors

Vol. 7

PETER LANG
New York • Washington, D.C./Baltimore • Bern
Frankfurt am Main • Berlin • Brussels • Vienna • Oxford

GATEWAYS *to* SPIRITUALITY

Pre-School through Grade Twelve

PETER W. COBB, EDITOR

PETER LANG
New York • Washington, D.C./Baltimore • Bern
Frankfurt am Main • Berlin • Brussels • Vienna • Oxford

Library of Congress Cataloging-in-Publication Data

Gateways to spirituality: pre-school through grade twelve / edited by Peter W. Cobb.
p. cm. — (Studies in education and spirituality; v. 7)
Includes bibliographical references and index.
1. Religious education of children—United States.
I. Cobb, Peter W. II. Series.
BL42.5.U5.G38 207'.5—dc22 2004010423
ISBN 0-8204-6815-0
ISSN 1527-8247

Bibliographic information published by **Die Deutsche Bibliothek**.
Die Deutsche Bibliothek lists this publication in the "Deutsche
Nationalbibliografie"; detailed bibliographic data is available
on the Internet at http://dnb.ddb.de/.

Cover photograph by Ann M. Thurber
Cover design by Sophie Boorsch Appel

The paper in this book meets the guidelines for permanence and durability
of the Committee on Production Guidelines for Book Longevity
of the Council of Library Resources.

© 2005 Peter Lang Publishing, Inc., New York
275 Seventh Avenue, 28th Floor, New York, NY 10001
www.peterlangusa.com

Printed in the United States of America

Most of all, there is my family. For me, the nature of their spiritual journey, and their participation in mine, is an ongoing source of faith and delight.

Thank you, Peter, Susan, and Heather, and most especially, thank you, Carolyn.
It is to you that I dedicate this book.

When it's over, I want to say: all my life
I was a bride married to amazement.
I was the bridegroom, taking the world into my arms.

~Mary Oliver, from *When Death Comes*

Contents

Acknowledgments

The genesis of this book dates to January 2001 when a group of organizations sponsored a conference at Union Theological Seminary, New York, to explore the emerging field of interfaith education. Many of the chapter contributors shared their perspectives about religious pluralism and spirituality in schools. I am indebted to Peter Laurence, Co-Founder of the Education as Transformation Project based at Wellesley College, for the invitation to edit a volume that complements the scholarly work in the Peter Lang Series on Spirituality and Education. Peter's careful and sympathetic review as Series Editor is deeply appreciated.

Gateways to Spirituality: Pre-School through Grade Twelve could not have been written without the inspired, passionate, and thoughtful visions of our authors. Their voices call us to be open to fresh discoveries and pedagogies that foster the spiritual formation of globally aware students who will meet with hope the challenges of the twenty-first century. Thank you.

I am deeply grateful to the many teachers, chaplains, colleagues, and students for the imaginative and patient ways in which they have guided and shaped my spiritual education. They are too numerous to mention personally, yet the understanding garnered during my sixty-one years reflects their wisdom. I think particularly of Charles C. Haynes who once advised me, gently but insistently, that "God just might not be a liberal Protestant." His words have enabled me to listen less judgmentally to myriad expressions of the Divine in intra- and interfaith conversations. Together with such wonderful friends and colleagues are the ministers and parishioners within the several churches in which I have grown up and have attended as an adult. They continue to inspire me by their faith and goodness.

The people at Peter Lang Publishing are truly an editor's pleasure. I sincerely appreciate the significant contributions made by Heidi Burns, Senior Editor, whose encouragement and punctilious approach reflects such a deep love of excellence and scholarship. My thanks to Christopher Myers, Managing Director; Jacqueline Pavlovic and

Sophie Appel, Production Coordinators, and Justin Pelegano, Editorial Assistant, for their helpfulness, guidance, and support.

However, this book would not have come to fruition had it not been for the careful and faithful labors of Ann Thurber. From the beginning, she has been the person on point to whom the authors turned, to whom I turned, for counsel. The finished work breathes with her ardor and her spirit of kindness.

My gratitude is expressed to the copyright holders for their permission to use the following copyrighted material:

From Ackland Art Museum, The University of North Carolina at Chapel Hill, for the illustrations of *Standing Vishnu,* 12th Century, Ackland Fund 82.6.1; *Head of Buddha,* 15th Century, Ackland Fund 91.2; *The Virgin and Child Enthroned with Saints,* ca. 1490, attributed to Jacopo del Sellaio, Italian, Florence, The William A. Whitaker Foundation Art Fund, 63.18.1.

From "When Death Comes," *New and Selected Poems* by Mary Oliver, copyright © 1992 by Mary Oliver, reprinted by permission of Beacon Press, Boston.

From "Knowledge...Shall Vanish Away" in *For the Inward Journey: The Writings of Howard Thurman,* copyright © 1984 by Sue Bailey Thurman, reprinted by permission of Harcourt, Inc.

From "Catch" in *The Orb Weaver: Poems* by Robert Francis, copyright © 1960 by Wesleyan University Press, reprinted by permission of Wesleyan University Press.

From "Burnt Norton" in *Four Quartets* by T. S. Eliot, copyright © 1936 by Harcourt, Inc., and renewed 1964 by T. S. Eliot, reprinted by permission of the publisher and by Faber & Faber Ltd.

From "I Would Like to Describe" from *Selected Poems of Zbigniew Herbert, Edited and Translated by Czeslaw Milosz and Peter Dale Scott,* English translation copyright © 1968 by Czeslaw Milosz and Peter Scott, reprinted by permission of Penguin Books Ltd. Introduction Copyright © 1968 by A. Alvarez, reprinted by permission of HarperCollins Publishers, Inc.

From *The Narrow Road to the Deep North and Other Travel Sketches* by Matsuo Basho, translated by Nobuyuki Yuasa (Penguin Classics 1966). Copyright © Nobuyuki Yuasa, 1966, reprinted by permission of Penguin Books Ltd.

From Small Group Reflection Sharing, Kairos Senior Retreat, Flintridge Sacred Heart Academy, permission given by Mollie Merchant, Class of 2000.

Finally, I acknowledge the contributions of student voices expressed throughout the book, trusting that their voices herald a future of spiritual awakening.

Peter W. Cobb

2005

Introduction

Peter W. Cobb

It is clear that spiritual formation, like cognitive and moral formation, begins early in life. It may well be that higher orders of spiritual discernment and choice require significant maturity; indeed there is every reason to believe this is the case. Still, the years when children are in elementary, middle, and high school are precisely the years when habits of spiritual understanding and practice, or their absence, take root. It is not only in the intellectual domain that Jean Brodie's words ring true: "Give me a child at an impressionable age, and she is mine for life."

Given such awareness of authority and impressionability, we need to take seriously the spiritual nature of children as it relates to their lives in schools, for children no more leave their "spirituality" at home than they do their book bags. They bring to each day a capacity for reverence, for faith and belief, for the experience of devotion, and for transcendence. Is it the place of the school to acknowledge, honor, and instruct to, or in relation to, those capacities?

This collection of essays posits that it is. We acknowledge the skittishness of the culture as it relates to religion, spirituality, and education, skittishness that is theological and political as well as curricular and pedagogical. Still, religious impulse and spiritual nature left unattended by schools risk substantively impairing a child's intellectual, social, aesthetic, and ethical growth. We are clear about the separation of church, synagogue, temple, mosque, and state. Nevertheless, we believe that spiritual neglect is deeply problematic, both in terms of the whole child and best educational practice. Spirituality is not an elective category of being and should not, therefore, be consigned to an elective status in our nation's schools.

Having made these assertions, what schools do about the spirituality of their students and how they do it is the subject for lively discussion and debate. This book is not intended to propose a template of spiritual instruction and engagement. Rather, it is to provide teachers in schools, students and professors in the field of education, together with those who are generally committed to taking seriously the spiritual lives of students, an opportunity to dwell in a conversation that too often has been strident, occasional, and marginal.

There is in the preface to *Education as Transformation: Religious Pluralism, Spirituality, & a New Vision for Higher Education in America*, a quote taken from Howard Thurman that bears repeating, for it speaks of innate spiritual impulses that do not await college and university to find expression, nurture, or instruction:

> There is a sense of wholeness at the core of man
> that must abound in all he does;
> that marks with reverence his ev'ry step,
> that has its sway when all else fails;
> that wearies out all evil things;
> that warms the depths of frozen fears
> making friend of foe;
> and lasts beyond the living and the dead,
> beyond the goals of peace, the ends of war!
> this man seeks through all his years;
> to be complete and of one piece, within and without.[1]

Transformation presumes formation. However ardent the desire of university and college professors to honor the potential for higher education to be spiritually transformative, not one of them would argue that transformation should require spiritual remediation. However, it seems clear by the experience on college and university campuses that if we do not attend to the role of K-12 schools in the spiritual formation of children and youths, that is precisely what we will leave for our colleagues in higher education.

For this volume, we have assembled a remarkable collection of scholars and school practitioners. It was the intention from the onset of this project to look first and foremost to persons who can draw on classroom and corridor experience for their insights into the spiritual nature of children and the cultural nature of schools. We have tried hard to offer a spirited mix of the philosophical and the practical. We have called on individuals from school and organizational settings and have invited persons from different faith traditions and perspectives to contribute. We have tried to find a good blend of new voices with voices already recognized in their respective fields. Many of these authors will be new to you, and we are proud to introduce them as provocative and stimulating colleagues in what we trust will be an ongoing conversation.

No neat categories or chronologies demarcate this volume. Each author has a distinctive slant on the issue of how schools are approaching the spiritual nature and lives of students. Each addresses one or more of the following themes: engaging religious difference and pluralism in schools; encountering spiritual practice in schools; attending to religious instruction/religious literacy in schools; and acknowledging issues of spiritual and religious formation in schools.

There is an overlap of interest and perspective; there is also divergence of opinion. There should be. There certainly is in the public square. The common thread woven among all the authors is the clear conviction that connections exist between spirituality, student learning, social and ethical consciousness, and community life. Schools need to find ways to honor these connections.

A *New Yorker* cartoon some years ago shows an elementary classroom. On the blackboard the lesson for the day reads: "The Path to Enlightenment." One young girl, raising her hand, asks the question, "Are we there yet?" Engaging the spiritual lives and natures of our nation's students may not get us there, but surely it will help.

Catherine Powell builds her essay on the theme of "spiritual gifts" and reflects on "what these gifts are and what they offer school communities." In a chapter called "Pre-School Spirituality: Children's Gifts and Our Response," she explores in a wonderfully anecdotal way the "sensorial/whole body nature of young children's experience and learning style, relational sensitivity of the young child, the child's gift of wonder, and the child's sense of time," using as her constructs the theology of incarnation, the theology of love, the theology of gratitude and abundance, and the theology of the eternal.

Amanda Millay Hughes has authored the chapter entitled "In Search of Attributes: Exploring the Potential of Sacred Objects in Teaching and Learning About World Religions." She poses the following five questions: "(1) What are the appropriate uses of art objects as primary source material in multicultural education within primary and secondary level classrooms? (2) What is the capacity of art objects for withstanding and sustaining respectful, non-threatening inquiry? (3) Might the search for attributes in objects of religious origin be a method for opening content-rich discussions of moral and ethical systems, as well as character education as it applies to decision making, critical thinking skills, and a fuller appreciation of and participation in a diverse American culture? (4) What are the limits and potentials for building empathy and understanding across traditions by examining common values represented in objects from diverse faith traditions? (5) How might educators establish uniform practices and processes when encountering familiar and unfamiliar cultural and faith systems represented in art objects?" The Five Faiths Project offers a remarkable resource to teachers who are looking for an innovative, imaginative and highly aesthetic point of entry into the study of world religions.

Arthur J. Schwartz asks in his chapter, entitled "Spiritual Giftedness: Identifying and Measuring 'Religious Genius,'" the compelling questions: "Are some of our young spiritually gifted? Might even a few be considered spiritual prodigies? How might we identify these young people? And how might we best nurture their 'gifts?'" His chapter relates the well-established field of gifted education to current research in the realm of spiritual intelligence.

Rachael Kessler, author of *The Soul of Education: Helping Students Find Connection, Compassion and Character at School*, has created a program entitled "PassageWays" which acknowledges adolescent "tipping points" with regard to spiritual concerns and purposes. The "yearning, wonder, wisdom, fear, and confusion of students" can become either a distraction from the curriculum or central to it. She regards the path to enlightenment as educational imperative, the need to be present for the multiple ways in which students awaken to their own truths. In her chapter "PassageWays: A Model for Fostering the Spiritual Development of Students and Teachers in Schools," she sets forth principles and practices "that can be infused into any classroom, any age level, any content arena." Her chapter is a reflection on, and recapitulation of, her experience using this framework in public and private schools across the United States.

Extending Catherine Powell's observations on spiritual formation, Sister Ramona Bascom, O.P., former Principal of Flintridge Sacred Heart Academy, La Canada, California, focuses her essay, "The Net of Faith: Religious Studies, Campus Ministry, and Christian Service in a Religious Secondary School," on "spiritual practices and the adolescent response/need to and for such practices." The context for her reflections is direct classroom instruction and "retreats, liturgies, and Christian service as the 'lab aspect' of the classroom." While Flintridge Sacred Heart is a Roman Catholic boarding and day school for girls, the students matriculated represent all the major religions. Sr. Ramona's understanding of adolescent need/response is thereby informed by a "larger understanding of spirituality" than that of one faith tradition.

Meera S. Viswanathan analyzes the experience of older students in boarding schools. Her chapter, "Resurrecting the Spirit: Acknowledging the Inner Life in the World of Boarding Schools," asks, "In the world of highly competitive, highly structured boarding schools, how do students grapple with ethical, moral, spiritual, philosophical, and religious questions, issues and values? How are we to understand the phrase *in loco parentis* with respect to questions of "the inner life?" Viswanathan uses her deep familiarity with Deerfield Academy as a context for juxtaposing a series of contrasts historically, regionally, and culturally to suggest what we might learn from how others have sought to answer these questions.

Manish K. Mishra urges a "Rethinking (of) High School World Religions: Pedagogical Options for Addressing Ethical and Cultural Relativism." Mishra takes ardent exception to traditional approaches to the study of world religions because he believes that they reinforce the adolescent predisposition to casually syncretistic or relativistic (if not nihilistic) thinking. He offers a new curricular design that acknowledges religious pluralism as the "preferred framework" for study while managing not to lapse into pedagogical neutrality that disallows critical discrimination between conflicting truth claims. He further wants to offer students the chance to investigate "non-conventional, non-institutional world religious traditions" as an antidote to student disinterest in religious studies.

Timothy L. Morehouse describes introducing students to the study of religion through a course entitled "Pilgrims and Pilgrimage." He shows how such a course may help achieve the mutually inclusive educational goals of "religious literacy, ethical reflection, cultural awareness, epistemological reflection, and spiritual discipline" in ways that are consistent with student experience and exploration.

As an introduction to the instructional possibilities of taking religion seriously, Mark Rigg entitles his chapter "In Our End Is Our Beginning" and examines models of religious education in terms of their long-term goals. His thesis is that "faith is a fundamental aspect of every human endeavor, hence of every academic department; thus schools engaged in religious education need to be explicit about what they believe and teach. Specifically, they need to avoid 'teleological blindness,' i.e., a failure to see where one will end up based on the course one has set." Reflecting his experience in independent schools as the context for religious instruction, he looks at four instructional models: catechetical, theological, religious studies, and Unitarian, and argues for private schools to take seriously the theological model. Recognizing that public schools live under different political constraints, he suggests that they need to ask a series of questions about "what religious knowledge is likely to be of most use to public school students," and to honor the understanding that not to teach about religion is to teach "some form of the Enlightenment dichotomy that reduces religion to a private matter."

John J. Roberts asks, "What would a class be like that took spirituality and education seriously?" He entitles his essay, "Walking the Talk: The Classroom as Spirituality Workshop." Mirroring the argument of Parker Palmer, he suggests that what we teach (or ought to teach) and what we remember in teachers is the "self" as much as any content. Indeed, taking partial and implicit exception to Mark Rigg's suggestion about the presence of the Enlightenment dichotomy in public school classrooms, Roberts postulates that even "if postmodern thinkers have discredited the Enlightenment notion of the objective observer, we are hardly doomed to nihilistic relativism." He goes on to suggest that, given the current educational obsession with reform and its emphasis on accountability via test taking, "scant energy is left for truly important matters, such as our desperate need to turn out moral graduates." He provides a classroom model for intentionally attending to the moral and spiritual life of students.

Warren A. Nord has given his chapter the title "Religion, Spirituality, and Education in a (Not Entirely) Secular Culture." He argues persuasively that religion is essentially marginalized in public education, and he carefully documents his assertions. He discusses the neglect of religion in textbooks and state standards. He maintains that the little discussion of religion that exists tends to treat it as an artifact, with virtually no mention of either contemporary theology or how religions have confronted modernity. He makes three arguments for the inclusion of religion in education. "First, a proper liberal education should initiate students into an ongoing conversation in which representations of various communities and traditions are allowed to contend with each other about how to make sense of the world and how to live their lives...And then there is the question of justice." Nord makes the analogy that, until the last several decades, "textbooks and curricula routinely ignored women's history and minority literature." He goes on to assert, "We are now (almost) all sensitive to the fact that this wasn't a benign neglect, but a form of discrimination, of educational disenfranchisement." His third argument is that public schools are constitutionally required to include religious voices as a matter of fairness and neutrality, and that neutrality is not a matter of uncritically privileging the secular point of view. His chapter concludes with suggestions how schools can take religion seriously.

In his chapter "Freedom for Narcissus, Too: Liberating the Spiritual Dimension of the Religious Student" Matthew Hicks uses the novel *Narcissus and Goldmund* by Hermann Hesse as a backdrop for his reflections. Hicks predicates his argument for taking seriously the religiously grounded student on the observation that "Goldmund-like students locate their spirituality in art, nature, or sport, and many of them accept and adopt a worldview grounded in materialism." He goes on to note: "The rub, unfortunately, is that contemporary education tends to be more comfortable with Goldmund than with Narcissus. In today's classrooms, those students who, like Narcissus, define their lives in terms of, and seek meaning within, a specific religious tradition are stifled, if not completely shut out."

What does one do about the stifling or sidelining of religious and spiritual instruction? Jonathan Vinson steps out of the school classroom to write about "Religion in the Public Schools: Released Time Reconsidered." He considers the legal and social history of programs that are specifically intended to offer public school children opportunities for off-campus religious instruction during the school day. He draws on his experience with release time programs to assess their value as a corollary to in-school spiritual and religious engagement and their place in the landscape of American education. He concludes by arguing for their continued inclusion in the school options available for integrating and taking seriously the religious and spiritual inquiry of young people.

Eboo Patel demonstrates how three trends in schools, service learning, education on world religion, and engaging religious diversity within our schools, can be integrated in one multifaceted pedagogical model. His approach to appreciative understanding of spirituality through social justice in his chapter "Interfaith Service-Learning" connects the multicultural context of our communities with current global needs and concerns.

Patricia M. Lyons begins her chapter, entitled "God's Autograph: Taking the Soul Seriously in the Classroom," with the tale of a young man who went to E-Bay to "sell his soul." She goes on to note: "To speak of the possibility of the soul is to carry the soul of a teenager out of a burning building. It is to whisper to them that the cry of their own soul is not fiction or wishful thinking; but rather, that it is the truth and the source of dignity in life." She extends a passionate invitation to make the learning process a lever against the spiritual reductionism, materialism, and nihilism of our culture, rather than letting pedagogy become its instrument.

Ann M. Thurber authors the conclusion to the book. Her point of view is a synthesizing one. She postulates that the human condition and historical convergence open the gate for schools to acknowledge religious literacy and spiritual formation in constitutionally and intellectually appropriate ways. Thurber maintains that the "spiritual work" of schools is to create connections between communities, to attend to students' mental tendencies toward the sacred, and to allow opportunities for sacred listening. She affirms, harkening intently and intentionally to the contributors of this volume, that religious and spiritual illiteracy are untenable for the future of responsible global citizenship. She welcomes research being conducted in the area of spiritual intelligence, knowing that informed conceptual frameworks are required for the ongoing credibility of the field. Finally, Thurber believes that spiritual formation and social transformation are related in a way that education needs to acknowledge and honor.

The Quaker secondary school I attended had as its motto, "For the honor of truth." If our often imperfect and provisional search for truth transforms, we must attend to the varieties of spiritual journeys toward truth as requisite for a full understanding of the human condition and of ourselves. In our nation's schools, we cannot amputate this dimension of human experience and history without crippling the education of our students. We have no wish to privilege a religious understanding of truth. Rather, this book is intended to honor all truths and to invite all truths into our nation's classrooms.

Note

[1] Howard Thurman, "Knowledge...Shall Vanish Away," in *Education as Transformation: Religious Pluralism, Spirituality, & a New Vision for Higher Education in America,* ed. Victor H. Kazanjian, Jr., and Peter L. Laurence (New York: Peter Lang, 2000), ix. Thurman penned these lines before language became gender inclusive. The editors concur that his intention was "to include all of humanity" in the verse.

Chapter 1

Pre-School Spirituality: Children's Gifts and Our Response

Catherine Powell

A four-year-old boy sat at the art table in our after-school program. He worked quietly, making a paper chain. Though his work did not seem responsive to the day's lesson on prayer, we adults left him to it. At the end of the afternoon, we called all the children to our regular ending time of prayer and song. Several children brought things they had made or symbols from throughout the room to be focal points for our prayer: a drawing, a statue, a globe. The boy dragged over his long paper chain. "Uh-oh," I thought, ready for trouble as other children turned interestedly toward him. He took the chain directly to the globe. As he wrapped it around and around, we saw that he had stamped a heart on every link. He sat down quietly and smiled as we sang the children's favorite song: "There's enough love to go all around the world…" When the other children were leaving, the boy took me by the hand and led me back over to our prayer area. He stuck his finger between the layers of paper chain and pointed to a spot on the globe. "This is where we are," he told me. Then he moved his finger around to the other side of the earth. "This," he said, "is where my father is." When she picked him up, his mother confirmed that his father was on a business trip to China.

Pre-school children have spiritual lives. They do not depend on us to give them spirituality. In fact, they have important spiritual capacities rarely found in adults. We adults, especially parents and teachers, need to recognize, protect, and develop these capacities of the children in our care. In her book *The Religious Potential of the Child,* Sofia Cavalletti invites us to explore children's innate spiritual characteristics, including their ability to be absorbed in the moment, their capacity for wonder, and their openness to love.[1]

Pre-school children have their own sense of time. A little girl might stay absolutely still for half an hour, squatting by a line of ants, absorbed in their journey. A little boy might be sent to the sink to wash up for dinner and be found there fifteen minutes later, still rubbing soapy circles on his hands. From an adult point of view, this absorption in the moment can be a problem. "Sense of time!" we might say. "They have *no* sense of time!" However, from a spiritual point of view, the little girl and boy have a wonderful sense of time. They have the ability to be absorbed in the moment. Adult practitioners of many religions spend hours and even years learning to be absorbed in the moment; young children do it easily, and invite us to join them. This ability includes both full awareness of the reality at hand and a sense of timelessness.

To be absorbed in the moment is important because such absorption counterbalances increasing pressure for children to do and to produce. Doing and producing are key elements of adult maturity, but they can be overemphasized. In our society, people are deemed either valuable or not based on what they do and what they have. Those who are not wealthy or talented may feel guilty. In this atmosphere, adults are prone to become driven, greedy, or filled with false pride. Alan Jones, in *Journey into Christ,* uses images from *Alice in Wonderland* to make the point that we must resist feeling a desperate need to achieve. This need can drive us at a breakneck pace: "Poor Alice in *Through the Looking Glass* has to run furiously in order to stay in the same place. We (who want to know Christ), on the other hand, have to learn to stand still in order to continue our journey."[2] Ambition and an overemphasis on achievement can skew a human being's perspective of himself in relation to God; learning to live in the present, on the other hand, opens a person to the experience of God. Abbot Anthony Bloom, author of *Beginning to Pray,* writes about needing to find inner peace, which includes release from a sense of time. "[We have] the subjective sense that time is running fast and that we have no time left...There is absolutely no need to run after time to catch it. It does not run away from us, it runs towards us."[3]

In a society in which information spreads rapidly, the pace of most aspects of life picks up. Stress is ubiquitous. The human body, brain, and spirit are pushed far beyond their optimal pace. It is inevitable that young children will feel some stress as they try to keep up with the adult world around them, but the level of that stress is increasing. When one of my daughters was about five, a psychologist showed her pictures and asked her to tell a story about each one as part of an evaluation. In the parents' feedback session later, the psychologist showed us a picture of a mother kangaroo, pocketbook over her arm, hat perched jauntily on her head, hopping down a pathway with her little kangaroo at her side. The sky was clear; flowers lined the path. I thought it was a lovely picture. Here is the story my daughter told about it: "The mother kangaroo is very busy. She has a lot to do. She's in a hurry. The little kangaroo has to keep up. She tries very, very hard, but she can't go fast enough. The mother is mad."

Parents today are faced with a huge range of opportunities for their children, as well as, for many, the income to take advantage of them. Music lessons, athletic teams, community service, and tutoring are only a few of the options. Children are hurried from one activity to the next. During the school day, each hour is packed as schools add to their curricula to keep up with new technology, scientific advancements, and higher standards. Children feel pressure from parents, teachers, and themselves to perform constantly. A common concern expressed by faculty groups across the country is that children are not just supposed to be "above average" like those in Lake Wobegon; they are supposed to be "excellent" in every endeavor. The fast pace is not likely to decrease as children get older; therefore, it is crucial that children hold on to their early ability to step out of linear time.

Regularly, in school or at home, we need to give children the opportunity to function free of time constraints. Even as we teach them to understand linear time and to be productive, we must also allow them time to hold onto their way of being lost in the moment. We adults must think carefully about creating an atmosphere in which there is space for unstructured being, for roomy transitions between portions of the day, and for organized, productive time. We must teach children to recognize and honor both timeless moments and periods of productive activity. In addition, we must teach them to find space for both in their days as they grow up. Learning how to take control of time, particularly how to say no to inviting opportunities when there are too many of them, is a crucial skill in our culture. Furthermore, learning that one must honor the human need for nonproductive time, for rest, for prayer, for the proper functioning of that which is beyond the conscious, is vitally important as well.

Another spiritual gift of young children is wonder. Just as children's sense of time counteracts our tendency to rush through life, so their ability to wonder counteracts cynicism and greed. By wonder, I do not mean fantasy or dreamy disconnection from reality. As Cavalletti so aptly states, "Wonder is a very serious thing that, rather than leading us away from reality, can arise only from an attentive observation of reality."[4]

When invited to pray, young children almost always demonstrate their capacity for wonder in their prayers of thanksgiving. They are amazed at colors, at nature, at people. "Thank you, God, for the tree, for the green grass...Thank you for the way the candles smell and Barney, my dog, and for the sky and for Halloween." Wonder cultivates gratitude. The world is not present to be judged or used. The world is present to be loved and enjoyed.

A young child's wonder is an experience of the whole self. It involves the body and the senses as much as the mind. We see it in the child who wants to smell the yeast again and again, breathing it in with eyes closed. We see it in the child who listens to acorns falling on the roof, grinning with pleasure with each ping. In my classroom after school, we light a candle before we pray. A child hurries to turn off the lights. Everyone sits for a moment silently gazing at the flame. I can hear sighs of satisfaction. In a world in which we adults know ourselves as separate from the things around us, wonder brings us back into relationship with them. A child brings a flower and puts it in a vase beside our prayer candle. It is a focus of pleasure and even awe. Children's wonder invites us to a more respectful stewardship of the earth. Many adults find their lives enriched by the observations of children who see the world with fresh eyes.

In Jewish and Christian thought God is fully present in the world. God's word in creation and God's incarnation in Jesus Christ teach us that God is inseparably connected to all that exists. The world is an expression of God's self. When we stand back from nature, from hands-on work, even from our own bodies, we stand back from God. When we take an attitude of dominance or mastery toward the things that express God, we lose our knowledge of ourselves as fellow created beings with the rest of the world. Charles Davis, a strong proponent of incarnation theology, mourns our objectification of the earth and advises a different attitude: "The world is to be affectionately caressed and embraced with a self-forgetting love."[5] Wonder moves us out of objectification and brings us back to the truth of creation's inter-connectedness.

Wonder also leads to joy. Cavalletti writes, "The nature of wonder is not a force that pushes us passively from behind; it is situated ahead of us and attracts us with irresistible force toward the object of our astonishment..."[6] It is all too easy for day-to-day activities to become rote or boring. Even young children, when hurried or pushed through the day, grow weary or jaded. Wonder preserves excitement and enthusiasm. It feeds energy and hope.

Adults need to respect a child's wonder. We should not respond to amazement, fascination, and absorption with patronizing smiles or admonitions to snap out of it and get down to business.

Demonstrating our appreciation for the divine invitation, we can join in the wonder and share our own delight in the marvelous. If we do not allow time to savor such moments, or if we artificially fill the environment with too many stimuli, we can crowd out wonder. Many a parent has watched a three-year-old surrounded by twenty birthday presents, but most interested in a scrap of shiny ribbon. We know so much and want so much for our children that it is tempting to offer more and more to their senses. Instead, we can cultivate wonder by letting them enjoy the world at their own pace.

A third characteristic of young children attesting to their spiritual aptitude is that of love. We accept as a psychological given that the giving and receiving of love is at the heart of early childhood development. Young children are uniquely open to it. Sofia Cavalletti asserts "...since the religious experience is fundamentally an expression of love, it corresponds in a special way to the child's nature. We believe that the child, more than any other, has need of love because the child himself is rich in love."[7] Jesus seems to agree. In the familiar narrative in the Gospel of Mark 10:14–1, Jesus becomes angry when children are kept from approaching him: "And he took them in his arms and blessed them, laying his hands upon them."

In our after-school program, I gathered a group of three- and four-year-olds together to tell them the biblical parable of the precious pearl. In the story, a pearl merchant buys and sells his wares until one day he finds a pearl more precious than any other. He sells everything he owns and happily buys that one precious pearl. "I wonder about this story," I said to the quiet listeners. "I wonder about that merchant. And I wonder about that pearl. Is it a regular pearl or something different? I wonder..." A pause and then a small girl speaks up. "I know," she says and then continues, "The merchant is God and the pearl is us."

Love is an antidote to spiritual maladies. We live in a mobile world of short-lived relationships. We live in a world in which different people and cultures constantly challenge us. Our way of life can lead to isolation, disconnection, and a valuing of competition over cooperation. Love and relationship, grounding young children early in life, are powerful foundations. Not only do they form a child's sense of self and self-esteem, they also offer a paradigm for making later decisions.

Religious educators, teachers, and parents are all concerned with a child's moral development. In fact, parents often articulate their reason for joining a community of faith in terms of their hope for their children's learning right from wrong, and how to behave nicely toward other people. However, moral development must be based on a foundation of love. In Cavalletti's words, "...the adult who wants to give children a moral formation should refrain from any promptings of the common kind in the moral order; instead the adult should announce God's love and help the child to experience and enjoy it in reflection and prayer. We believe that the more profound, deeply felt, and enjoyed the child's religious response is, the more ready, autonomous, and genuine will be the (moral) response of the older child."[8] Alan Jones writes of the negative image of God envisioned by many adults because they were first introduced to God as moral judge. He says, "Most of us still confuse Christianity with morality and cannot discern it as Gospel, Good News. It is only after the experience of Gospel, grace, Good News that implications for behavior can be discerned."[9]

With her back to the room, a four-year-old girl sat in front of a wooden depiction of The Last Supper. She was still and silent for so long that I finally went over to join her. We sat there together until she turned toward me. "You know," she offered, "Jesus could give a friend-party and invite the whole world." Her experience of the freely given love Christians name "grace" had already moved her to assume an inclusive attitude toward others.

The adults in a young child's life need to value love as expressed in relationship. An act as simple as listening to a child can support his or her natural gift for love. This means setting aside our adult agendas in order to receive the love offered by the child, as well as being prepared to give love. Dr. Viola Brody, pioneer of developmental play therapy, trained adults to form relationships with children through the language of touch. Her understanding of the nature of touch offers a striking analogy for the nature of love. Dr. Brody wrote: "In order for a child to experience herself touched, a capable adult must touch her."[10] If we replace the word "touch" in this quotation with the word "love," we are struck by its message: "In order for a child to experience herself loved, a capable adult must love her. A capable adult is one who has had the experience of feeling loved. Because she knows what it feels like to be loved...[s]he knows how to provide the relationship needed for the child to be loved, too."[11] If we want to allow a child's love to come to its fullness, we must truly receive it and truly return it. In receiving the love of a child, we adults come to know the kind of love God offers, and are thus able to love more fully in return.

Children's spiritual gifts compel our respect. Our role is to recognize them, protect them, and reflect to our children the value of what they offer. It is also up to us to offer something of worth to them. To the children who show us timelessness, wonder, and love, we offer the words and images that we have come to know as containers for the eternal, the wondrous, and the infinitely loving. We offer religion. We make a mistake if we think that being broadly spiritual is enough for children. Again Cavalletti speaks, "To want to stay on a level of religiousness deprived of content would be tantamount, as Santayana stated, to wanting to speak a language without using a spoken tongue. If we intend to talk about God we must use a language, and the language with which we speak of God takes the name of an actual religion."[12] A specific spirituality, a religion, provides a foundation and structure for children's rich experience. In a lecture on his recent book entitled *The Good Life: Truths That Last in Times of Need*, Peter Gomes emphasized the need to go beyond individual spirituality to participation in a religion. Especially in times of weakness, he asserted, a human being "requires the framework, the companions, and the worship of his religion; the whole armor of the household of God."[13] We are grateful for our children and what they have to teach us, and we are responsible for their care. We commit ourselves to recognizing and nurturing their spiritual lives, and to offering them the timeless, wonderful, loving God in the very best ways we know.

Notes

[1] Sofia Cavalletti, *The Religious Potential of the Child: Experiencing Scripture and Liturgy with Young Children* (Chicago, Illinois: Liturgy Training Publications, 1993).
[2] Alan Jones, *Journey into Christ* (New York: Seabury Press, 1977), 96.
[3] Anthony Bloom, *Beginning to Pray* (Mahwah, NJ: Paulist Press, 1988), 82.
[4] Cavalletti, *The Religious Potential of the Child,* 139.
[5] Charles Davis, *Body as Spirit: The Nature of Religious Feeling* (New York: Seabury Press, 1976), 79.
[6] Cavalletti, *The Religious Potential of the Child,* 138.
[7] Cavalletti, 44.
[8] Cavalletti, 153.
[9] Jones, *Journey into Christ,* 63.
[10] Viola Brody, *The Dialogue of Touch: Developmental Play Therapy* (Northvale, NJ: Jason Aronson, 1997), 7.
[11] Ibid., 7.
[12] Cavalletti, *The Religious Potential of the Child,* 27.
[13] Peter Gomes, Lecture on *The Good Life: Truths That Last in Times of Need,* Washington National Cathedral, Washington, D.C., May 14, 2002; Event video archive: http://www.cathedral.org/cathedral/video/spring02.html.

Works Consulted

Bloom, Anthony. *Beginning to Pray.* Mahwah, NJ: Paulist Press, 1988.
Brody, Viola. *The Dialogue of Touch: Developmental Play Therapy.* Northvale, NJ: Jason Aronson, 1997.
Cavalletti, Sofia. *The Religious Potential of the Child: Experiencing Scripture and Liturgy with Young Children.* Chicago, Illinois: Liturgy Training Publications, 1993.
Davis, Charles. *Body as Spirit: The Nature of Religious Feeling.* New York: Seabury Press, 1976.

Gomes, Peter. Lecture on *The Good Life: Truths That Last in Times of Need.* Washington National Cathedral, Washington, D.C., May 14, 2002. Event video archive: http://www.cathedral.org/cathedral/video/spring02.html.

Jones, Alan. *Journey Into Christ.* New York: Seabury Press, 1977.

Chapter 2

In Search of Attributes: Exploring the Potential of Sacred Objects in Teaching and Learning about World Religions

Amanda Millay Hughes

Twenty-eight fifth-graders from a local, private, Christian elementary school arrive for a two-hour guided tour at the Ackland Art Museum on the campus of the University of North Carolina at Chapel Hill. It is ten o'clock on Wednesday morning, and as it happens, Holy Wednesday in the Christian tradition. The classroom teacher and five chaperones escort the class. They have come for a Five Faiths Tour. These young people are not as homogenous a group as one might expect in the Bible Belt of America, all enrolled in a Christian academy with bright green circle stickers on their shirts marking them as members of the group. There are children of Asian and Latino descent, African Americans and Anglos in the mix. Divided into two groups, each assigned a gallery teacher, one group heads to the North Gallery, where fifteenth-, sixteenth-, and seventeenth-century works from the Roman Catholic tradition will serve as the focus for their discussion of Catholic Christianity. The other group heads to the Asian gallery, to begin by sitting in a semi-circle on the floor near *Standing Vishnu* and *Vishnu in His Boar Incarnation*.

Over the course of the next two hours, these students will rotate through three spaces in the Museum and look at objects from faith traditions with which they are, more or less, unfamiliar. They will consider Hinduism, Judaism, Buddhism, Catholic Christianity, and Islam by focusing on works of art within the Ackland's Five Faiths Collection. In just under two hours, they will span more than five thousand years of human thought and belief.

FIG. 1. *Standing Vishnu,* Ackland Art Museum,
The University of North Carolina at Chapel Hill, Ackland Fund.

The students have received some classroom instruction in preparation for this visit. They recognize the face of the Buddha and know that Muhammad is the prophet of Islam. Despite the religious affiliation of the school, the students are unfamiliar with St. Catherine and St. Lucy. They guess that the silver chalice set in among other Jewish ritual objects must be a special cup for wine, but they know next to nothing about Sabbath, Havdallah, or Kiddush. They do not recognize the script used in the illuminated manuscript pages of the copy of the Qur'an on display, nor do they know the significance of calligraphy in Islam. These young people know that last Sunday was Palm Sunday and next will be Easter, but they are not so sure about Passover, or when Ramadan will come this year. They have never heard of celebrations of the Buddha's birthday.

Each gallery teacher begins with a welcome and brief overview of the lesson and the museum. When asked what the rules might be in the museum, the students answer with a predictable list: don't run, don't touch, don't lean on the walls, don't write with a pen. The gallery teachers explain the reasons for the rules in an attempt to make them more meaningful. When asked if there are any other rules, one student answers with a slightly questioning tone, "Don't talk?" and another says, "Don't talk loud?"

Visiting groups often add this rule to their list: Don't talk, or at least don't talk loudly. More often than not, student groups must be cajoled into a free exchange of ideas, fast flowing questions and answers, inquiries and explorations. When a gallery teacher asks visiting students the first question, a few may tentatively raise their hands hoping to be called on, and hoping to possess the right answer. As it was in the grade school classes from which we all emerged, there are often one or two who eagerly answer for the whole group and another one or two who refuse to speak at all. One may choose to be silent in a museum, to engage only one's own thoughts, but there is no rule that prohibits the visitor from speaking, asking, answering, or talking to and about the objects themselves. In fact, the opposite is true. Museums are routinely understood as centers of discourse. Conversations with and about objects are encouraged.

Nevertheless, there is something about the atmosphere in a museum, much like that of a library, which seems to suggest that silence is the expected response. The space is quiet and impeccably clean, both of which are rare commodities in today's world. Security guards reinforce the undisclosed value of the objects. Visitors feel it. They wander, pause and look, move on, and look again. Only rarely do they speak and when they do, the speech is offered as a whisper. In a museum gallery, even young visitors recognize on levels commensurate with their experience that they are in the presence of works of art valued by the culture, even if they cannot articulate why. The museum context implies objective merit. The works have been selected for display by often-invisible criteria. They are rare, precious, and singular. More mature visitors often stand in front of certain paintings or sculptures lost in a kind of reverie, what John Armstrong describes as attempting to hold "something in your mind, caressing it so to speak, with a succession of thoughts."[1] Younger visitors may appear less inclined to participate in this reverie, but their behavior often belies their resistance. They stare, wonder, imagine, and perhaps even caress the ideas present with silent attention. However, without help, they are loath to speak. One possible path for educators, particularly when dealing with art objects, may be to honor that instinct for silence, enter the reverie and share the experience. Once we have participated in the experience, we can encourage speech. Standing side by side with our students, we look at the object that has invoked this silent response and begin to engage it with questions.

However, it may be that other motivations fuel the perception that silence must be a rule in the museum. Visitors arrive with their own expectations for the experience. Enculturation informs participation. Along with backpacks, they carry with them the rhythms and expectations of the classroom and the culture at large. While there are classrooms in which open inquiry is valued and brainstorming and guessing are prized as necessary pieces of the learning process, there are also classrooms in which these things are devalued and discouraged. Our current educational climate in America, with its emphasis on content mastery and high-stakes testing, may be the cause of some of these children's silence. Why answer at all if you do not know the right answer? Why risk being wrong when right is so highly valued?

While it is merely speculation, it seems possible that students add the "don't talk" rule to the list as a way to protect themselves from error. Surely, if the students wait long enough, the museum educator will begin to lecture, to instruct, to orate answers to unasked questions. Perhaps young visitors know this and wait for someone else to speak, tell the truth, offer a story, and give the key information. If everyone remains silent, this tacit agreement implies that the works will speak for themselves.

In the culture at large, there are other pressures and expectations that inform the museum visitor. Religious belief and practice are widely understood as matters for private contemplation and participation. Along with politics and money, religion is discouraged as a subject for open discourse. There may be some value to this assertion, but for young people whose dynamism for spirituality is not only undeniable but well documented, the stubbornness with which the culture asserts its reluctance to allow conversations of faith, meaning, religious practices and questions of devotion seems only to reinforce the general malaise of our youths. The rule of silence is fallacious. Not only can visitors speak in the galleries but, even more, young people must be encouraged to give voice to their first questions and the subsequent questions that emerge. Students are to be encouraged to ask questions of human meaning and understanding in every context of their lives. These are questions worthy of deep attention in secular and religious settings alike.

In developing lesson plans for Five Faiths Tours, Ackland staff members have dedicated time and resources to examine the potential and the limitations of works of art as catalysts for open inquiry, teaching, and learning in both the museum and classroom settings. Engaging works of art as primary source material in the study of world religions, as well as allowing time for careful observation, open-ended questioning strategies and multiple interpretive and interpolative voices, deepens our understanding of the religious landscape in America. Students are allowed to give voice to their questions of meaning and faith regardless of the environment in which these strategies are applied.

Three fallacies of museum culture may be at the root of the inhibition some educators feel in their efforts to incorporate objects into their classroom teaching. First, objects must be seen up close and in person in order to be truly appreciated. While it is a pleasure to be in the presence of works of art, modern reproduction capabilities, the Internet, and high-quality videotapes make it possible for students to have access, including up-close access, to works of art that otherwise might be unavailable to them. In some cases, technology allows students to see details and aspects of the object that would not be visible in the museum setting. The second fallacy is that works of art can speak for themselves and finally, that museum educators know all the answers. Unless the object has an audio component, works of art cannot speak at all. They may function as receptacles for stories, deities, and truths, but they cannot speak any more than a wine glass can drink the wine. Unless the viewer possesses a certain amount of information about the object, it is unlikely that she will be able to unpack all the details and implications of any one piece. If we all remain silent, it will be difficult to discover what the object can offer with regard to human potential, lived experience, material culture, and human heritage. Museum labels help, but like the caption on a photograph in a textbook, the information is reductive at best. Museum educators can assist and often do offer contextual information and insight, but they do not have all the answers. In the best-case scenario, museum educators, like their classroom counterparts, facilitate learning. The educator welcomes many voices together: the object and its label, the student and stories from the tradition, passages from the sacred texts. When all are deeply engaged in conversation, consideration, and careful and accurate observation, students are given a richer experience of the tradition as well as a learning experience that mirrors the rich cacophony of spirituality, belief, and faith present in all religious traditions.

Museum educators, like all educators, need strategies that begin and sustain this process of respectful exploration. These strategies create structures that allow students to explore ideas of religious significance, regardless of whether the prayers and the practices of the traditions are unfamiliar or their own. During the Wednesday morning tour, the classroom teacher requested something more than a "look and see" experience. She wanted her students to have the opportunity to engage works of sacred art in a meaningful way. She hoped that while looking closely at these works, her students might be introduced to the core beliefs and practices of these five faiths. However, that introduction can only happen through conversation. Someone must ask. Another must share. The focus must be the objects. The museum is not the only place where these lessons are possible; the classroom can also accommodate this style of inquiry. The necessary piece is the object. Whether the original work is viewed in a gallery, on the screen of a computer, or through a slide projector, or whether it is a replica that students may touch, it is the object that invites the inquiry and provides a catalyst for discussion.

For the past seven years the Ackland Art Museum has been engaged in an ongoing exploration of the potential and limitations of sacred art objects to serve as catalysts for teaching and learning about world religions. The *Five Faiths Project* is founded on the conviction that museums with multicultural collections can serve as centers of discourse on diverse faith traditions. It was through watching the experience of school groups, like the 28 students from the Christian Academy as they encountered images of Mary, the mother of Jesus, and Parvati, the mother of Ganesha, that the education staff became convinced of the project's potential. At its inception, North Carolina was experiencing rapid cultural diversification, resulting from the changing immigration laws of the early 1970s, and akin to the diversification of the nation as a whole. As the population boomed, the proverbial Bible Belt had to expand a notch or two to create room for mosques, bhavans, temples, and synagogues. Even within the dominant Christian tradition, new masses were offered in Spanish at local Roman Catholic churches in order to support and sustain Hispanic and Latino families in their faith. In response to this changing demographic of visitors, the museum began to acquire objects, either by gift, purchase, or long-term loan, that would offer visitors a glimpse into the religious beliefs and practices of faiths that were no longer far away, but right next door.[2]

In the first years of the *Five Faiths Project*, it became clear that specific target audiences might benefit from its approach. Despite a limited number of resources available to teachers, education about world religions is mandated in every school system in the country in which there is a standard course of study defined by state and local agencies. The United States Supreme Court has upheld the notion that teaching and learning about the world's religious traditions are integral parts of a well-rounded education. Nevertheless, the challenges for the museum have been comparable to those of the classroom educator: How might we give voice to the deeply held beliefs of people of faith? How can we appropriately address the spiritual component of human life and human experience?

First, we learned that many of these traditions are vibrant and living, even if the objects in our collection represent only the historical presence of the faith. We began to appreciate the necessity of acknowledging the context in which an object is engaged. We began to ask: How is the object changed by its context? How essential is it for the viewer to understand the original context and the current context in order to appreciate the object? If the context is fundamentally religious in nature, such as a sanctuary or a mosque, the object receives regard appropriate not only to itself but to the context in which it is found. The same may be true of the museum context. The museum context creates a certain regard for objects that they might not receive in a different environment. By entering into a relationship with faith communities and individual believers, we learned that these communities could be an invaluable resource to any educator seeking to offer students a richer understanding of the complexity and significance of original context. Storytellers and faith leaders enrich our understanding of the original uses of ritual and devotional objects. In addition, these communities may be able to provide comparable objects that students can touch and examine more closely. By including their voices in exhibition planning, label writing, and public programs as well as in classroom settings, visitors and students receive a richer interpretation of the object and the faith from which it emerged.

In the presence of members of faith communities new questions emerge: How is the object displayed, handled, cleaned, and employed in the course of sacred observances? What does this object mean to you? How does a museum object compare to objects used in your faith observances? One central question can only be answered by a faith practitioner: What do people of faith experience in the presence of this object? By focusing our conversations on the objects, the museum was able to amass a wealth of information about faith practices that might otherwise have been unavailable to us.

Second, we have discovered that through conversations that center on objects, teaching and learning are uniformly enhanced. The inquiry itself, as well as the subsequent knowledge and understanding, deepen because the objects are able to withstand critique and questioning strategies that individual believers may not be able or willing to withstand. While looking at the *Head of Buddha*, a Thai bronze prominently on display in the Ackland's Yeager Gallery, Buddhist practitioners are unfazed by questions about the size of his ears, the snails on his head, or the shape of his nose. They are able to share how these artistic constructions represent certain attributes of Buddha nature, carefully defined by the Pali Canons.

By freely asking questions such as "What does that mean? What is that? Why is the Buddha sitting like that?" students open a discourse of discovery into a wider range of fundamental beliefs and practices.

FIG. 2. *Head of Buddha,* Ackland Art Museum,
The University of North Carolina at Chapel Hill, Ackland Fund.

This is accomplished without indoctrination. As the teachings of Buddhism are transmitted through study of the object, the educator retains a necessary distance from the core content.

Opportunities to practice this kind of inquiry are invaluable. Information about objects in the collection, including date, location of origin, and materials used in manufacture can be taught by rote memorization, but in working with students, the persistent questions of divine value, human response, and historical and contemporary significance may be more important. Educators and students benefit from experiences that reinforce the notion that this faith exists not only as a historical fact, and not merely as a phenomenon worthy of study within the framework of academic inquiry, but as a living tradition with objects serving as reflections of passages or stories from sacred texts, possibly as vessels of divine energy and certainly as a part of the continuous stream of believing alive and well in contemporary culture. Introductions to core beliefs, ritual practices, selections from sacred texts, combined with visits to local centers of worship and insights available only from lay and ordained members within each faith, enrich student appreciation of the vibrant complexity of each tradition. Rather than becoming overwhelmed with more facts and data pertaining to the faith, students are given the opportunity to witness its fundamental import. The object becomes the catalyst for sustained inquiry. By being provided with a broad selection of information of varying type and style, students are able to grasp those aspects most salient to them while being assured that there are additional resources at their disposal.[3]

As educators engage multiple voices and points of view in order to deepen our appreciation of a particular object or faith, complexity and diversity emerge. Even with core beliefs shared and firmly held, culturally specific practices abound in each faith heritage. All the traditions are engaged in some form of reflexive consideration. With this in mind, statements of uniformity such as "All Christians believe..." or "All Muslims express their devotion by...." become less important than questions of inquiry. Because no individual can be expected to speak for all of a particular faith's beliefs and traditions or be held up as the solitary exemplar for that tradition, it is in the confluence of voices that core beliefs emerge. A mainline Protestant must not be expected to articulate the uses of icons in the Eastern Orthodox tradition, even though both are undeniably Christian in sensibility. Nevertheless, certain central figures in the icons may be recognizable: Jesus, Mary,

John the Baptist. The Protestant Christian may offer stories about the lives and significance of these more familiar figures. All Buddhists may not be prepared to outline the distinctions between Mahayana and Theravada Buddhism, but they may offer a more personal understanding of the teachings of the Buddha.

Similarly, object-based study introduces the limitations of any given object in explicating the depth of the tradition. Educators use the objects to introduce discussions of core truths and often find the conversation moving quickly to questions of meaning, memory, faith, and practice. This is desirable in that it expands the students' appreciation beyond facts to lived experience. These conversations often deepen the experience of those for whom the faith tradition is familiar, while providing foundational information for those for whom the tradition is completely unknown.

By returning to the object as a common point of reference, educators and students can explore questions of spirituality in many varied human endeavors without violating the boundary that constrains public school educators in particular from proselytizing or teaching religion, rather than teaching about religion. For those in religious private schools, these same strategies allow educators within a certain tradition the possibility of empathetic understanding of other faiths without the threat of minimizing their own beliefs or those of the supporting institution.

Over time, the Ackland recognized that, as a public institution with objects from many different traditions, we were uniquely positioned to model respectful pluralism. Moving through the galleries might be understood as a metaphor for moving through contemporary culture. Objects from diverse traditions stand in neighboring galleries in much the same configuration which individuals in America experience as they encounter diversity in their home neighborhoods. The museum is able to offer educators and student groups, as well as individual visitors, a venue in which they may learn about unfamiliar faith traditions while learning how to engage that difference in a respectful and productive fashion. The objects do not threaten one another. They exist side by side in the museum, as these diverse traditions stand side by side in our society. In effect, we were able to provide a venue in which students and educators might learn and practice living with diversity.

By the time the fifth-grade students arrived for their Wednesday visit, the Museum had established certain practices that were applicable in both museum and classroom settings.

Explore More Than One Tradition

In order to fulfill our obligation to remain neutral in our presentation of religious objects, the museum rarely, if ever, conducts a "One-Faith" tour for a school group. If students come to see works from the Islamic tradition, they will also visit the Asian gallery. Moving from one faith to another, students can experience the tensions created by difference, note certain commonalities, and enjoy an environment in which claims of uniqueness are not challenged.

Krister Stendahl, Andrew W. Mellon Professor of Divinity Emeritus at Harvard University, explains that learning about other faiths while living deeply into his own Christian calling enabled him to experience "more than tolerance, more than reluctant recognition of the actual pluralism that surrounds us…" He goes on to say that Christian calling "allows me to sing my song to Jesus with abandon and that without speaking negatively about others."[4] Put in another way, knowledge about other traditions may have a widely unrealized potential to deepen, rather than threaten, the faith of believers in all traditions. By beginning with diverse objects from diverse faiths, we practice skills we will use in encounters with people of diverse faiths. In addition, knowledge about faith traditions may well enrich the experience of those who claim or desire no faith tradition at all. By refusing to privilege one tradition or no tradition, educators model the possibility of communities living well with diversity. In *Knowledge and the Sacred,* Seyyed Hossein Nasr writes, "…if there is one really new and significant dimension to the religious and spiritual life of man [sic] today, it is this presence of other worlds of sacred form and meaning not as archaeological or historical facts and phenomena but as religious reality."5 By adopting parallel practices and employing them with more than one tradition, educators and students experiment with ways of interacting with diverse and often contradictory religious realities.

Make Consistent Language Choices

In using works of art as objects of study, references to central figures within each tradition are virtually unavoidable. The Ackland has determined to remove all honorifics in our discussions with student groups. References are made to Jesus or Mary, not Christ or the Virgin. Likewise, educators refer to Ganesha and Buddha, not Lord Ganesha and Lord Buddha. This decision does not represent a desire on the part of the museum to demote any individual or deity, nor to deny the honor given by believers to these figures, but rather precisely because we recognize the use of honorifics as rooted in devotional sensibilities. Believers acknowledge the lordship and express it by including the title in their discourse. By removing the honorific, museum and classroom educators remain neutral on the devotional worthiness of individual or deities.

In addition, we strive to use appropriate language drawn from inside the tradition whenever possible. Worship centers, often the original context for works of sacred art, have specific names. A cathedral is not a mosque and a synagogue is not a stupa. Calling these centers by their appropriate names reinforces a respect for difference. Similarly, a surah is the correct name for a section of the Qur'an, Bible is not a term that can be applied to the Vedas, and the priest, imam, guru, rabbi, or taitaku deserve to be acknowledged by their appropriate title. Using distinctive and precise language helps to establish each religious tradition as distinct, even when sharing common narratives or values. Each tradition deserves acknowledgment of its particularity.

Learning to use the correct language choices for texts, objects, and roles within the traditions also prepares students for interfaith conversations in which these distinctions may play an important role.

Employ Sacred Stories

We have determined to frame all narratives from religious traditions as sacred stories, rejecting the use of the word "myth" as undeniably suspect. Many sacred objects are made as visual communicators of sacred stories. Often the objects contain symbols and visual metaphors that are only discernable through sacred story. If students are ignorant of the story, they are more likely to reject the object's significance. David Carr, Professor of Information and Library Science at the University of North Carolina at Chapel Hill, puts it this way, "Among objects of faith, a tension is present between our formative knowledge and its opposite: our formative ignorance, which may involve fear and confusion."[6] Sacred stories bridge the gap between the known and the unknown along a narrative thread. Stories reduce fear and unravel confusion. When asked if the stories are true, educators may remind students that sacred stories emerge from a number of sources: sacred texts, other religious texts, and the oral tradition. Individuals within the traditions believe the stories to contain important lessons and truths and have retained the stories across generations. If only in that sense, the stories are true. However, are these narratives describing real events? The honest answer is "We don't know." Sacred stories envelop more than facts, they also hold belief. For our purposes, it is less important to determine the factual accuracy of any given story than to acknowledge its fundamental veracity for believers and verify its heritage through reliable sources.

While it is important to learn sacred stories in order to tell them as answers to questions about sacred objects, the Ackland encourages educators to refrain from putting words into the mouths of religious figures unless the words can be verified from a reliable text. For example, storytellers should avoid putting common American vernacular into the mouth of Buddha. An individual Buddhist practitioner may do so within the context of a story learned from a grandparent, but an educator puts integrity at risk when making up sayings or adding words in order to capture the attention of students. Allowing the stories of the tradition to come forward without added embellishment, particularly in the words of central figures, models the appropriate regard necessary for interfaith dialogue.

Ask Open-Ended Questions

When searching for meaning and understanding in a work of sacred art, open-ended questions generate meaningful discussions, while at the same time, they generate new questions and prompt continued inquiry. In the study of world religions, it is essential that educators leave the path of inquiry open. There is no destination point at which the richness of the tradition is fully realized nor is there any test that can demonstrate full knowledge of its practices and expressions. The best practices allow for continued investigation. Look at Vishnu, what do you see? What else? What else? What words might you use to describe him? Focusing on the physical qualities of the objects engages students in careful observation and critical thinking. Inviting students to compare one image of Vishnu with others, watching for similarities and differences, provides a tangible example of the multiplicity and diversity present within the tradition. Students are encouraged to ask comparable questions of members of faith communities and educators as well. David Carr offers a few questions that are appropriate when considering objects from one tradition or many:

- What is the object's conventional place and use in ritual pattern and practice?
- What is the object's meaning in observances of birth, death, initiation, or transformation?
- What is the object's relationship to sacred text or narrative, symbol, or deity?

- What is the object's comparative complexity among other objects of its kind? [7]

Each of these questions stimulates other questions and presses the students to examine their own understanding of the object's significance and their response to it. Students may then ask questions about how these objects and faiths define the path of the human toward the divine, assist human beings on that path, and define the human being in the cosmology of the faith.

Explore the Implications

By consistently returning to the objects for consideration, students are bound to uncover their own questions of meaning and value. After looking at the Torah Scroll and a pointer, one of the fifth graders announced, "I have things I don't want anyone to touch." When asked why, he continued, "Because they're important to me, really important." As we examine the object and listen to stories, "we want to know the mystery and the inspiration in ways that illuminate the faith."[8] Works of sacred art are portals to this exploration. It is not surprising that when students and visitors attend to the works of art and are provided with contextual information, often they will find points of commonality with their own experiences, and, on that common ground, begin to practice respect for what only minutes earlier appeared as insurmountable difference.

Give Voice to Questions

Many educators express concern that by choosing to give voice to students' and museum visitors' deepest questions of meaning, a floodlight will illuminate the limitations of their knowledge. It seems better to lecture and avoid questions altogether. However, finding the limits of our knowledge may be one of the necessary goals in this mode of inquiry. When we reach the limits of our knowledge, we return to wonder. When we touch the limits of our knowledge of the sacred, we inch closer to a kind of sacred knowledge. This sacred knowledge does not readily fall under a rubric for examination, nor is it consistent with the standard course of study or the museum's primary goals: preservation of works of art and access to those works. Nevertheless, in an increasingly diverse society, true pluralism will honor the presence of sacred knowledge and refuse to denigrate it or deny its existence. If sacred knowledge borders our commitment to teach about world religions, how might a responsible educator respect that boundary?

One of the greatest challenges of teaching about world religions rests squarely in this question. Educators, whether teaching in public or private classrooms, lecture halls or galleries, must acknowledge the boundary and recognize the differences between knowledge of the sacred and sacred knowledge. Educators travel with their students as they move from basic understanding to more complex application. At certain points, the teacher must retreat and allow the student both the autonomy and the freedom to move into previously unknown territory. Similarly, in teaching about world religions, educators are wise to step back whenever students cross the boundary to enter their own experience of faith and devotional practices. The teacher does not disappear, but rather distances herself from the discovery. This stepping back is most meaningful when true education has occurred in advance. It may be tempting for educators to offer their own sacred knowledge in times of crisis or discomfort, but students need knowledge of the sacred more certainly than any sacred knowledge a public or private educator might offer. The dispensation of sacred knowledge falls to imams, priests, sages, and other leaders of faith communities.

Currently, educators often express concern about teaching religion, even imparting information about the world's religions, fearing that students, parents, and administrations may misunderstand and confuse it with indoctrination and teaching sacred knowledge. The distinction is subtle, but highly potent. As teachers draw this distinction, they point their students back to communities of faith, families, relatives, and others better positioned to assist in individual inquiry. Educators are able to offer this redirection most effectively when they have already established themselves as trustworthy sources of information and of "knowledge about" rather than insider revelations. By informing students of the influence of religious systems on critical thought, exploration, moral and ethical systems, economics, medicine, and even mathematics, educators offer students another set of facts with which to inform their own life choices. By acknowledging the necessity of multiple voices and perspectives, educators indicate a path for students to use in their own quest for meaning.

A two-hour visit to the galleries is only a brief encounter with the potential of objects to serve as catalysts for this kind of education. Teachers are well advised to include images of objects from religious cultures regularly in their classrooms, precisely because they instill awe and awaken wonder. The objects represent to students the mastery of the human hand as well as the possibility of the divine's influence within the hand's work. The objects stir our ignorance and generate the creation of new and varied conditions for learning and response. The objects themselves challenge and deepen our understanding of the significance of human experience, beckoning us to reckon with the challenges of our own lived experience, our values, our ethics, and our commitments.

In object-based study, students and educators find a workable beginning and a meaningful end. Any given object is finite, and while the inquiry it generates may be sufficient to a lifetime, it too is finite. This finitude points the student to other resources, other voices, and ultimately other objects that open up new areas of inquiry. By returning to the objects, we experience both the limits and the potential of education about the world's religions. In search of the attributes of objects from faith traditions, students and educators may find the core values needed for contemporary society as well.

The 28 students who came to the Ackland that Wednesday morning left with a few stories to tell. They looked at the objects. They

FIG. 3. Attributed to Jacopo del Sellaio, *The Virgin and Child Enthroned with Saints,* ca. 1490, Ackland Art Museum, The University of North Carolina at Chapel Hill, The William A. Whitaker Foundation Art Fund.

learned about the board incarnation of Vishnu in which the world was saved from devastating floods, and of Muhammad's wise strategy for replacing the Black Stone of the Ka'ba. They heard a story of the Kiddush Cup and another about St. Lucy.

They heard about the snails that covered Buddha's head to protect him from the sun and rain. All the stories were prompted by questions raised while looking closely at the objects. However, even more, the students left the museum without having raised their voices. No one shouted. No one condemned. No one attempted to convert anyone from one faith to another, from no faith to one. However, the students asked, wondered aloud, gave voice to their own questions. At its best, object-based teaching and learning affords students the chance to speak, to ask, and to have their questions honored with appropriate answers while pointing them down a path of continued inquiry. It provides a foundation for respectful exploration of the human experience and the new American landscape of religious pluralism.

Notes

[1] John Armstrong, *Move Closer: An Intimate Philosophy of Art* (New York: Farrar, Straus and Giroux, 2000), 74.

[2] Ray Williams, now Director of Education at the Peabody Essex Museum in Salem, Massachusetts, continues to be revered for his initial vision of this program. Many hours of research and effort were required to establish relationships with local faith communities and public and private school educators as key partners in the first phase of Ackland Museum's *Five Faiths Project.*

[3] There are numerous Web sites that offer contextual information in the study of objects. The Pluralism Project at Harvard, http://www.fas.harvard.edu/~pluralism/ assists educators in finding local faith communities and www.sacred-texts.com offers English translations of hundreds of sacred stories.

[4] Krister Stendahl, "Religious Pluralism and the Claim to Uniqueness," in *Education as Transformation: Religious Pluralism, Spirituality & a New Vision for Higher Education in America,* ed. Victor H. Kazanjian, Jr., and Peter L. Laurence (New York: Peter Lang Publishing, Inc., 2000), 183.

[5] Seyyed Hossein Nasr, *Knowledge and the Sacred* (Albany, NY: State University of New York Press, 1989), 292.

[6] Taken from David Carr's presentation, "A Conversation in the Galleries," during the Ackland Museum's first *Five Faiths Colloquy* held on August 20, 2002.

[7] Ibid.

[8] Ibid.

Works Consulted

Armstrong, John. *Move Closer: An Intimate Philosophy of Art.* New York: Farrar, Straus and Giroux, 2000.

Carr, David. "A Conversation in the Galleries." *Five Faiths Colloquy: Year One.* Chapel Hill, NC: Ackland Art Museum.

Nasr, Seyyed Hossein. *Knowledge and the Sacred.* Albany, NY: State University of New York Press, 1989.

Stendahl, Krister. "Religious Pluralism and the Claim to Uniqueness." In *Education as Transformation: Religious Pluralism, Spirituality, & a New Vision for Higher Education in America,* ed. Victor H. Kazanjian, Jr., and Peter L. Laurence. New York: Peter Lang, 2000.

Chapter 3

Spiritual Giftedness: Identifying and Measuring "Religious Genius"

Arthur J. Schwartz

After three days Joseph and Mary found Jesus in the Temple courts, sitting among the teachers, listening and asking them questions. Everyone who heard Jesus was amazed at his understanding and his answers.
Luke 2:46–47

Biblical scholars, in their efforts to discern the significance of Luke's story about the twelve-year-old Jesus in the Temple, have debated for centuries what so "amazed" the rabbis. One group of scholars posit that Jesus was simply profoundly "learned" in the traditional sense, possessing an uncommonly mature intellectual grasp of the Torah, especially for a twelve-year-old. Other scholars suggest that the rabbis (as well as Joseph and Mary) were "amazed" because this pre-adolescent from Bethlehem was communicating a new, if not revolutionary, understanding of God and God's nature.

Although this debate may rage on for centuries to come, what is clear is that Luke sought to portray Jesus as a religious or spiritual prodigy. The notion of spiritual prodigies is well established in many religions. In Judaism, for example, Baal Shem Tov, founder of Hasidism, was widely acknowledged as a religious prodigy, especially his mystical (and nonrational) orientation to God and Torah. It is difficult to understand the theology of Buddhism, especially Tibetan Buddhism, without recognizing that each of the fourteen Dalai Lamas possessed at birth and throughout childhood extraordinary spiritual gifts and proclivities.[1]

This essay seeks to explore the nature and nurturing of spiritual giftedness. Does it exist? If so, how might it be identified and measured? Moreover, even if research could develop an empirically valid measurement tool to examine this aspect of human difference, why undertake such an effort? Don't we all have the capacity to be spiritual prodigies in different ways or according to our "callings?" Hasn't God provided each one of us with our own unique spiritual gifts? Furthermore, in this age where the pervasive yoke of radical egalitarianism abounds, it is problematic to suggest that some of us are more spiritually gifted than others?

However, if we examine other domains, it is clear that individual differences do exist. Quite frequently these God-given attributes, qualities, and skills are exuberantly praised and celebrated. Tiger Woods made a guest appearance on "The Tonight Show" with Johnny Carson at age six because of his extraordinary ability to hit a golf ball. Most of us, I would venture to say, if asked to define the term "prodigy" conjure up the genius of Mozart and the manifestation of his musical gifts at such a tender age. History is replete, moreover, with examples of gifted chess players and mathematical virtuosi whose profound talents and skills became apparent during their first decade of life.

Indeed, whether it is in the academic classroom or on the athletic field, educators and coaches are clearly identifying and nurturing individual differences. Throughout much of the world, gifted education has become a well-established and significantly funded component of schools, whereby students who possess even "moderate" academic talents (in disciplines ranging from science to history to the arts) are offered a smorgasbord of enrichment programs and challenging curricula. Who can deny that coaches in almost all sports have become adept at identifying and cultivating athletic "giftedness" in very young children? My own son, along with one hundred and fifty peers, was evaluated at age eight for his ability as a soccer player. After assessing his soccer ability, he was placed on the township's "A" team. For the past five years, his team has practiced more frequently than teams deemed less "gifted," and the team has been given the opportunity to learn from highly knowledgeable and expert soccer coaches. Is there any doubt that these highly structured "interventions" have helped to maximize my child's athletic gifts?

Perhaps the reader has already raised in his or her mind the following question: Why is it necessary to identify and measure "giftedness" in any domain? Indeed, readers may be recalling stories they have read about talented tennis players or piano prodigies who suffer "burnout" before they are old enough to drive a car. Why must we be so focused on identifying and nurturing the skills and talents of our young people? It is a fair question to ask.

The answer is deceptively simple: Research has shown that we "soar with our strengths." While the risk of burnout is real, the reality is that young people who are gifted in a particular domain often want to exercise and strengthen their talent. Scholars from a wide variety of research disciplines have demonstrated a strong correlation between what we are good at and what we like doing. That is to say, kids who are especially talented at solving mathematical problems tend to enjoy math and readily seek out opportunities to improve their math skills. In the realm of athletics, scores of articles have been written about talented basketball players, labeled "gym rats" at an early age because of their love and passion for the game.

In other words, no matter how much raw talent and innate skills a young person may exhibit, these abilities will wither unless there exists what researchers describe as a "rage to master."[2] Once again, the research is clear: There is no substitute for hard work and the intrinsic motivation to excel at a particular task or domain of activity, no matter how much natural ability is prevalent. While it may be stretching the research to suggest that high achievement is more a function of tenacity than talent, deliberate practice is a critical and necessary ingredient. Prodigies practice—and often quite a bit. For example, while Mozart could play the clavier by his fourth birthday and began to compose little keyboard pieces by age five, it was not until he was fifteen that he began to produce significant musical creations.

It is doubtful that Mozart thought of practicing as an arduous or painful enterprise; rather, it is more likely that he found his time at the piano a positive (if not joyful) experience. Indeed, a considerable body of contemporary research shows that children like to practice and strengthen their God-given "gift," especially when their practices are viewed as preparation for a "performance" or "final project" (whether it be an athletic competition or building a model rocket). Professor Mihaly Csikszentmihalyi suggests that during these practices and performances individuals may experience what he calls "flow," a biological term to describe how people feel when they are involved in a sustained activity worth doing for its own sake. Flow occurs, he suggests, when an activity challenges the individual to fully engage his or her capacities. Furthermore, as these capacities grow, staying in flow requires taking on increasingly greater challenges (e.g., more complex equations or rocket designs).[3]

Thus, while there may be multiple reasons why societies focus on identifying and nurturing the skills and talents of our young people, one very compelling reason may be that parents and educators clearly recognize that children thrive when they have the opportunity to develop their God-given skills and talents. It is a simple calculus: Kids like to do what they are good at, and what they are good at they tend to like to do. Furthermore, ample research suggests that when given the opportunity to "soar" with their strengths, kids are more intrinsically motivated, happier, less at risk, and, if one asks almost any educator, fun to teach![4]

It is clear as well that contemporary educators, whether within the domain of science or soccer, utilize (roughly) the same set of pedagogical strategies:

- identify a "gifted" child through a range of assessment tools;
- determine the child has an intrinsic motivation to acquire new skills in that domain; if so,

- provide opportunities, through sustained practice, for the children to strengthen their natural talents and skills in that domain; and,
- offer a scaffolding of increasingly more difficult challenges, such as performances or projects, whereby the children can self-assess their acquisition and mastery of skills compared with the recognized "experts" in the domain.

The question that frames the final section of this chapter is whether the principles and pedagogical strategies outlined above can be applied to the domain of religion and spirituality. Developing a range of assessment tools to measure spiritual giftedness is a challenging task. It is difficult to envision a pencil-and-paper test that captures the validity and essence of a young person's religiosity or spirituality, although a number of researchers have begun to develop and refine such empirical instruments.[5]

Perhaps the first step is to identify more precisely what I mean when I suggest that someone is religiously or spiritually "gifted." Am I referring to the person's religious piety? Alternatively, should we measure selfless acts of compassion for those less fortunate? What about those children who possess extraordinary knowledge of sacred texts? While these are clearly elements of religiosity that need to be more closely investigated and measured, none of these exemplify, at least for me, the core dimension necessary to explore empirically and to understand more fully the nature and development of spiritual giftedness in childhood and adolescence.

The foremost dimension denoting spiritual giftedness is a positive and significant relationship to God. Moreover, for many of us, and here I include practitioners of most major religions, this relationship is best understood within the context of one's prayer life. In his book *God and You: Prayer as a Personal Relationship*, the Catholic priest William Barry illuminates the essence, if not the universality, of this relationship: "People engage in prayer as conscious relationship because they want to know and love God better. Of course, we may want God's help in difficult crises. We may want to be healed of a disease, for example, but at the deepest level our desire is for a relationship. What surprises people who let God come close is that God, too, wants a relationship."[6]

In many ways, a positive relationship to God reflects the same qualities as a significant relationship with another human being (parent, sibling, friend, or spouse). First, a positive relationship is satisfying and never toxic or aversive in nature (e.g., dangerous or destructive). Second, there is the sense of intimacy. When we feel close and connected to others we are willing to reveal central aspects of ourselves, especially our emotions and feelings. Moreover, we experience intimacy when we feel understood, validated, and cared for. However, intimacy is a fragile quality, and thus we are most likely to experience intimacy within a long-term relationship.

Finally, there is the dimension of commitment. We all know too well that as a relationship develops there are moments when one chooses (or not) to "invest" in it. Indeed, researchers have noted that there is a strong correlation between investing resources (time, effort, emotions, and so on) and an individual's enhanced commitment to relationships. A committed one, therefore, is understood both as an intention to persist in the face of obstacles or doubts as well as the development of a long-term orientation or allegiance to the relationship.[7]

In defining spiritual giftedness as a significant relationship to God, I am clearly drawing on and extending the ideas of Howard Gardner and the rapidly growing number of emotional theorists and researchers. In Gardner's theory, two of his eight primary intelligences are interpersonal and intrapersonal. Interpersonal intelligence denotes an ability for a person to understand other people (what motivates them, how to work effectively with them, how to lead or follow or care for them). Intrapersonal intelligence means knowing oneself as Socrates affirms in his well-known maxim "Know Thyself." Emotional intelligence, as defined by Salovey and Sluyter, involves "the ability to perceive accurately, appraise, and express emotion; the ability to access and/or generate feelings when they facilitate thought; the ability to understand emotion and emotional knowledge; and the ability to regulate emotions to promote emotional and intelligent growth."[8]

Any effort to develop an empirically based understanding of spiritual giftedness will need to employ these theories and research. However, neither Gardner nor emotional intelligence scholars adequately address or discuss one's "relationship to God" as the core dimension of spiritual giftedness. Indeed, Gardner has recently rejected the phenomenology of "spiritual intelligence" while emotional development scholars, at least to my knowledge, have yet to explore the link between an individual's relationship to God and how this relationship serves as an emotional appraiser and regulator. More specifically, emotional intelligence researchers have yet to examine how one's relationship to God and the core religious teachings and precepts of a religious tradition (e.g., turning the other cheek, forgiveness, emphasis on peace) might serve to facilitate particular behaviors and actions.[9]

A positive and significant relationship to God is a spiritual idea that animates the world's faith traditions and theological literature. Furthermore, we know from the writings of spiritual geniuses, ranging from Meister Eckhart to Maimonides, that striving for a meaningful relationship with God is at the very core of the religious experience. However, how might religious educators and parents assess a young person's relationship to God? How might we begin to measure the validity and reliability of the construct, let alone identify adepts who have developed an extraordinarily secure attachment to God?[10]

Certainly this challenge is not as simple as denoting how far a golf ball is hit or how fast and elegantly a complex algebraic equation is completed. Perhaps we ought to be guided by the challenge that George Gallup once shared with me: "Just because we don't yet know how to measure something, doesn't mean it doesn't exist."[11]

Therefore, let us begin by acknowledging that some young people most probably have a (statistically) more meaningful and significant "prayer life" and relationship with God than others in their age cohort. Furthermore, few religious educators would disagree that some kids simply have a stronger, more deeply felt attachment to God. In other words, there is a phenomenological truth to the reality of spiritual giftedness as a significant relationship to God that simply has never been researched. For example, in my review of the literature, I have yet to identify a single book or article (in any religion) that explores the concept of spiritual giftedness in ways analogous to mathematical or athletic giftedness.

Clearly, spiritual giftedness must denote more than a significant relationship to God. A spiritually gifted child or adolescent should be able to use his or her relationship and attachment to God to "perform" a variety of spiritually inspired actions and behaviors (my use of the term perform is analogous to an athletic competition or building a model rocket). A spiritually gifted young person has the ability to forgive and not bear grudges. She has the ability to feel or sense awe, wonder, and beauty. She affirms the joy and sweetness of life, even in the face of challenging or negative external circumstances. Thus, a young person who possesses a secure attachment to God should exhibit and inhabit daily a wide constellation of virtues and human strengths. While she will surely experience doubts about her relationship to God and will likely experience times of profound spiritual dryness compared to most of her peers, we can only understand and describe her life, and the person she is striving to become, as fueled by prayer and dynamically powered by Divine purpose and meaning.

Perhaps during the twenty-first century we will witness the radical acceleration of interest and enthusiasm for discovering new methods to identify and measure spiritual giftedness in young people. This is not to suggest that only spiritually gifted children should learn how to pray, any more than I would advocate that only mathematically precocious children learn geometry. However, I forward the possibility that by taking more seriously the identification and nurturing of the spiritually gifted, we may be entering a century in which spiritual adepts are as cherished and praised as mathematical prodigies, a century in which houses of worship (across religious traditions) provide sustained opportunities for spiritually gifted children to practice and strengthen their innate ability to communicate with God, a century in which it will be commonplace for spiritually gifted children to learn from "experts" and "masters" about the practices and methods by which to develop a deeper and more meaningful relationship with God.

I share this vision without any hope or expectation that we may one day educate an "Einstein of the Spirit" who radically revolutionizes our understanding of God and of God's divine purposes. Rather, the ideas embedded in this essay have been developed, at least in part, to illuminate and underscore a truth common to (almost) all religions: the primacy of prayer as a core spiritual practice. For as Parker Palmer suggests, in prayer "we touch that transcendent Spirit from which all things arise and to whom all things return."[12]

Notes

[1] For research on the Baal Shem Tov, see Isaac Bashevis Singer, *Reaches of Heaven: A Story of the Baal Shem Tov* (New York: Farrar, Straus and Giroux, 1982). For an illuminating history on the process undertaken to identify each of the fourteen Dalai Lamas, see Glen Mullin, *The Fourteen Dalai Lamas: A Sacred Legacy of Reincarnation* (Santa Fe, NM: Clear Light Publishers, 2001).

[2] The phrase "rage to master" is used by Ellen Winner, "The Rage to Master: The Decisive Case for Talent in the Visual Arts," in *The Road to Excellence: The Acquisition of Expert Performance in the Arts and Sciences, Sports and Games* (Hillsdale, NJ: Lawrence Erlbaum Associates, Inc., 1996), 271–301.

[3] For a comprehensive overview of the "flow concept," see Mihaly Csikszentmihalyi, author of both *Finding Flow: The Psychology of Engagement with Everyday Life* (New York: Basic Books, 1998) and *Flow: The Psychology of Optimal Experience* (New York: Perennial Publishers, 1993).

[4] Nicholas Colangelo and Gary Davis, *Handbook of Gifted Education* (Boston, MA: Allyn and Bacon, 2003).

[5] A thoughtful overview of the current status and future challenges regarding the measurement of religiosity and spirituality is found in W. Slater, T. Hall, and K. Edwards, "Measuring Religion and Spirituality: Where Are We and Where Are We Going?" *Journal of Psychology and Theology* 29.1 (2001): 4–21.

6 William A. Barry, *God and You: Prayer as a Personal Relationship* (New York: Paulist Press, 1987), 71.

7 Researcher Caryl Rusbult studies positive relationships and willingly discussed at length her research on the topic. Although a professing agnostic, Rusbult nonetheless expressed disappointment that none of her colleagues in the field of relationship studies, at least to her knowledge, have ever examined the individual-God relationship. For an explanation and statistical analysis of her "investment model," see Caryl Rusbult, J. Martz, and C. Agnew, "The Investment Model Scale: Measuring Commitment Level, Satisfaction Level, Quality of Alternatives, and Investment Size, *Personal Relationships* 5 (1998): 357–91.

8 Peter Salovey and David J. Sluyter, *Emotional Development and Emotional Intelligence: Educational Implications* (New York: Basic Books, 1997), 10.

9 Howard Gardner, *Multiple Intelligences* (New York: Basic Books, 1993); Gardner's explicit rejection of a "spiritual intelligence" can be found in H. Gardner, "A Case Against Spiritual Intelligence," *International Journal for the Psychology of Religion* 10 (2000): 27–34. While Daniel Goleman's 1997 book *Emotional Intelligence* has had considerable impact in the fields of education and youth policy, I encourage the reader to review P. Salovey and D. Sluyter's work cited in the endnote above.

10 In order to more fully understand a relationship to God that is satisfying, intimate, and committed, a growing number of social scientists in the field of religion are using the term "secure attachment to God." Following the ethological theories of attachment developed by John Bowlby in the 1970's, "secure attachment" is a biological and emotional capacity to love and to feel loved. Thus, from an attachment perspective, a positive and significant relationship with God vivifies a deep and emotional bond (summed up succinctly in the universal maxim "God is love"). When an individual inhabits this secure attachment, she or he experiences God both as a "safe haven" (in times of stress or when in need of security) and as a "secure base" (to explore one's inner and outer environment). Professor Lee Kirkpatrick is widely considered the leading "attachment to God" researcher. For an overview of his theory and empirical studies, see W. Rowatt and L. Kirkpatrick, "Two Dimensions of Attachment to God and Their Relation to Affect, Religiosity, and Personality Constructs," *Journal for the Scientific Study of Religion* 41.4 (2002): 637.

11 Personal conversation with George Gallup, June 2000.

12 Parker Palmer, *To Know As We Are Known: Education As A Spiritual Journey* (San Francisco, CA: Harper and Row, 1993).

Works Consulted

Barry, William A. *God and You: Prayer as a Personal Relationship*. New York: Paulist Press, 1987.

Colangelo, Nicholas, and Davis, Gary. *Handbook of Gifted Education*. 3rd ed. Boston, MA: Allyn and Bacon, 2003.

Csikszentmihalyi, Mihaly. *Finding Flow: The Psychology of Engagement With Everyday Life*. New York: Basic Books, 1998.

———. *Flow: The Psychology of Optimal Experience*. New York: Perennial Publishers, 1993.

Gardner, Howard. "A Case Against Spiritual Intelligence." *International Journal for the Psychology of Religion,* 10 (2000): 27–34.

———. *Multiple Intelligences.* New York: Basic Books, 1993.

Goleman, Daniel. *Emotional Intelligencce.* New York: Bantam Books, 1997.

Mullin, Glen. *The Fourteen Dalai Lamas: A Sacred Legacy of Reincarnation.* Santa Fe, NM: Clear Light Publishers, 2001.

Palmer, Parker. *To Know As We Are Known: Education As A Spiritual Journey.* San Francisco, CA: Harper and Row, 1993.

Rowatt, W., and Kirkpatrick, L. "Two Dimensions of Attachment to God and Their Relationship to Affect, Religiosity, and Personality Constructs." *Journal for the Scientific Study of Religion* 41.4 (2002): 637–51.

Rusbult, Caryl, Martz, J., and Agnew, C. "The Investment Model Scale: Measuring Commitment Level, Satisfaction Level, Quality of Alternatives, and Investment Size." *Personal Relationships* 5 (1998): 357–91.

Salovey, Peter, and Sluyter, David J. *Emotional Development and Emotional Intelligence: Educational Implications.* New York: Basic Books, 1997.

Singer, Isaac Bashevis. *Reaches of Heaven: A Story of the Baal Shem Tov.* New York: Farrar, Straus and Giroux, 1982.

Slater, W., Hall, T., and Edwards, K. "Measuring Religion and Spirituality: Where Are We and Where Are We Going?" *Journal of Psychology and Theology* 29.1 (2001): 4–21.

Winner, Ellen. "The Rage to Master: The Decisive Case for Talent in the Visual Arts." In *The Road to Excellence: The Acquisition of Expert Performance in the Arts and Sciences, Sports and Games.* Hillsdale, NJ: Lawrence Erlbaum Associates, Inc., 1996.

Chapter 4

PassageWays:
A Model for Fostering the Spiritual
Development of Students and
Teachers in Schools

Rachael Kessler

It is that time in our Senior Passage course when we celebrate and honor childhood before the challenge of letting it go. We are asking the students to sift and sort, as they stand on the threshold to adulthood: What do you want to take with you? What do you want to leave behind because it no longer serves you?

All students are invited to share something precious from their own childhood that they want always to take with them. The almost musky scent of nostalgia wafts through the room as we all scan our memories for these precious moments, people, and places from childhood. A twilight glow seems to surround us as the stories are shared:

> "I would take with me the innocence of childhood, when I didn't even know that other people were different from me."
> "I would take my friend with whom I shared so much of my childhood; many good moments, and even bad ones."
> "I would take my village in the Sudan; my language, culture, all those things that everyone thinks I have forgotten, but I have not."
> "I would take the moonlight, and the truth of my imagination."
> "I would take my dress-up box and all the times I spent trying on so many ways of being."
> "I would take the song of the meadowlark, the smell of grass and the wet earth in the greenbelt behind my house where I spent so much of my childhood."[1]

Poised on the brink of huge decisions, departures, loss, confusion, and emergence, these sophisticated eighteen-year-olds are basking now in the sweetness of childhood that they have brought into the room. We have created together a space that is safe enough for tenderness.

Minutes later, we tell them it is time to come into the present, to explore in anonymous writing what they are wondering and worried about, curious, and afraid of. We give them paper and pencils to write their "personal mysteries," those thoughts they have when they lie awake at night. The moment they take hold of the pencils, the atmosphere in the room shifts. A flood has been unleashed. They turn their chairs every which way to separate from each other and begin to pour out onto the page for twenty minutes. I rest into the silence in the room, the soft sounds of lead on paper. I feel transported to a sense of deep trust. We have created together an atmosphere that is safe enough for the soul to speak.

Classrooms That Welcome Soul

Attention shifts when soul is present in education. We listen with great care not only to what is spoken but also to the messages between the words and tones, while watching gestures and the flicker of feelings across the face. We concentrate on what has heart and meaning. The yearning, wonder, wisdom, fear, and confusion of students become central to the curriculum. Questions become as important as answers.

When soul enters the classroom, masks drop away. Students dare to share the joy and talents they have feared would provoke jealousy in even their best friends. They risk exposing the pain or shame that might be judged as weakness. Seeing deeply into the perspective of others, accepting what has felt unworthy in their selves, students discover compassion and begin to learn about forgiveness.

For almost twenty years, I have worked with teams of educators around the country in both private and public school settings to create curriculum, methodology, and teacher development that can feed the awakening spirit of young people as part of school life. I call this approach "The PassageWays Program."[2] It is a set of principles and practices for working with adolescents that integrates heart, spirit, and community with strong academics. This curriculum of the heart is a response to the "mysteries" of teenagers: Their usually unspoken questions and concerns are at its center.

I first discovered this approach at the Crossroads School in Santa Monica, California, where I worked for seven years as Chair of the Department of Human Development and built the team that created the "Mysteries Program." In the 1990s, I began to take the gifts of "Mysteries" into schools around the country, adapting, refining, and expanding the curriculum to include what I learned from colleagues in the new and growing field of social and emotional learning. In those first years, I could not explain how our classes invited soul into the room. We were not, and are not, practicing religion or even talking about religion. Even so, the students reported that there was something "spiritual" about our classes. We had to figure out what they meant.

Most adolescents grapple with the profound questions of loss, love, and letting go; of meaning, purpose, and service; of self-reliance and community; and of choice and surrender. How they respond to these questions, whether with love, denial or even violence, can be profoundly influenced by the community of the classroom. When students work together to create an authentic community, they learn that they can meet any challenge with grace, love, and power; even wrenching conflict, prejudice, profound gratitude, or death. Creating authentic community is the first step in the soul of education.

How Can Classroom Teachers Invite Soul?

Safety in the classroom is essential to create the conditions for spiritual formation and to help students make the choices that build and sustain a life of compassion and integrity. Students need to feel safe:

- to feel and know what they feel;
- to tolerate confusion, uncertainty;
- to express what they feel and think;
- to ask questions that feel "dumb" or "have no answers;
- to take risks, make mistakes, and grow and forgive; and,
- to wrestle with the "demons" inside that lead us to harm.

To achieve this safety and openness, students and teachers in a classroom informed by PassageWays work together carefully for weeks and months to build the healthy relationships that lead to authentic community. Early in the semester, we collaboratively create agreements[3] that state conditions named by students as essential for speaking about what matters most to them. In classroom after classroom, across the country and the age span, students call for the same qualities of behavior: respect, honesty, caring, listening, fairness, openness, and commitment. As teachers, we add "the right to pass" and the willingness to learn about forgiveness.

PassageWays uses play to help students focus, relax, and become a team through laughter and cooperation. In addition to strengthening community and helping students become fully present, games and expressive arts engage them in body movement that is essential for the unwinding of the nervous system which can help them deal with over-stimulation and stress. Both play and the arts provide opportunities for young people to express the creative drive that is one essential avenue to nurturing the spirit of students.

Often at the beginning of class, we use silence as a way to help students "settle," to digest what they have been learning, to honor for a moment what is distracting them, to rest, daydream or pray so that they come refreshed and fully present to this new subject. Students learn to make friends with silence. An eighth-grade teacher who has integrated PassageWays practices for community building and increasing focusing abilities, calls this five to ten minute period a "solo time." Her students have responded with immense gratitude. "Why are your students so much more focused than mine?" asked a colleague in her department. A new math teacher reported that in the middle of a very difficult class in which students were frustrated and stumped, one student raised his hand and said, "What we need to solve this problem is a 'solo time.'" In the past year, four teachers in her school have adopted the use of silence because of her work and its impact on her students.

Teachers who integrate the PassageWays model spend weeks providing practice in the art of deep listening and authentic speaking, first in dyads and then in the larger circle. Students learn to let go of their own agenda and simply bear witness to what the other is saying. When speaking, they learn to look to themselves for what they want to say and not be so dependent on cues from others.

Symbols that students create or bring into class allow teenagers to speak indirectly about feelings and thoughts that are awkward to address head on. In PassageWays, we find that symbols are a powerful way to help students move quickly and deeply into their feelings. "Take some time this week to think about what is really important to you in your life right now," we ask the high school seniors in the course designed to be a rite of passage from adolescence to adulthood and described in the opening paragraph. "Then find an object which can symbolize what you realize is so important to you now."

This raggedy old doll belonged to my mother. I have been cut off from my mother during most of high school. We just couldn't get along. But now that we know I'm going to leave soon, we have suddenly discovered each other again. I love her so much. My relationship to my mother is what is really important to me now.

I wear this ring around my neck. It belongs to my father, but he has lent it to me. It's his wedding ring, and my parents are divorced. My father travels a lot and I worry about him. It feels good to have his ring close to my heart. And it reminds me of how precious relationships are. And how fragile.[4]

A principal in Canada shared a story from her days of teaching a first- and second-grade class where she also worked with symbols:

> I talked with my students about life being like a journey. As little as they were, they seemed to understand. They drew pictures about their journey. We talked about their journeys. Then I asked them to look for an object in nature that reminded them of themselves and of their journey. A first grade girl brought in a tiny pinecone. She said, "This pinecone is at the beginning of its life as a tree. It reminds me of me because I'm at the beginning of my journey as a person."
>
> A second-grade boy brought in two jars filled with shells. "I call these 'brain shells,'" he said pointing to the first jar. "They remind me of me because I'm very smart." Then, he held up the jar in which the same shells were crushed. "These crushed shells remind me of me too. They remind me of how hard I am on myself when I don't do things just right."[5]

While symbols are particularly important for adolescents because they allow an indirectness of expression at a time when young people need to create a separate sense of self, we can see that even for young children, symbols lead to profound self-awareness. Self-awareness, what Daniel Goleman considers the foundation skill of emotional intelligence, is essential to deep connection to the self and to meaningful communication that allows deep connection with others.[6]

Symbols can also be used as a private exercise in self-awareness. "Draw or sculpt a symbol of what you are feeling right now. You don't need to show it to anyone else. It's just for you." Here is another example: "Write a metaphor about what friendship means to you. You can share it with the group or keep it for yourself, putting it in your folder to look at when the semester ends."

"Questions of Wonder" or "Mysteries Questions" are another PassageWays tool for encouraging students to discover what is in their hearts. Once trust and respect are established in the classroom, we give students the opportunity to write anonymously the questions they think about when they cannot sleep at night, or when they are alone or daydreaming in class. Why am I here? Does my life have a purpose? How do I find it? I have been hurt so many times, I wonder if there is a God? How does one trust oneself or believe in oneself? How can I NOT be a cynic? Why this emptiness in this world, in my heart? How does this emptiness come, go away, and come back again? Why am I so alone? Why do I feel like the burden of the world is on my shoulders? Why do I feel scared and confused about becoming an adult? What does it mean to accept that this is my life and I have responsibility for it? Why was I given a divorced family?

These are some of thousands of questions I have gathered from teenagers 12 to 18 years of age since the mid-1980s. When students hear the collective "mysteries" of their own classroom community read back to them in an honoring voice by their teachers, there is always one student who says, "I can't believe I'm not alone anymore." Then another will say, "I can't believe you people wrote those questions." Sharing their deep concerns, their curiosity, wonder and wisdom, students begin to discover a deep interest in their peers, even the ones they have always judged to be unworthy of their attention and respect. The capacity for empathy has been stirred, and the search for meaning, so essential to spiritual formation, is validated and stimulated.

Into this profound interest in their peers we introduce the practice of council, the core of the PassageWays approach and several other programs as described in Jack Zimmerman and Virginia Coyle's *The Way of Council*.[7] With everyone sitting in a circle where all can see and be seen, the council process allows each person to speak without interruption or immediate response. Students learn to listen deeply and discover what it feels like to be truly heard. As each student reflects on the same theme, or tells a story from their life that illustrates how they currently think or feel about the theme, students who listen deeply find themselves "walking in another person's shoes." This structured practice for "multiple perspective-taking" provides a skill and an experience that lead to critical and creative thinking, as well as to the development of empathy and compassion. In council, students also experience stillness and silent reflection practiced in the company of others. Silence becomes a comfortable ally as we pause to digest one story and wait for another to form, or when teachers call for moments of reflection, or when the room fills with feeling at the end of a class.

> "I remember you guys, and I bet you remember me," said one, his voice quavering as he said his good-byes to the students in his Senior Passage course. "I was the guy you threw food at in the lunchroom. I was the kid you hurled insults at, like geek and dork. Well, you know what? I'm still a geek. I'm still a dork. I know that and so do you. But I also know something else. In the weeks and months of listening to your stories, and you listening to mine, I've seen that even the most beautiful girls in this class, the most beautiful girls in the world, have suffered with how they look or how others see them. I've shared your pain and you've shared mine. You guys have really taken me in. You've accepted me and respected me. I love you guys, and I know you love me."[8]

"Apprehending the other's reality, feeling what he feels as nearly as possible," says Nel Noddings in *Caring: A Feminine Approach to Ethics & Moral Education* "is the essential part of caring from the view of the one caring. For if I take on the other's reality as possibility and begin to feel its reality, I feel also that I must act accordingly."[9] In the young man's story above, we can see clearly the possibilities for compassion and caring that arise when students have the opportunity to meet as a group in ways that go beyond civility, beyond cooperation, to discover a genuine communing heart to heart, soul to soul. Even those who are estranged, alienated, or who see themselves as enemies have experienced through PassageWays the joy of transcending mistrust, stereotypes, and prejudice that once felt like permanent barriers.

A sixth grade team is discovering that Passages allows their students to enter middle school without the usual descent into cruelty. "I have never had kids who treated each other with such kindness," said a first-year teacher implementing PassageWays and shared the following story of reconciliation and forgiveness that emerged during their weekly PassageWays hour:

"I feel like a lot of you don't even know my name," said one student. "When we do stuff together, you don't look at me most of the time...and you never call me by my name. It makes me feel invisible."

It was already February in this sixth grade class. The teacher listened as each of the students in the circle took turns speaking. Working for the first time with the PassageWays program, she and her partner had never seen sixth grade students learn to treat each other with such kindness. But the class was taking a downward turn. Students were having hurt feelings, especially from the actions of the more "popular crowd." Responding to this decline in morale, she had organized a council around the simple questions: "How are things going in our classroom? Is there anything you have felt hurt about that you want to share? What do you need to help you heal, and for this to be a better place to learn?

"Sometimes I feel people are making fun of me because of the clothes I wear...I can't afford the Abercrombie clothes that some of you wear, but that doesn't mean you have a right to make fun of me."

"What hurts me is that the big jock gods don't seem to think that the rest of us matter," said a sad-eyed boy. "I feel like some of you are saying mean things behind my back, and laughing at me."

As the council continued, the teacher felt sad, but not surprised. During the first semester, this class had avoided the usual descent into the now common cruelties of early adolescence. Since the new year, a coldness had begun to creep in. Using one of the methods she learned in the PassageWays course, the teacher decided it was time to try to turn things around. She had cautioned the students not to name names—to speak specifically about the behaviors that felt hurtful to them, but to avoid being hurtful to others.

When the round was completed, one of the "popular" boys spoke up: "I want to know if it was me that hurt some of you because I would want to apologize." He seemed genuinely upset. It was as if he was getting a window into the hearts of those he had dismissed. The teacher encouraged him to approach students privately if he thought he had caused them harm.

"Thank you all for your honesty and courage," the teacher said to the group after the final person in the circle finished speaking. "It feels so much better to have these feelings out in the open, doesn't it?" She paused as several heads nodded. "I really appreciate the way you have listened to each other." She paused again, noting that the group was completely still and present. "I wonder if any of you would be willing to say something more about what you need in order to go forward with the school year and feel better about being in the class."

"I wish..." one student began, but stopped, unsure how to put into words what she was feeling. "I wish you would not look at the clothes I wear, and just find out who I am."

"I need to be called by my name. If you don't remember it, ask me. I will be happy to tell you."

"If you don't like me, that's okay," said a girl who had chosen not to speak in an earlier round. "But *please* don't try to get other people to side with you. *Please* let other people just decide for themselves, okay?"

The teacher was impressed that everyone remained silent while the girl who had just spoken wiped away a tear. As a teacher, those little signs that students were attending to each other's needs meant so much to her. Taken together, those small shifts made the difference between a group of strangers and a community of learners.

"I want to ask you not to whisper and laugh when you are around me," said the boy whose eyes no longer seemed sad but filled with an intensity never seen before. "Maybe you're not making fun of me, but it feels that way. So I'd appreciate your helping me deal with that."

The teacher closed the council by thanking the students once again, and also encouraging them to apologize to each other if they felt they had hurt someone, even unintentionally. If she had any doubts that the council had an impact, they vanished in the coming days.

"I feel so good—so clean!" said one student a few days later. "I apologized and now it feels so good between us."

"I had no idea some of the things I was doing would feel so awful to others," confided one of the more popular girls at the end of a school day.

A few other students learned that apologies were not panaceas.

"I tried..." said one of the boys. "I apologized and he just walked away."

"Sometimes healing takes time. He's probably waiting to see if you really mean it or not. Let your behavior show that you have had a change of heart."

As the class came back together during the spring months, the teacher traced back the shift to that day of the council. She was grateful that, instead of watching helplessly as the class came apart, she had known what to do.[10]

Gateways to the Soul of Students

Listening to the stories of students over fifteen years, reading thousands of "Mysteries Questions," I began to see a pattern of what nourishes the inner life of children and youths. As we seek ways to foster spiritual formation in our students while respecting the separation of church and state, these "gateways" provide clues to the opportunities we can create.

1. Search for Meaning and Purpose

The search for meaning and purpose concerns the exploration of existential questions that burst forth in adolescence. "Why am I here? Does my life have a purpose? How do I find out what it is? What does my future hold? Is there life after death? Is there a God?" I've read these questions time and again when students write anonymously about their personal "mysteries" involving wonder, worries, curiosity, fear, and excitement.

This domain of meaning and purpose is crucial to motivation and learning for students. However, it can also be paradoxically simple and uncomfortable for teachers to deal with. Teachers who predicate their authority on the ability to "know," or to have the "right answer" are profoundly uncomfortable with questions that appear to have no answers. In most schools "purpose" is primarily taught through goal setting and decision-making, often with strictly rational techniques. However, when the spiritual dimension is omitted, or if the inner life of the adolescent is not cultivated as part of the search for goals or careers, they will most likely base their decisions on external pressures from peers, parents, teachers. One student writes:

> So many of my friends are so clueless. They don't know what they want to do; they know what they're supposed to do. They don't know how they feel. They know how they're supposed to feel. And here I find myself in a group of people going through all my same stuff, and although I don't have the answers to all the questions, I find myself feeling like everything is perfect and right...I have this "community" that gives me a home base and a sense of security.

Educators can provide experiences that honor the big questions. They can also allow students to give their gifts to the world through school and community service, through creative expression, or academic or athletic achievement. In the way we teach, we can help students see and create patterns that connect learning to their personal lives. A student helps explain:

> When I go over to the local elementary school to tutor two Spanish-speaking children, they are so excited to see me. I guess they don't get too much attention from a teacher and a classroom that is strictly English speaking…When I am with them, I feel special. I am an average student at my school; I don't hold any elected positions, I am not on any varsity team. I do not stand out in any way, and that is okay with me. It is okay with me because for 3 hours each week, Maria and Miguel make me feel like I am the most important person in the world.

2. Longing for Silence and Solitude

The longing for silence and solitude can lead to identity formation and goal setting, to learning readiness and inner peace. For adolescents, this domain is often ambivalent, fraught with both fear and urgent need. As a respite from the tyranny of busyness and noise that afflicts even our young children, silence may be a realm of reflection, calm, or fertile chaos; an avenue of stillness and rest for some, prayer or contemplation for others. A student writes:

> I like to take time to go within myself sometimes. And when I do that, I try to take an emptiness inside there. I think that everyone struggles to find their own way with their spirit and it's in the struggle that our spirit comes forth.

3. Urge for Transcendence

The urge for transcendence describes the desire of young people to go beyond their perceived limits. "How far can I be stretched, how much adversity can I stand?" writes one student. "Is there a greater force at work? Can humans tap into that force, and bring it into their daily lives?" writes another. Transcendence includes not only the mystical realm, but also secular experiences of the extraordinary in the arts, athletics, academics, or human relations. By naming this human need that spans all cultures, educators can help students constructively channel this urge and challenge themselves in ways that reach for this peak experience.

4. Hunger for Joy and Delight

The hunger for joy and delight can be satisfied through experiences of great simplicity, such as play, celebration, or gratitude. "I want to move many and take joy in every person, every little thing," writes one student. Another asks: "Do all people have the same capacity to feel joy and sorrow?" Educators can also help students express the exaltation they feel when encountering beauty, power, grace, brilliance, love, or the sheer joy of being alive.

5. Creativity

The creative drive is perhaps the most familiar domain for nourishing the spirit of students in secular schools. In opportunities for acts of creation, people often encounter their participation in a process infused with depth, meaning, and mystery. Asked if she felt there was any connection between creativity and her spirit, an eighth-grade girl responded, "Of course there is. Creativity is the outreach of your spirit into form so you can see it, touch it, feel it."

6. Call for Initiations

The call for initiation refers to a hunger the ancients met through rites of passage for their young. As educators, we can create programs that guide adolescents to become conscious about the irrevocable transition from childhood to adulthood, give them tools for making transitions and separations, challenge them to discover the capacities for their next step and create ceremonies with parents and other faculty that acknowledge and welcome them into the community of adults.

Students who have had the opportunity to experience the support of a school program designed to be a rite of passage learn that they can move on to their next step with strength and grace. "A senior in high school must make colossal decisions whether he or she is ready or not," writes one fellow, describing the impact of the program on his life. He adds:

The more people can be honest about and aware of their own needs when making these decisions, the healthier the decisions will be. This class has provided me with an environment that allows me to clear my head, slow down, and make healthy choices for me.

A young woman from Colorado described it this way:

It is difficult for me to express the depth and meaning of this group in a way that does it justice. It has taught me that I have the power to control my destiny, but also to let it guide me when necessary. I have learned to see the beauty in myself, others, the world. Along with this I have become more accepting of my weaknesses. The group has created an environment for all of us to see and learn things that have always been present, just not recognized.

In addition to the Senior Passage course, the PassageWays Institute is currently creating curricula for supporting students through the completion of elementary and middle school, and through the challenges of entering the cultures in secondary schools. Our Newcomers Transition Program provides a structured opportunity for students who are recent immigrants and refugees to grieve their losses, celebrate their new goals and explore a new sense of self that integrates who they have been in the past with who they are becoming as citizens of a new culture.[11]

7. Yearning for Deep Connection

The common thread is deep connection. As my students tell stories about each of these domains, I hear a common thread: the experience of deep connection. This seventh domain describes a quality of relationship that is profoundly caring, resonant with meaning, and involves feelings of belonging, and of being truly seen or known.

Through deep connection to the self, a student encounters strength and richness that are the basis for developing the autonomy central to the adolescent journey, discovering purpose and unlocking creativity. Teachers can nourish this form of deep connection by giving students time for solitary reflection. Classroom exercises that encourage reflection and expression through writing or art can also allow a student access to the inner self while in the midst of other people. Totally engrossed in such creative activities, students are encouraged to discover and express their own feelings, values, and beliefs.

Connecting deeply to another person or to a meaningful group, young people discover the balm of belonging that soothes the profound alienation that fractures the identity of our youths and prevents them from contributing to our communities. Students feel a sense of belonging when they are part of an authentic community in the classroom, a community in which they feel seen and heard for who they really are. Many teachers create this opportunity through "morning meetings," advisory groups, weekly councils or sharing circles offered in a context of ground rules that make it safe to be vulnerable. The teacher must continue to support the autonomy and uniqueness of the individual while fostering a sense of belonging and union with the group. The more that young people are encouraged to strengthen their own boundaries and develop their own identity, the more capable they are of bonding to a group in a healthy, enduring way.

Some students connect deeply to nature: "When I get depressed," revealed a young woman to her "family group" members in a school in Manhattan, "I go to this park near my house where there is an absolutely enormous tree. I go and sit down with it because it feels so strong to me."

"It was my science teacher who awakened my spirit," said a teacher about his high school days in Massachusetts. "He conveyed a sense of awe about the natural world that would change me forever."

And some students discover solace in their relationship to God or to a religious practice. Writes one, "I try to practice being present. That's what Buddhism has given to me that I really cherish. It's really the most important thing to me now." Another writes, "I became a Christian a few years back. It's been the most wonderful thing in my life. I can't tell you what it feels like to know that I'm loved like that.

Always loved and guided by Jesus. And it's brought our family much closer."

When students know there is a time in school life where they may give voice to the great comfort and joy they find in their relationship to God or to nature, this freedom of expression itself nourishes their spirits. The First Amendment actually protects students' rights to freely express their own religious beliefs. However, we teachers must be careful not to share our religious beliefs because, given the power and public nature of our role, students may experience a teacher's sharing as proselytizing. However, in our fear and confusion about violating the law, we have actually suppressed student freedom and the rich exchange that comes when such an important part of their lives is acknowledged and respected.

Students who feel deeply connected do not need danger to feel fully alive. They do not need guns to feel powerful. They do not want to hurt others or themselves. Out of connection grows compassion and passion: passion for people, for students' goals and dreams, for life itself.

Teachers Who Welcome Soul

Because "we teach who we are," teachers who invite heart and soul into the classroom also find it essential to nurture their own spiritual development. This may mean personal practices to cultivate awareness, serenity, and compassion, as well as collaborative efforts with other teachers to give and receive support for the challenges and joys of entering this terrain with their students.[12]

We can have the best curricula available, train teachers in technique and theory, but our students will be unsafe and our programs hollow if we do not provide opportunities for teachers to cultivate their own spiritual formation and their own emotional intelligence. Students are reluctant to open their hearts unless they feel their teachers are on the journey themselves, working on personal as well as curriculum integration. Here I will briefly summarize "the willingness to care" that is one dimension of what, in PassageWays, we call "The Teaching Presence."[13]

The capacity of the teacher to care deeply for students is the foundation of all of the classroom practices described above. When students do not trust adults, a common phenomenon in today's society, they are not motivated to learn from us and will certainly not embrace our values or ethical beliefs. "The bonds that transmit basic human values from elders to the young are unraveling," write Brendtro, Van Bockern, and Clementson as they describe why so many youths are wary of adults. "If the social bond between adult and child is absent, conscience fails to develop and the transmission of values is distorted or aborted."[14]

Nel Noddings adds another dimension to understanding the crucial role of the caring bond between teachers and students: "Kids learn in communion. They listen to people who matter to them and to whom they matter.... Caring relations can prepare children for an initial receptivity to all sorts of experiences and subject matters."[15] The receptivity Noddings speaks of which grows out of authentic caring from adults is critical not only to academic learning but to the "transmission of values," the willingness of our students to embrace the values and caring behavior we practice and preach.

In 2002, I had the opportunity to speak about *The Soul of Education* in Beijing to administrators from international schools. My host was extremely nervous that if I spoke of anything that suggested religion, the authorities could close down the conference. I was reminded of the preciousness of our rights, our freedom of spiritual exploration and expression back home. More than ever I see that in a pluralistic society, educators can provide a forum that honors the many and diverse ways individual students nourish their spirits. We can offer activities that allow them to experience deep connection. In the search itself, in loving the questions, in the deep yearning they let themselves feel, young people will discover what is sacred in life, what is sacred in their own lives, and what allows them to bring their most sacred gifts to nourish the world.

Notes

[1] These childhood memories are representative of the many personal stories shared during years of facilitating Senior Passage courses. While the voices of students expressed throughout the chapter are based on real discussions, names and identities are naturally protected with utmost care and confidentiality.

[2] The PassageWays Program has three roots: (1) the Mysteries Program at Crossroads School for Arts and Science, Santa Monica, California, where core methods in a program for high school seniors, developed by Jack Zimmerman, were expanded into a curriculum for Grades 7–12 by a team of teachers I led as Chair of the Department of Human Development, 1985–1991; (2) teacher-training programs that I have offered over the last decade through the PassageWays Institute (formerly the Institute for Social and Emotional Learning); and (3) discussions with colleagues through the Collaborative for Academic, Social & Emotional Learning (CASEL).

[3] In the language of adult groups, agreements would be called "ground rules" or "norms." We find the former term more effectively engages students in a sense of empowerment over their classroom.

[4] The two vignettes are examples of the powerful symbolic nature of certain objects in the lives of secondary school seniors.

[5] This story came from a member of the audience at a keynote I presented in Calgary, Alberta, for school principals. She was correcting my assumption that working with symbols may not be appropriate for younger children since I worked only with adolescents.

[6] Reference to Daniel Goleman's significant work in the field of emotional intelligence is found in my book, *The Soul of Education* (Alexandria, VA: Association for Supervision and Curriculum Development, 2000), 83.

[7] Jack Zimmerman and Virginia Coyle, *The Way of Council* (Las Vegas: Bramble Books, 1997).

[8] This comes from a young man speaking during the closure phase of a Senior Passage Course. It is described in *The Soul of Education* as an example of how students create and experience moments of "transcendence" when they overcome long-standing prejudice and conflict they had believed to be intractable.

[9] Nel Noddings, *Caring: A Feminine Approach to Ethics & Moral Education* (Berkeley, CA: University of California Press, 2003), 16.

[10] Adapted from the PassageWays Journal of Mrs. Cindy Matthews, Sixth Grade Teacher, Platt Middle School, Boulder, Colorado, 2002–2003, Passages Curriculum Team Teacher.

[11] Programs are now available for the completion of elementary school and for entering the culture of middle school. The "Newcomers Transition Program" is currently being developed, as is the completion of middle school and the entry passage into high school.

[12] For a series of reflection questions and group exercises designed for teachers to work on their own formation in each of the gateways, please see my article "Soul of Students, Soul of Teacher: Welcoming the Inner Life to Schools," in *Schools with Spirit,* ed. Linda Lantieri (Boston, MA: Beacon Press, 2001).

[13] See http://www.PassageWays.org for the latest version of this article or "The Teaching Presence," *The Virginia Journal of Education* 94.2 (November 2000), 7–10.

[14] Larry Brendtro, Steve Van Bockern, and John Clementson, "Adult-wary and Angry, Restoring Social Bonds," *Holistic Education Review* 8.1 (March 1995), 35–43.

[15] Nel Noddings, *The Challenge to Care in Schools* (New York: Teachers College Press, 1992), 36.

Works Consulted

Brendtro, Larry, Steve Van Bockern, and John Clementson. Adult-wary and angry: Restoring social bonds. *Holistic Education Review* 8.1 (March 1995): 35–43.

Goleman, Daniel. *Emotional Intelligence.* New York: Bantam Books, 1997.

Kessler, Rachael. Soul of Students, Soul of Teacher: Welcoming the Inner Life to Schools. *Schools with Spirit: Nurturing the Inner Lives of Children and Teachers,* Ed. Linda Lantieri. Boston, MA: Beacon Press.

——. *The Soul of Education: Helping Students Find Connection, Compassion, and Character at School.* Alexandria, VA: Association for Supervision and Curriculum Development, 2000.

——. The Teaching Presence. *The Virginia Journal of Education* 94.2 (November 2000): 7–10.

Noddings, Nel. *Caring: A Feminine Approach to Ethics and Moral Education.* Berkeley, CA: University of California Press, 2003.

——. *The Challenge to Care in Schools: An Alternative Approach to Education.* New York: Teachers College Press, 1992.

Zimmerman, Jack, and Virginia Coyle. *The Way of Council.* Las Vegas, NV: Bramble Books, 1997.

Chapter 5

The Net of Faith:
Religious Studies, Campus Ministry, and Christian Service in a Religious Secondary School

Sister Ramona Bascom, O.P.

In "Understanding and Guiding Teenage Spirituality," Sister Carole Riley contends that "teens dream of truth, authenticity and integrity" and that it is the privileged role of the adult "to assist the adolescent to honor the dream."[1] Reflecting on more than thirty years of high school administration and teaching, I see in my mind's eye hundreds of young women who are achieving this dream. I honor the many educators, both lay and religious, who have assisted them, and the schools which have provided the necessary tools, including a giant safety net,[2] that encourage the risk taking necessary to their growth.

The great adventure and task of our lives is the journey with one another on the road to Ultimate Truth, to and with God. Conscious of this adventure, teens are at a stage in their lives when they are asking some of the ultimate questions. To help them discover the answers or the other necessary questions, adolescents need environments that offer both the theory and practice of their spiritual tradition, as well as adult models to guide them in this great adventure of the spiritual life. One's relationship with God is of the utmost importance. In their growth toward independence, young people are open to and searching for ways to claim God as their own without becoming indifferent to, or having to reject, their spiritual religious heritage. Religious schools provide settings that nourish the faith development of the youths entrusted to them in a spirit of reverence for the mystery of God's interaction with the individual. The pedagogical goals of religious education are to present solid doctrine, morality, and values; to help with the understanding of sacred scripture; to present and to practice models of personal and communal prayer; and to offer opportunities for compassionate service to others. These goals must be sustained while preserving the sacredness of the individual conscience in a spirit of faith and trust, respecting God-given individual freedom and allowing open-ended questioning in an authentic atmosphere that encourages students in the achievement of their dreams.

One such religious school is Flintridge Sacred Heart Academy, a small, day and resident Catholic, independent girls' school in Southern California, owned and operated by the Dominican Sisters. The 400 member student body is ethnically diverse, including young women of African American, Asian, Hispanic, and Native American ancestry, and represents most major religions, although most students are Catholic. The 800-year-old Dominican tradition is to preach the gospel and to seek Truth while giving to others the fruits of one's contemplation. It is a flexible tradition that honors diversity and walks hand in hand with others in the life quest for Truth. I mention this only because it has helped us develop a holistic approach to the education of young women. "The faith life of the school community is nourished through a comprehensive program of instruction, service and spiritual experiences, thus rendering it living, conscious and active, in the school, the family, and the local and world communities."[3]

Some issues that teens face in their development include: a great need to belong, seeing themselves as different, constantly dealing with friendship issues, laboring under enormous stress, self-doubt, and perhaps finding themselves on an emotional roller coaster. They need to feel safe and empowered, know that they are not alone and realize that, though unique, they are not the only ones asking the question, at least interiorly, "Who am I?" It is our privilege to help them in these developmental tasks and, through our own lives as well as our teaching, help them to discover and to know God, not as the child knows but as the young maturing adult knows.[4]

This chapter discusses the Religious Studies curriculum and the Campus Ministry program that directs the retreats, Christian service, liturgies, LIFE (Living in Faith Experience), and other spiritually centered activities. Together, these areas help to promote the giant safety net in which students can feel safe, empowered, and unique within a community of faith. The Campus Minister and the Religious Studies Department Chair work closely to oversee and integrate each area into the total school program. The administration, faculty, and staff support this endeavor because it is intrinsic to the philosophy, goals, and mission of the school.

Religious Studies Program

The Religious Studies curriculum is a four-year sequential curriculum, designed to give the student "a strong knowledge of lived faith that finds its center in the experience of Jesus."[5] Throughout their four years the students learn that theology interacts with the culture and that capitalism and materialism are values within mainstream American culture. Critical thinking skills are necessary for our students to look at their culture and criticize it in order to be able to practice their religion, holding fast to the gospel values. They need to be able to stand apart and be counter-cultural when such a stance is necessary, as well as to embrace cultural goodness.

A religious tradition gives a set of values by which to critique and then to make decisions in the light of this tradition. Students need to learn what to accept and what to reject. This, of course, has enormous implications for the adolescent in light of: friends, integrity, false values, drugs, alcohol, and risky sexual activity. It can help them realize that "not everybody is doing it." For example, media in the form of videos, CDs, movie or TV clips are presented during discussions about cultural values—some of which are antithetical to most religious traditions. In addition, students are taught to respect each other through learning about other religious traditions and gaining an appreciation of cultural diversity.

Sacred Scripture is used throughout for study, prayer, reflection, and in the celebration of the liturgical year. The girls keep journals in which they relate personal experience to a particular passage in scripture. Sometimes a question is used relative to a particular theme: "When did you suffer most? Reflect on suffering in current culture using *The Gospel of Mark*, the *Book of Job* and Frankl's *Man's Search for Meaning*." It is imperative that the students see their faith tied to their personal experience in order for them to make it their own.

Each year the girls are taught and practice a variety of prayers. Prayer precedes classroom instruction, activities, games, assemblies, and meetings. The students are exposed to prayer styles such as adoration, praise, thanksgiving, and petition, both formal and informal, spontaneous and prepared, some of which are centuries old. Meditation and contemplative prayer are also practiced often including centering prayer and reflection on a scripture passage or one from a mystical writer. The rich spiritual heritage of Julian of Norwich, Catherine of Siena, Meister Eckhart, John of the Cross, Theresa of Avila, and Teilhard de Chardin are treasures for today's world. The annual retreats and days of recollection also give them opportunity to practice other prayer forms. The goal is to help them find a way of prayer that most suits them at this time in their life as well as give them something else to draw upon as they mature. Each religious studies classroom has a prayer table and the students are encouraged to have one of their own at home. The campus has many religious symbols throughout, including works of art, statues, and posters. It is important to help the girls see and find God in all things, all places, and all people.

The Sacraments are also part of the yearly curriculum. The world and the universe are the Sacrament of God, no less than Sacred Scripture. Anywhere we encounter God is a Sacrament. Students study the meaning and importance of signs and symbols. They make use of the prayer of ritual; they study the Seven Sacraments and see how each parallels the major rites of passage in our lives. They study the history of the sacraments over the past two thousand years and try their hand at composing prayers that would be appropriate. In the classroom, they reenact the Sacraments of Baptism, Healing of the Sick, and Matrimony.

Curriculum

Freshman Year: An overview of the Judeo-Christian tradition through the lens of Catholicism. The student is introduced to the Catholic understanding that the life of faith is a journey and that the beginning of high school usually marks a new level of faith development. The course is designed as a survey of the Scripture and Tradition that comprise the Catholic heritage. The first section is an exploration of identity and development. The second semester is a survey of the world's major religions. The approach is one of global awareness and sensitivity. It is an objective survey meant to focus on the truth about religion rather than the truth of a particular religion. The drama teacher became a powerful, living sermon when he changed the dates of one of our productions because one of the leading ladies was Jewish and the production date conflicted with a major Jewish holiday. Here was respect in action from a well-loved and highly respected teacher.

Sophomore Year: The first semester is entitled "Sacraments." The student discovers how human life itself is a sacrament, and how the rituals of the seven official Sacraments celebrate God's presence, especially in the major stages of our lives. Students will come to understand "sacrament" through the rituals and symbols of their lived experiences and to see that the clearest and fullest Sacrament of God's love comes to us in the person of Jesus Christ. The second semester focuses on ethics and morality and is a course about moral decision-making, applying Catholic Christian principles toward the resolution of ethical dilemmas in life. It strives to empower young women to learn how to discern what is morally right even in complex situations.

The girls are encouraged to recognize that all of life is a sacred gift from God and that moral decision-making is a choice to respond responsibly to God's free gift. Over the years I have had girls, both individually and in small groups, come to my office to describe, somewhat indignantly, an immoral situation (stealing from the lunch truck, bad example at a party, and the like) and ask "What are you going to do about it? You can't let them get away with it." After a discussion about their responsibility as well as mine we have come to a positive solution. What has pleased me each time is the freedom the girls felt to come and talk, as well as their recognition of something wrong that needed to be corrected. One student, caught cheating in class, wrote me a note of gratitude for what she had learned and followed it up after graduation again describing her appreciation for the life lessons she learned at the school.

Junior Year: This year is dedicated to the study of Sacred Scripture, both the Hebrew Scriptures and the Christian Scriptures, through which we are able to touch God, to listen to God, and to respond. The tools of literary genre and of literary criticism are taught in the junior English class and go hand in glove with their study of scripture. Because the girls are also studying foreign languages, they are aware of the difficulties of works in translation. The history and social customs of the times are also taken into account so that the students may approach the scriptures intelligently and prayerfully.

Senior Year: In Applied Theology and Faith Issues the seniors are invited to explore and re-examine all that they have learned to date in their religious studies courses. They are asked to integrate it all through more sophisticated theological reflections on their own personal faith experiences and the personal faith experiences of others. The second semester is Christology. The girls begin with an understanding of the historical Jesus, and explore the evolution of Christology from the early Christian Church's first experience of Jesus to modern understandings, including feminist and liberation Christology.

On each level the individual teachers are vital because not only are they teaching the subject matter, but they are also sharing their faith life with God. Teens are wonderful at detecting any falsity in the teacher of any subject area, but none more so than this. We have all experienced the great "hypocrisy detector" of the adolescent. The religious studies teacher must be one who not only relates well, but also has a passion for the subject and is imbued with deep faith and love, while at the same time being able to share with the adolescent the struggles of the faith journey.

The Campus Ministry Program

The Campus Ministry program is the laboratory component of religious education and encompasses retreats, liturgies, days of recollection, prayer services, and Christian service. It is directed by the Campus Minister, a mature, committed Christian woman, who serves as leader, role model, mentor, and spiritual director. A key role, the Campus Minister is aware of the needs of the faith community and seeks multiple ways to meet these needs. She works closely with the administration, the counseling department, the faculty and the religious education teachers. She trains and works with the student campus ministers in their leadership roles, particularly as retreat team members.

Liturgy

The all-school and class liturgies involve dance, together with instrumental and vocal music, that are used as prayer. Both drama and dance were used in the liturgy during the Middle Ages and have enhanced liturgical worship ever since. It is important for the student to realize that as humans our body is part of our worship and prayer. Gestures, standing, kneeling, singing, and dancing are all prayer. The liturgies are planned by the students under the direction of a teacher and include music, songs, dance, petitions, theme, and homily. Liturgies for the entire student body offer the opportunity for the "school as local church" to come together and worship God. Communal prayer nourishes the individual as well as the community. These services must meet the needs of the adolescent and help to deepen their faith, give them leadership roles in planning the liturgy as well as encourage them to participate in it in a meaningful way. The liturgy meets the needs of the seasons and events of the school community. The girls learn to bring everything to prayer and to the praying community.

This was apparent in three recent events: 9/11, the death of a beloved science teacher, and the death of a junior suffering from cancer. For a remembrance of 9/11 the girls, together with the liturgy coordinator, planned a very meaningful ecumenical prayer service with representatives from all of the major religions. It gave to the entire school community a sense of belonging to something so much bigger than our local selves. The unexpected death the following week of a beloved science teacher was a terrible blow to everyone. His wife wanted the funeral memorial service to be held at Flintridge Sacred Heart Academy because this was his home away from home. She asked for our priest chaplain to say the Mass of Resurrection. Alumnae came from far and near as did parents and students. It was a beautiful, moving tribute, all the more touching because neither the teacher nor his wife was Catholic. The junior class put together a beautiful memorial service for their classmate who died out of season on her seventeenth birthday. She had fought cancer valiantly since the end of her freshman year. Her classmates spoke, sang, and danced their prayer in an auditorium at Forest Lawn to over a thousand assembled people. Her parents had asked that the girls be a major part of the service.

Retreat Experiences

Annual class retreats are invaluable as the "laboratory component" of the religious studies class. In a relaxed atmosphere, off-campus, the students and the retreat team have an opportunity to pray, to listen to the word proclaimed by both students and adults, to give witness to the faith that is within them, to discuss and question, in short to form a faith community which is both supportive and nourishing. As with the religious studies program, each retreat is designed and structured to meet the developmental needs of the students. The major topics of each year's retreat also dovetail with the major themes and topics of the religious studies class, while the individual teacher of the grade is a retreat team member.

The Freshman Retreats: There are two one-day retreats, one at the beginning of the school year and one at the beginning of the second semester. Their themes include transition to high school and membership in a faith community.

The first semester focuses on being a part of a faith community. Topics covered include identity and development, faith as a response to God's call, and Church as a gathering in the Spirit of Jesus. The day includes both large and small group presentations, periods of reflection and discussions. Older students give presentations about their own transitions to high school. The opening prayer is a scripture reading with reflection and petitions with the large group. The small groups do shared prayer and the group leaders pray personal blessings upon the members of their group. Journaling is an important part of this day.

In the early part of the second semester the freshmen have their second day on campus but away from the school classroom building. The theme is "bloom where you are planted" and the format is much the same as the first semester. The girls are told that they are planted in a specific faith community in this particular school. Flintridge Sacred Heart, though predominately Roman Catholic, enrolls students 25% of whom represent other traditions including Protestant, Buddhist, Jewish, Sikh, and Muslim. There is no attempt to proselytize. Rather the focus is on God and one's relationship to God, using one's own faith tradition. We can always be a faith community, as long as we respect one another's faith tradition. At her admissions interview the parents of one recent graduate explained that they realized their daughter needed to be in a religious environment because they had not given her one. They said that they had mistakenly thought to let her be and choose her own religion. Her mother was Presbyterian and her father Jewish; neither of them practiced. Their daughter was a great asset to the school and soaked up everything, especially the arts. Shortly after her Kairos retreat in her senior year, she confided in me that she had decided on her religion. When I asked her which one, she replied "Jewish. I want to have my Bat Mitzvah." Both her parents and the school community rejoiced with her.

The focus of the second semester is World Religions, which allows for open discussion, exploration, and sharing of one another's faith traditions. The girls reflect on Divine Providence as well as on their individual gifts that are to be shared for the good of the community. There is an emphasis on the recognition of each individual as gifted by God. As a symbol of this, the freshmen plant seeds, following their growth throughout the rest of the year. (Yes, occasionally the plants die which is not to be taken as a negative sign. The plant is replaced, amidst some teasing.)

The Sophomore Retreats: The retreat theme includes the Paschal Mystery of life, death, and resurrection, the Sacramental Awareness of the Seven Sacraments, and the sacraments of daily life. These topics are the focus of the first semester of the students' religious studies course.

A two-and-one-half day off-campus retreat with the entire class occurs during the second semester. Because the topics of friendship and relationships are so integral to this age level, especially for girls, there is an emphasis on friendship. Meditation walks, prayer in small groups, and guided meditation in a large group are part of the first day. Morning and night prayers are held; presentations are made by the LIFER's on understanding God as our primary relationship in life, and the need to make decisions in the light of this relationship. The second semester religious studies focus is on morality and ethics. Needless to say young people at this age need all of the help they can get in making their decisions based on strong moral principles rather than on the influence of the group or on the spur of the moment. The sophomore year seems to be a particularly difficult transition year for adolescent girls.

The Junior Retreats: In mid-September, while the weather is still wonderful, the entire junior class goes to Howland's Landing on Santa Catalina Island, some 20 miles off the coast of Los Angeles. The staff at Howland's Landing is knowledgeable in ecology, marine biology, and the flora and fauna of the island, which is largely undeveloped. Howland's Landing is a small cove inaccessible to others, except by boat, so it is an ideal place for an extended four-day retreat allowing the retreatants to focus on the topic at hand with no outside distractions. The retreat theme is that of journey, our relationship to nature and to the God of Nature, and learning to see God in all of creation. There is an emphasis on ecological spirituality and our responsibility as stewards to care for Mother Earth, our home and God's creation. We need to see all of creation as an interrelated community. There is an added emphasis on developing and recognizing one's inner strength. On this retreat the student leaders are juniors, trained to lead the small group discussions, making sure that their group is at the appointed place on time. The staff of Howland's Landing is responsible for the activities of each day. These include snorkeling, kayaking, hiking, handling an obstacle/ropes course, star-gazing, and composting. There are lectures by the staff before each event and comments during the event. Each activity is done in small groups with a Howland's Landing staff member plus a faculty member in attendance. Everything is outdoors; simple cabins provide the sleeping area.

Each day begins with morning prayer. There is a reflection by an adult leader, small group discussions, journaling, short readings by mystics such as Teilhard de Chardin, Henry David Thoreau, Ralph Waldo Emerson, Meister Eckhart, Julian of Norwich, Anne Morrow Lindbergh, Thomas Merton, and Catherine of Siena, to name a few. Because the juniors study Advanced Placement Environmental Studies and American Literature, there is an attempt to coordinate some of the readings to reflect interdisciplinary ecological and philosophical perspectives. During an evening talent show, the girls are able to see the interconnectedness of their studies of literature, science, and scripture. The more the students can see that all that they are studying is integral to living, the better. Each day ends with small group reflection and night prayer, while on the last day, there is a celebration of the Eucharist. The retreat is followed up with a one-day gathering of all participants in the spring. It is a particularly meaningful experience for the juniors, giving them a jump-start as upper-class women. It integrates fully the international students, helping them to realize their own unique gifts and contribution to the class. They know they belong.

The Senior Retreat: The seniors have a four-day retreat called Kairos. Half of the class attends at the end of the first semester and the other half attends at the beginning of the second semester. There are both adult and student leaders. The two student directors are graduates, usually from the last two graduating classes, who are attending college in the Southern California region. They bring a maturity and experience that meets the needs of the seniors. Several weeks prior to the retreat, the adult retreat director trains the senior leaders. Different teachers mentor the individual leader as she prepares her major talk. This retreat focuses on one's relationship with God and on the gift and responsibilities of that relationship. The Kairos retreat has lifelong significance for students. One graduate, a Kairos leader in her senior year, was killed in an auto accident shortly after her marriage.

Her Kairos medallion was hanging in her car. Both her husband and her parents wanted her buried with it. Her husband said that she always had the medallion with her and had told him all about the retreat.

Like most of the retreats there is a sequential development. This one starts with knowing oneself and one's background, then knowing one's values based on gospel values, the importance of friends, God as our primary friend, obstacles we encounter in our friendship with God, signs of God's friendship, and putting our love into action, while living out the retreat each day of our life. There are major talks given by both adults and student leaders; most of the discussion occurs in small groups led by the student leaders. Music is integral; some media are used; prayer is part of each activity, with a major session of shared prayer. Parents participate in this retreat, and the girls, as a result, have the opportunity to come to a greater understanding of their parents. A great deal of healing and bonding occurs between parents and daughters, often accompanied by tears and hugs. At the homecoming session one father, who had been estranged from his daughter, got right up and embraced her as she was addressing the group. One parent said that his daughter had learned so much about herself, citing that such emerging selfhood was the reason for having chosen to enroll in the Academy.

The retreat program, which gets fine-tuned each year, has been such a blessed success in helping to meet the spiritual and moral growth needs of our girls that the school considers it essential to the Academy experience. The girls are expected to attend. In fact, the retreats are so much a part of their experience that in an eleven-year time span only two girls have asked not to attend. Most students look forward to them. As one senior said during our small group sharing, "It's not easy but I want to be God's Mollie, not Mollie's Mollie."[6] This young woman, speaking from a Presbyterian tradition, taught us so much that evening.

Christian Service Program

Compassion is one of the basic components of the major religions. It is certainly a mandate of the Gospels. Young people are inherently generous. Organized mandatory community service opportunities nurture this generosity and help to educate them in the broader context of the needs of their society. From a pragmatic viewpoint, service can help some find careers and, at the very least, point them toward a life-long commitment to service. In the school's service program a minimum of 15 hours is required in 9th through 11th grades. These hours must be spent with the poor or needy persons, and they must be interpersonal. The girls serve in hospitals, juvenile camps, convalescent homes, homes for unwed mothers and battered women, or they tutor in schools or are involved in similar activities. The purpose is to follow the gospel messages "As often as you did it to one of the least of these, you did it to me" (Matthew 25:40) and "love one another as I have loved you" (John 15:12). The student realizes her responsibility for others and the unconditional love that is required of us, leaving judgment to God alone.

The seniors spend a week of service (5 days, 7 hours each day) after the Advanced Placement/final exams. They go to schools for the developmentally handicapped, Habitat for Humanity, tutor in inner-city schools, help in convalescent homes, and work with teenage mothers and their babies. One evening mid-week is spent sharing experiences and in theological reflection: "How do I see God in this experience?" Parents and faculty are invited to attend. Seniors may often find themselves doing much more voluntary service both as individuals and in small groups. To their surprise, some of them have found themselves enjoying the experience and learning from it.

The service program has made the generous more so and helped the self-centered reach outward. There is a great realization of how different we all are and how some are more fortunate than others. Many years ago the school adopted an inner-city elementary school in East Los Angeles, raising money for scholarships and tutoring there.

Each year the girls invite the entire student body and staff to our school to share a Christmas party with entertainment provided by both schools and Santa, as well as gifts and refreshments offered by the FSHA girls. The girls are called to be both gift and blessing to others and to realize that they meet God in others and are thereby blessed in the encounter. One sophomore was so taken by a local article on a young boy who needed a bone marrow transplant that she organized both her church and her entire community to participate in a possible bone marrow match not only to this one patient but on a regular basis. It has become an annual event, and this young woman has been enriched and nurtured in her own generous leadership.

Two clubs, open to all members of the student body, support the service program: Christian Action Movement (CAM) and Amnesty International. Both of these organizations specifically and intentionally promote service to and justice for others. They give the girls an opportunity to put their values and religious beliefs into practice.

At a meeting with a recent graduating class, my personal beliefs about our work as a school faith community were confirmed. Talking about their high school years, the school, and what they had gained, the students told me that they felt safe and loved. They felt empowered because they were treated as young adults capable of responsible decision-making. They felt free to express themselves artistically, athletically, socially, and spiritually. They believed themselves loved and respected for who they had become, not just for what they had done. Their class has formed a strong bond, rejoicing in each other's good fortune and sharing in each other's pain. Unquestionably they belonged to a loving, caring community of faith. These experiences have made them go out of themselves to be of service to others, not because they had to, but because they wanted to. Their retreats were a source of strength and growth in faith. They knew they were on the journey and that God was the road, the companion on the way, and the destination. They were so grateful that the school had provided them with a giant safety net that had allowed them the freedom to take risks and to discover their own strengths. Now they were eager to meet the challenge of the next step.

Notes

I am indebted to the Religious Studies Department and to the Campus Minister for sharing with me their own experiences in the classroom as well as on retreats. As principal, I made it a point to participate in both the Junior and Senior Retreats, as well as to visit the Sophomore and Freshmen Retreats, each year.

[1] Carole Riley, *Understanding and Guiding Teenage Spirituality* (Canfield, Ohio: Alba House Cassettes) Tape 1, Side 1. This tape offers an excellent overview with practical applications and provides material for good staff discussions.

[2] The Class of 2003 used this metaphor of a giant safety net to describe the school that allowed them to take risks knowing that they would be safe and honored. They felt that the school gave them enough latitude and trust to experiment while providing enough boundaries to make them feel secure and free.

[3] Religious Studies Department, *Department of Religious Studies Handbook,* Flintridge Sacred Heart Academy, 2002–2003, p. 1.

[4] Riley, Tape 1, Side 1.

[5] *Department of Religious Studies Handbook,* 1.

[6] The quotation from Small Group Reflection time during the Kairos Senior Retreat is used with permission from Ms. Mollie Merchant, Class of 2000.

Works Consulted

Religious Studies Department. *Religious Studies Handbook.* Flintridge, CA: Flintridge Sacred Heart Academy, 2003.

Riley, C. *Understanding and Guiding Teenage Spirituality.* Canfield, Ohio: The Society of Saint Paul, Alba House Cassettes, General Prayer and Meditation, n.d.

Chapter 6

Resurrecting the Spirit: Acknowledging the Inner Life in the World of Boarding Schools

Meera S. Viswanathan

From the world of Mr. Chips to that of Harry Potter, boarding schools traditionally conjure up the vision of neatly trimmed lawns, immaculate blazers, and orderly education, removed from the hurly-burly of everyday life that remains stable or quiescent, depending on your vantage point. However, the challenges and flux confronting public education (academic curriculum; chemical dependency; sexuality and pregnancy; health; violence; information technology) in the United States are both directly and indirectly affecting independent schools as well.

Additionally, many independent boarding schools over the last twenty or thirty years have had to deal with questions of co-education, issues of diversity, financial aid, and most significantly the concerns surrounding the phrase *in loco parentis* (in place of the parent) the mandate, explicit or tacit, of every primary and secondary boarding school.

It was not until my husband was appointed headmaster of a New England boarding school ten years ago that I began to appreciate the subtle difficulties implied by having to stand in the place of six hundred sets of parents. As a university professor I was accustomed to instruction in a residential environment, but of course the notion of *in loco parentis* along with ideas such as parietals would strike most college students as naively quaint and positively antediluvian.

Whereas at boarding schools, even if one eschewed the now-suspect paternalism of the older school model, one still had to acknowledge the formidable obligation of shepherding students through the rigors of adolescence through the twenty-four hours of the day. For the day students it was somewhat simpler in this respect. After a full day of classes, meals, sports, clubs, and a host of other opportunities and responsibilities, the day students could at last "go home," though of course they faced many other singular hurdles. However, what of the other five hundred twenty for whose intellectual, social, and emotional lives we became almost solely responsible, who could not "go home" at night, for whom school had necessarily become home?

The role of parents in children's lives is an especially evocative topic for me as I recollect my early life in India. My grandfather in Madras would regularly regale my sister and me with tales of the Hindu divinities, ostensibly as entertainment. The earliest story I recollect involved the family of Shiva, his wife Parvati, and their two sons: Ganesha, the chubby elephant-headed god of knowledge and understanding; and his handsome, martially inclined brother, Karthikeya, the god of war. One day, the two parents decided, as is the wont of parents, to set a challenge before their sons in order to determine who of the two truly had understood the teachings of his parents thus far. Calling the boys before them, they explained that the contest involved circling the universe. Whoever of the two could most quickly circumambulate the universe, that son would be deemed the principal heir.

Hearing this, Karthikeya crowed with glee, delighting in his athletic build and the speed of his peacock mount. Departing from the house, he straddled the peacock and began his sojourn around the world. Ganesha by contrast was bemused and befuddled. Ruefully considering his girth and the minuscule proportions of his animal mount, the small rat who could ferret out secrets and hidden truths, Ganesha realized that he had no hope of catching up with his brother by conventional means even if the latter had not had a head start. Pondering the quest set by his mother and father, he wondered why they would offer a challenge that was so clearly biased in favor of his brother, or if indeed that was their intention.

Suddenly an idea came to him and he asked his parents to stand together in the middle of the room. Slowly he began to walk around them in a circle clockwise and just as he was completing the circuit, a cry came from outside the door, "I've won, I've won." As Karthikeya breathlessly returned before them, triumphantly certain that he had won the contest, Parvati and Shiva shook their heads and said "No, in fact Ganesha has succeeded first." Outraged, Karthikeya demanded to know how that could be when it was obvious that Ganesha had not even stepped one foot outside the house, much less circled the universe. Parvati and Shiva smiled at their disappointed son and explained that it is parents who give birth to us and who represent the heart of our world. To circle them symbolically is to comprehend them and thus the universe itself. Ganesha realized the lesson his parents were trying to teach him and sought the ultimate, not in the unknown out there, but rather here and now through the source of his being, his parents.

Of course, as a child I recognized this as a wonderful story and cheered on the stalwart Ganesha, but I had little understanding of what it all meant or, more significantly, why my grandfather was telling us this narrative. To stand in the place of a parent, *in loco parentis,* is a daunting undertaking, not merely feeding and clothing offspring, but nurturing and teaching children about the deepest and most significant questions and truths. In his book, *Taking Our Places,* Norman Fischer remarks, "Each of us has a place in the world. Taking that place, I have come to feel, is our real job as human beings...To take our place is to mature, to grow into what we are."[1] Later he elaborates, "Spiritual practice, I gradually came to feel, is in essence the practice of maturity."[2] Already, Fischer has noted, "Taking our places as mature individuals in this world is not work we can do alone. We need others to help us, and we need to help others."[3] This is the challenge of *in loco parentis* that we can neither discount nor ignore; the act of mentoring human development in our children, which in itself is a gesture of the spirit, both for them and for us.

Over the years, I have become accustomed to comforting, consoling, and encouraging homesick students; students who did not have a date for the prom; students who felt that they were too fat, too thin, too short, too tall, too anything; students who agonized about a death or divorce in the family; or who were not accepted by the college of choice; or simply felt that they did not "fit in." Having had no children of my own, my model for these encounters was the stellar example provided by the faculty of our school. We have a splendid set of substitute parents available: deans, school physician and nurses, psychological counselors and experienced, compassionate faculty and staff for whom boarding school life truly is a vocation, a calling rather than a mere profession.

As I observed and participated in the life of the school, one question continued to trouble me: In the world of highly competitive, highly structured boarding schools, how do students grapple and, just as importantly, how are they taught to grapple with abstract ethical, moral, spiritual, philosophical, and religious questions, issues, and values? In other words, how are we to understand *in loco parentis* with respect to questions of "the inner life?" Obviously, as a secular independent school, we do not observe a specific creed or doctrine. Even so, at the same time we wish to give students at this critical time in their lives the freedom to practice the faiths they brought with them from home as well as to learn and ask questions about other belief systems and general philosophical and ethical issues about life, death, and human being. Like Shiva and Parvati's sons, our students revolve around the world we lay out for them embodied in ourselves.

Our dining hall works hard to accommodate the dietary requirements of our various students, whether for health, religion, or reasons of principle, offering vegetarian meals, *halal* meats, and kosher food for students who request them. We have a two-term philosophy and religion requirement that can be met by a host of different courses ranging from ethics to world religions to Judeo-Christian thought. We note that we offer transportation for interested students to religious services of their choice on appropriate days. There exist a few student groups centering around religious practices. However, is this in fact enough?

When my family immigrated to the United States from India some forty years or so ago, there were relatively few Indians in our area, certainly not enough to constitute any kind of "community." My mother would observe Hindu holidays and festivals at home, teaching us sacred chants (*slokas*) and prayers, but she realized that the world was becoming bifurcated for us: Religious practices and beliefs were part of our Hindu life inside the house and within the family, but they had no counterpart outside.

She decided that we needed spiritual and ethical training and guidance outside as well and so sent us with our various school friends to Protestant Sunday School (we attended weekly for over a decade) and Catholic Mass; we lit Shabbat candles on Friday nights with Jewish friends as well as going to High Holy Day services at the reform synagogue; we went regularly to the Hana Matsuri and O-bon festivals at the local Buddhist temple.

These experiences were significant from my mother's perspective and enhanced the teachings that she gave us at home. My only regret from childhood was that reciprocal interest in my beliefs and those of my family seemed nonexistent then. Looking back, I realize how critical these assorted encounters with religious practice and belief were to the development of my "inner life"; that sphere encompassed by moral, ethical, spiritual, religious, and philosophical truths. Especially in my teenage years, I remember asking questions about the purpose of life, the significance of death, whether divinity existed, and whether morality was understood universally.

Ironically, it seems easier and less a breach of good taste in our present-day world to admit to a host of unsavory practices than to admit publicly to an interest in religion and spirituality or even more culpably, to belief in a faith-system. That many horrific acts have been committed ostensibly in the name of every religion there is no doubt. Moreover, surely, as I experienced firsthand, those of a minority belief-system can face considerable bias, resentment, and hostility. However, quite a few of us seem incapable of distinguishing between human actions on the one hand and the issue of the sacral on the other.

Many students of different faiths confided in me that when they first started boarding school, they imagined attending the kind of religious services they attended at home or freely identifying themselves as Jewish, or Christian, or Muslim, and so on. However, they quickly understood that other students might regard them as peculiar or weird or not worthy of interest if they did so. "What about the beliefs of others?" I asked. "Yes," they admitted that they would like to understand the thinking of others, but alas, the pace of life at boarding school did not allow for any time to consider and learn about these things, however interesting and culturally important they might be.

Until the 1970s our school, like many others, while not centering on a particular sectarian creed, nevertheless required all students to attend Sunday services at the brick church in the village. (Jewish students were required to attend; Catholic students received a dispensation to attend Mass with a faculty member in a nearby town.) In addition, every Sunday evening there would be a mandatory "Sing," in which all students along with the faculty and headmaster would sing Protestant hymns. An invited speaker, often an itinerant preacher, would share his thoughts on some topic not necessarily spiritual but morally uplifting before the school would retire Sunday evening in preparation for the beginning of the academic work week. While almost everyone associated with the school recognizes now the spiritual bias implicit in these practices and their leveling qualities, almost all of the alumni of whatever faith mourn the passing of those Sunday Sings. These were, the alumni explain, chances for the school to assemble to share a moment of convivial unity, and they also offered a time of some reflection about things beyond quotidian life and classes. It is not that the speakers were necessarily gifted or eloquent, for some were remembered as remarkably turgid and prosaic. Rather, it is that the weekly ritual offered a brief respite from daily affairs and set a rhythm for the coming week. In addition, Sunday night sings were complemented by ritual Saturday night secular songs that were sung before the weekly movie.

Like so many social practices that were indifferent to racial, ethnic, social, economic, and religious differences outside what was perceived to be the "norm," these in some senses appropriately were dismantled during the tumultuous times of the sixties and seventies. For a while, there was a conflation of the weekend singing. For a few years, there was a secular Sunday night sing centering on college songs, ditties from musicals, and American folk songs along with a thoughtful talk given by a faculty member, generally without reference to spirituality or religion. However, this practice too petered out, and the ritual was abandoned.

The pity of it is that nothing was constructed to replace in a meaningful fashion the benefits conferred by these rituals, and while individuals at the school sought to address the lacuna on an *ad hoc* basis, there was a programmatic void. However, as my colleagues in other schools inform me, even in schools organized around a particular sectarian belief that did not do away with required services, there frequently remains a gap between the rituals undertaken and the ethical-spiritual needs of students.

Therein lies the real challenge: How are we to fulfill our obligation to stand in place of parents with respect to nurturing the inner life without being reductive, assimilative, or perhaps even sacrilegious, thereby arrogating to ourselves decisions about faith and truth that belong within the actual family? At the same time, how could we construct a view of the inner life that did not necessarily presume belief in divinity, transcendence or religious doctrine, i.e., a pluralistic view that included the non-religious as well as the various religious and spiritual positions?

As I spoke anecdotally about my conversations with students to other members of our school community, quite a few expressed a similar set of concerns. Parents admitted to some discomfort about our explicitly articulated attention to the academic curriculum and the physical and psychological well-being of our students, and their future college placement, but our putative silence about those areas that resisted normative calibration along the spectrum of failure and success. Given the adherence to traditions (even those in existence only for the last twenty or thirty years) and the understandable reluctance to embrace such an admittedly fuzzy area, the school clearly could not address by fiat the inner life question. More significantly, what to do and how to do it seemed less like sequential decisions than imbricated ones; how we undertook to answer these concerns was integral to whatever path we chose to follow.

The modern Japanese philosopher Tetsuro Watsuji argued that the basis of ethics derives from our very humanity. The characters with which one writes human being in Japanese (literally 人間 *ningen*) he noted could be etymologically deconstructed as the space between (間がら *aidagara*) people (人 *hito*); in other words, human being consisted not of a series of individuals in rapt isolation but rather our humanity derives from our social condition; it emerges from the interactions between people.[4]

Analogously, I have learned recently about the Zulu expression emblematic of sub-Saharan Africa known as *ubuntu*.[5] *Ubuntu* is said to derive from the folk saying "*Umuntu ngumuntu nagabantu,*" literally, "A person is a person because of other people."[6] Norman Fischer uses as the epigraph for his book Martin Buber's comment "All real living is meeting."[7] What is intriguing about the commonality of all three observations is that there is no distinction drawn between end and means, and each functions as a way of affirming our mutual humanity. That is to say, we are not meeting merely in order to achieve something else, or meeting to facilitate real living, or that the purpose of human being is other than discovering human being.

Would that I had grasped this profound idea much earlier!

Rather ingenuously, I assumed that we might assemble a committee at the school consisting of all relevant constituencies (students, faculty, parents, and alumni) to focus on students and the issue of the inner life. The rubric committee itself was somewhat problematic, suggestive as it was of a corporate or governmental hierarchy or some other such official authority. At the same time, its very bland neutrality afforded a measure of ease as we contemplated a leap into the abyss. I should admit that in the recesses of my heart I dread committee work, which seems so often to be a clumsy, unresponsive mechanism that consumes vast amounts of time with seemingly so little to show for it. However, here again I betray my disinclination and impatience for the necessary "messiness" and "inefficiency" of human encounters. Needless to say, for nearly two years, we committee members found ourselves embroiled in the thickness of every controversy.

First there was the issue of the composition of the committee. Obviously, only those who already shared a similar view (i.e., that the inner life was an important topic) would be likely to devote a few hours every other week to such an enterprise. What I had not realized was how some students who faced other challenges at the school (social, economic, cultural) might feel disinclined to join a group that might further emphasize their apartness. However, rather than trying to enforce an agenda of representativeness, we sought to create a conversation about spiritual and ethical life at the school.

We began by providing some general assurances to one another. There was no preconceived program in place; the goal was not to create consensus about spiritual beliefs or engage in evangelism, but to try to understand our reactions and responses to the central questions. Also, though we were a private school, we acknowledged the importance of a separation between church and state and the need to address the needs of all in our community, not simply the vocal few. We consisted of Jews, Catholics, Protestant Christians, a Syrian Christian, a Muslim, a Hindu, and several others who might be grouped as agnostic or atheist. Some were steeped in their beliefs and others simply identified themselves as such culturally.

Our first meeting was rather tense as we all wondered silently and out loud what was going to happen. More out of nervousness than anything else, we began by telling our stories, literally whence we came, geographically, ethnically, familially. Looking back, I wish I had had the prescience to record or note down these narratives in some fashion, but mesmerized, I simply sat and just listened. The stories both of young and old spoke of ancestral homes and journeys, remembrances of grandparents and lineages, cultural encounters and alienation, language and memory, sacred texts and rituals, dreams and cherished beliefs. All of us sat rapt as we heard the unfolding dramas of those whom we imagined we knew so well and now saw as both stranger and kin. It was this initial experience that allowed us later to speak with fervor and tenderness toward one another even as we disagreed about issues or saw the world differently.

Over the next year and a half, as a group we discussed our affection for the school, our experiences, our disappointments and our aspirations. Some of these conversations bore directly on the question of spiritual matters and others only indirectly. For example, at times we spoke of the need for students to have a place on campus which stood apart from ordinary life, a place to reflect, to meditate, to pray, and perhaps to mourn. While a Congregational church abuts the campus, many felt that they needed a place not associated with that or any specific sectarian focus, a place that belonged to the school and to the students. At other times, we discussed the ubiquitous problem of every boarding school: the problem of pace, i.e., the extraordinarily impacted rhythm of life in which prescribed activities seem to be structured by the minute.

Several committee members noted that it was not enough to take an additive approach to school life as we contemplated the role of spiritual and ethical concerns. Simply to layer more endeavors on top of the already hectic demands of the academy would be to relegate these critical matters of the heart and spirit to the realm of yet another club or school organization. Rather they argued that we needed to re-think wholesale the life of the school as we sought to understand the role of the spiritual/philosophical perspective in the lives of students.

A marvelous thing took place in the course of our meetings. Students who seemed painfully shy or prone to stammering suddenly developed remarkable eloquence and fluency as they passionately put forward a position. Adults learned to be silent and give way to students as they mused and groped their way toward realizations. One student, who seemed to affect deliberately a surfer-bum persona for much of the time, broke forth with a torrent of praise for Thoreau's *Walden* and "the need to live life deliberately," recognizing perhaps for the first time the power and truth of books read in the context of classes. Another patiently and thoughtfully explained to the group how the natural environment, especially mountains, allowed him the experience of transcendence, a truly spiritual encounter for him.

Students who might have seemed giddy or unconcerned about metaphysics gave evidence of a profoundly developed inner life. Nevertheless, each meeting unnerved me as I contemplated it, realizing that I had little idea what was to occur, no matter what the neatly printed agenda might say. This was my lesson to learn: to realize I was not in control and that it was the aggregate pulse of the group that drove the dialogue. Meanwhile our group created some little stir on campus and even some angst. Though the meetings were open to all, some felt that it constituted a private clique engaged in kabbalistic matters.

I, and later the students as well, spoke about the committee to parents, students, faculty, and alumni as did several members of the group. Parents were thrilled and excited and wanted to encourage the effort in any way they could. (There may well have been parents who disagreed or who felt indifferently about our activities, but none articulated those positions to us.) Alumni waxed nostalgic about their experiences at the school and saw these endeavors as a positive step for the school. Trustees thought it was an important area of concern.

Students were mixed in their reaction; some were enthusiastic about the possibilities; some felt we needed to take stronger measures; some worried about the school losing its secular and ecumenical character; and some were downright hostile to our committee's concerns, claiming that these were private matters involving the individual and had no place in official school life. Some were just confused about the whole business.

Perhaps the most surprising reaction was that of the faculty, who constitute some of the most thoughtful and dedicated individuals in the field of education that I have encountered in my life. They expressed as a whole the least interest and the greatest number of reservations about these concerns. While several championed the idea of talking about these issues in a concerted fashion, the majority seemed apprehensive and wary of the committee's intention and goals. Though somewhat taken aback at the time, I realize now that it was perhaps at heart a protective and nurturing response. It was the faculty after all who day in and day out saw, encouraged, and nurtured our students the most closely, much more so than parents or alumni. Given the heavy responsibilities weighing on them, they were correct to be wary about any change that might disturb the delicate balance necessary for a liberal education.

Interestingly, their concerns were not uniform. That is to say, many of the faculty members entertained different doubts as "secular intellectuals." Was it really necessary, they wondered, for the school to intervene in this manner; was it not enough to accommodate as we had been doing the specific needs of students who professed a particular faith?

While I had anticipated finding some reservations or even opposition among those espousing secularism, I had thought that faculty who identified themselves strongly with a particular religious creed would evince some interest and support. I was misguided as it turns out. Some of the faculty, as evangelical Christians, explained their angst about the school intervening in these matters, noting that their primary spiritual responsibility was to nurture those students sharing their beliefs. One extremely gifted and thoughtful faculty member of this persuasion took the trouble to have lunch with me to share his reactions to my comments. Pointedly, he noted that while it perhaps was the administration's responsibility to worry about the general climate regarding spiritual plurality for students, this was not his concern. This did not mean he did not care for and cherish the students who were not "born-again," but it did mean that he was not necessarily going to support ventures that encouraged the practice of all faith-systems or even issues related to the inner life apart from his doctrinal beliefs.

Nevertheless, the committee soldiered on as a movement toward reflection. We brought in a few lecturers on a variety of established religions (Buddhism, Christianity, Islam) and even distributed a survey on the subject produced by the students on the committee for the entire school. This was a fascinating exercise both for the range of written responses it produced as well as for the experience of pulse-taking itself. The committee continued its deliberations amidst these activities, though our own discussions often threatened to bog down with, for example, the question of distinctions among the notions of religion, spirituality, and questions of the inner life. However, owing to the pragmatism of the students, who plaintively inquired whether all we planned to do was talk, we eventually produced a set of recommendations that we presented to the headmaster.

Our central recommendations involved first, the establishing of an office of spiritual and ethical life, overseen by a dean who would work closely with other offices as well as directly with students to focus on matters of the heart and spirit. This individual would recognize her or his role first and foremost as a teacher to all students as well as an advocate and resource for the varied spiritual and ethical concerns of our community. We recommended a two-year preliminary appointment because this was admittedly an experimental venture in which the dean would need to work with our school community to chart out a possible trajectory. Second, we also noted the need for a spiritual space or spaces on campus that would allow opportunity for introspection, meditation, and prayer that was not biased in favor of a particular community of believers or non-believers. Third, we stressed the need for ongoing, extracurricular opportunities for us as a school to learn about different religions and belief-systems in the world today. It should be stressed that none of the activities would be mandatory for students. Finally, and this was certainly the most far-reaching of our recommendations, we wondered how to incorporate these suggestions not merely in an additive approach, but rather by using these recommendations as an opportunity to rethink radically how we function as a school. That is to say, what would it mean to use our concerns to rethink questions about pace, the structure of school life, and its fundamental aims?

To borrow Roger Williams's comment about the founding of the state of Rhode Island, our "lively experiment" continues. As a school, we have appointed a superbly gifted and thoughtful individual to the post of dean of spiritual and ethical life. There have been wonderful discoveries for us as a community owing to her untiring efforts, but it has not been easy and the fracture lines are many. As she embarks on her second year, having moved us to a new place of understanding as well as questioning during the first, we look forward to her help and guidance in helping us to see ourselves both as we are and as we wish to be.

As my good friend and academic colleague Hilary Matthews has written, "Let's do a good African thing in our schools! '*Indaba!*' 'Come let us talk together!' This is a process of open discussion rather than debate, where issues of import can be aired from a variety of under-standings, with the purpose of acquiring new understanding."[8] I con-cur. As faculty and administrators, we must be determined to seek out new ways to be responsive to the intellectual, social, physical, and spiritual needs of the students entrusted to our care, ever mindful of the dignity and importance to be conferred on each belief system and the individuals professing it.

Notes

[1] Norman Fischer, *Taking Our Places: The Buddhist Path to Truly Growing Up* (San Francisco, CA: HarperSan Francisco, 2003), 2.

[2] Ibid., 4.

[3] Ibid., 2.

[4] Tetsuro Watsuji, *Fudo,* trans. Geoffrey Bownas as *Climate and Culture: A Philoso-phical Study* (Westport, CT: Greenwood, 1988), 142–49.

[5] I was introduced to this concept by the Reverend Elizabeth Clement.

[6] Peter M. Senge, Art Kleiner, Charlotte Roberts, Rick Ross, Bryan Smith, *The Fifth Discipline: Strategies and Tools for Building a Learning Organization* (New York: Currency, 1994).

[7] Fischer, Frontispiece.

[8] Hilary Matthews, Bicentennial Fellow, Deerfield Academy, 2002–2003, and Direc-tor, Global Connections Foundation, "What Citizen for Tomorrow?" Paper presented at the annual Global Connections Conference, Paris, July 2003, and subsequently published in *Crossing Frontiers: Culture, Language & Bilingualism,* Global Connec-tions VII Seminar, ed. Peter D. Pelham and Eric Widmer (Deerfield Academy Press, 2004).

Works Consulted

Fischer, Norman. *Taking Our Places: The Buddhist Path to Truly Growing Up.* San Francisco, CA: HarperSan Francisco, 2003.

Matthews, Hilary. "What Citizen for Tomorrow?" Paper presented at the annual Global Connections Conference, Paris, July 2003, and subsequently published in *Crossing Frontiers: Culture, Language & Bilingualism,* Global Connections VII Seminar, Pelham, Peter D., and Eric Widmer, Deerfield, MA: Deerfield Academy Press, 2004.

Senge, Peter M., et al. *The Fifth Discipline Fieldbook: Strategies and Tools for Building a Learning Organization.* New York: Currency Publications, 1994.

Watsuji, Tetsuro. *Climate and Culture: A Philosophical Study.* Trans. Geoffrey Bownas. Westport, CT: Greenwood, 1988.

Chapter 7

Rethinking High School World Religions: Pedagogical Options for Addressing Ethical and Cultural Relativism

Manish K. Mishra

The importance of understanding the larger global community, and the religions that exist within it, has never been greater. The events of September 11, in particular, underscored the woeful lack of knowledge within American society of Islam and, through indiscriminate acts of hatred, even Sikhism and Hinduism. While colleges, universities, and particular religious communities have typically taken the lead in educating the American public about the realities of religious pluralism, secondary schools are increasingly playing a greater role in such efforts. Independent schools have long led the charge in providing quality course offerings in World Religions at the high school level, and more public school systems are examining ways to directly and sometimes indirectly address this subject matter as well. We have begun to understand as a society that continued illiteracy vis-à-vis religious pluralism is untenable and, in fact, undermines the religious freedom and tolerance we hold so dear.

Juxtaposed with this desire for greater literacy in World Religions is the reality that curriculum development for religious studies at the secondary school level generally lags behind the academy. Whereas universities are moving away from the "World Religions" course format in favor of "Religious Pluralism," a move that intentionally supplements factual description with analytical frameworks, many secondary schools are still making the transition from "Comparative Religions" to "World Religions," an earlier paradigm shift away from subjective comparison to objective description. In addition, the curricular needs at the secondary level frequently do not map one-to-one with those of the college or university level. The academy's approach to religious pluralism is often characterized by an assumption that participants in the pluralist dialogue come to the table with a firm faith background of some kind, typically Christian. What does one do when confronted in a high school setting, as I have been, not with "true believers" but with students enamored by the notion that all truth is relative?

The subject matter and pedagogical structure of World Religions lends itself to the fostering of such relativism amongst adolescents. World Religions students are presented with competing truth claims rooted in differing cultural realities. Given time limitations (typically a term or a semester) and the inevitable decision to cover a certain number of religious traditions within that short time period, foundational work is usually eschewed in favor of more applied, fact based, descriptive instruction. Students are, thus, not necessarily armed with sufficient intellectual tools to mediate the competing truth claims with which they are presented. In the absence of such tools, some students avoid the question of contradictory truth claims altogether. They arrive at the conclusion that all truth is relative.

I believe that we need to do a better job at more directly addressing the challenge that ethical and cultural relativism poses to our work. By neither adequately understanding the factors contributing to such relativism, nor crafting pedagogies that respond, we inadvertently reinforce the sense that Truth, with a capital "T," does not exist. In my opinion, such moralistic nihilism is an unfortunate place to leave students.

This chapter examines the nexus between relativism and the instruction of World Religions at the secondary school level. We will first examine the developmental and pedagogical factors that contribute to the emergence of relativism. The remainder of the chapter will then elaborate an alternate approach to the instruction of secondary school World Religions. This alternate model proposes that we reframe the core World Religions curriculum, address head-on the implications of ethical and cultural relativism, move toward the analytical framework provided by the collegiate "Religious Pluralism" model, and open up the curriculum by offering students the opportunity to explore non-conventional, non-institutional faith traditions.

The Developmental Context

The attractiveness that relativism holds for adolescents is accounted for in Lawrence Kohlberg's work on moral development. Kohlberg postulated six stages of moral development ranging from early childhood through adulthood: Stage 1, Punishment and Obedience Orientation; Stage 2, Instrumental Relativist Orientation; Stage 3, "Good Boy-Nice Girl" Orientation; Stage 4, Law and Order Orientation; Stage 5, Social Contract Legalistic (Utilitarian) Orientation; and Stage 6, Universal Principle Orientation.[1] Kohlberg's research indicates that while different individuals progress through these stages at their own pace, there are generally specific age ranges during which individuals move through a particular stage. For the purposes of this essay, we are most interested in the stage Kohlberg calls Stage 4 ½ . John Gibbs describes this stage as one of "meta-ethical sceptical relativism and [a] philosophy of non-imposition."[2]

Kohlberg considered Stage 4 ½ a transitional stage marking the shift from conventional Stage 4 moral reasoning to Stage 5 postconventional reasoning. As the individual is exposed to the diversity and frequent irreconcilability of competing truth claims, all truth is considered subjective, i.e., relative to the truth-seeker. Kohlberg described Stage 4 ½ as a college-aged phenomenon, while Larry Nucci, a contemporary interpreter, categorizes it as occurring between ages 17 and 20. [3] Transition from one stage of moral development to the next is typically caused by "disequilibria" of some kind. The moral framework and limits of the individual are tested in new ways, which in turn fosters the development of new, more sophisticated understandings and a transition to the next higher stage of moral reasoning.[4] James Fowler describes the events that typically fuel the jump from Kohlberg's Stage 4 to Stage 4 ½ and subsequently to Stage 5:

> First, the young person must leave home emotionally and perhaps physically, and encounter experiences of conflicting values in a context of moratorium. Then, second, the young adult...must have undertaken two further steps...the experience of sustained responsibility for the welfare of others and the experience of making and living with irreversible moral choices which are the marks of adulthood personal moral experience...research suggests that all young adults...who do develop post-conventional moral outlooks and commitments have experienced and resolved [this] adolescent identity crisis.[5]

Thus, emotional independence and a high degree of autonomy are necessary to create disequilibrium with Stage 4 reasoning.

The question then arises as to whether this disequilibrium with Stage 4 need occur only in late adolescence, as Kohlberg and even Nucci imply. It would appear that mid-teens and even some very mature early teens are capable of shifting toward Stage 4 ½ . Ronald Duska and Mariellen Whelan's analysis of Kohlberg's work underscores the conclusion that "...[d]evelopment is not governed [precisely] by age. Rate of development varies. Some young people achieve higher stages than older adults...certain ranges of ages...are good predicators of stages...but the important point is that the rate will vary even within the same family."[6] Kohlberg himself also acknowledged that the rate of progression through the six stages was unpredictable: Some might reach a particular stage faster, and others slower.[7] Contemporary American society, as well, is vastly different from that of the late 1960s, early 1970s when Kohlberg published much of his work: Teens today are faced with adult realities much earlier than they were thirty years ago. This encounter with greater responsibility and more sophisticated moral decision-making at a younger age can foment earlier stage progression. Finally, the academic literature on Kohlberg's stage theory does not account for the lived reality at independent residential secondary schools. The environment at such schools necessarily involves a high degree of emotional independence and autonomy, presenting teenagers as young as twelve or thirteen with the key disequilibria criteria required to move beyond Stage 4. The above factors point to the probability of a higher number of younger secondary-school aged youths reaching Kohlberg's Stage 4 ½ than has been traditionally presumed.

Such developmentally related relativism, as described by Kohlberg and others, is frequently reinforced by young persons' encounters with the world around them. Youths begin questioning the source of, and authority behind, societal norms. According to Nucci, "Moral positions espoused by these 'sophomoric' relativists rest on the justification that morality stems from societal norms that have force only within the context of particular social systems. Systems of norms are themselves arbitrary; thus, morality is a matter of what seems right to the person in his/her situation."[8]

Not just our own society's, but all systems of norms are questioned and viewed as arbitrary. James Fowler notes that Stage 4 ½ relativism "...arises out of the person's recognition of the relativity of law, customs, and group experiences from one society or group to the next."[9] The course content for World Religions, which introduces students to a variety of culturally rooted, meaning making systems, can inadvertently support the "sophomoric relativism" to which many of our teenaged students are developmentally predisposed. The cultural and intellectual encounter with "the Other," which we have helped bring about as teachers, can be used to self-justify Kohlberg Stage 4 ½ assumptions.

Prevailing High School Pedagogies

Given the popularity of relativism among some adolescents, the question must be asked whether our current pedagogical approach to World Religions is taking this into account. Mary Boys notes that there is a distinction "between *content*—that which is being handed on—and the *process* of handing on. There is both the *traditium*, the material being transmitted, and the *traditio*, the process of passing material from one generation to the next."[10] It is possible to critique the current World Religions approach in both its *traditium* and *traditio*.

World Religions courses tend to be fairly uniform in structure at the high school level. While teachers do frequently have flexibility in terms of presentation, particularly at independent secondary schools, the content typically focuses on the five large, modern-day institutional religions: the three Abrahamic faiths, Islam, Christianity, and Judaism, and the two great Indic-origin religions, Hinduism and Buddhism. To the extent time permits, some courses may also cover an additional religion or two, such as Confucianism and/or Taoism. This chosen *traditium* reflects a bias that is not sufficiently examined. We, as academics, are institutionally establishing the religions examined in our courses as normative. Inadvertently or advertently, we send the signal that other religions are peripheral and/or irrelevant. Many of our students already question or feel disillusioned with mainstream institutional religion. By providing an inflexible *traditium* that typically only covers larger mainstream traditions we create an approach that will not speak to many students.

While no single pedagogy can possibly account for all faith traditions, the stereotypical *traditium* of most World Religions courses thus contributes to the relativistic reaction of some students. The developmental work of William Perry, cited by Charles Shelton, sheds some additional light on this. Perry understands teenage relativism as emerging out of the adolescent's encounter with multiplicity and pluralism, the exact academic content of World Religions courses. He, in turn, categorizes and describes several different adolescent experiences of relativism. For example, multiplicity-related relativism occurs in response to exposure to competing values and ideas. In response, the individual internalizes a relativistic stance and uses it as a way to negate the absolutist claims of any one source of authority. Other teenagers embrace relativism more broadly as a legitimate way of thinking: all thought, all knowledge is considered relative.[11] According to Perry, the adolescent emerges out of these relativistic possibilities by way of making "commitments."[12] Teenagers discover that they must decide what they believe in and what they are willing to stand up for. This gradual articulation of values, of a belief system, represents a "commitment" on the part of the adolescent. Charles Shelton describes this scenario as follows:

> The importance of commitment cannot be overstressed when we are discussing the spiritual growth of the adolescent...Commitment arises after the adolescent perceives th[e] relativistic world and accepts it. Commitment means personal decision-making in a world of many choices and possibilities...The adolescent personally decides the extent to which previous values and behavior will now form a part of his/her personal commitment.[13]

The lack of choice with the predetermined, inflexible exploration of five or so major institutional religions closes off the possibility of commitment for at least some students. These students feel a lack of personal engagement with the material because the *traditium* is, in essence, fixed. Unless they are already committed to one or more of the religions studied, or become committed to them in the process of study, none of the course material will evoke deep-felt engagement or empathy. All of the traditions examined will be studied from a position of equal disinterest or detachment. This lack of commitment contributes to the relativizing of truth claims: in the negative, "they all equally don't get it," or in the positive, "they are all equally as good."
The *traditio,* the process by which we teach World Religions, presents us with certain challenges as well. Katherine Simon notes that educators have typically responded in four ways to the reality of pluralism:

- affirming the status quo by avoiding the issue of conflicting truth claims;
- teaching only those values that appear to be universally held;
- encouraging all points of view by adopting a "values clarification" approach;
- adopting a position of "pedagogical neutrality" by teaching all relevant positions.[14]

The subject matter of World Religions presumes the existence of competing truth claims that cannot be resolved by merely emphasizing commonly held values. As such, secondary school World Religions courses are usually taught using the values clarification approach or pedagogical neutrality.

The values clarification approach avoids comparing one set of norms or truths to another. The goal here is to send the message that no one tradition is normative or superior (even if the closed nature of the *traditium* symbolically attests otherwise). Students are encouraged to reach their own conclusions about the material presented and to verbalize those freely formed opinions. This approach, however, is highly problematic. As Simon explains:

> Although the [values clarification] approach is attractive for its openness to a range of opinions and the value it places on student's voices, its drawbacks are overwhelming. In its effort to acknowledge the diversity of views, it provides no criteria to help students distinguish better from worse moral decisions. Bent on ensuring that everyone can arrive without pressure at his or her own viewpoint, the approach provides neither theoretical basis nor practical strategies for conducting thoughtful discussions.[15]

Values clarification, thus, provides only a superficial encounter with multiplicity, lacking a conceptual framework for understanding or categorizing the diversity encountered. The relativity of individual opinion reigns supreme.

The pedagogical neutrality approach is characterized by teachers presenting, with equal diligence, different or even contradictory perspectives related to the subject matter at hand. Simon advocates the pedagogical neutrality approach as inherently superior to that of values clarification:

> Pedagogical neutrality, like values clarification, may seem to tend toward relativism—everyone's and anyone's views merit a hearing...pedagogical neutrality [does] require that opposing views be treated respectfully and in their best logic. However, it does not promote the idea, as values clarification tends to do, that one view is as good as another. In its advocacy for critical inquiry into a wide range of views, pedagogical neutrality goes far beyond values clarification in affirming that all positions are *not* equal. Some opinions stand on more solid intellectual ground than others, and rationality is to be highly prized...pedagogical neutrality [does not] require that the teacher abdicate or refrain from stating his or her own moral positions...There is no inherent contradiction in a teacher's holding a strong belief and yet promoting honest and thorough exploration of the strengths of opposing positions.[16]

While strongly advocating pedagogical neutrality, Simon acknowledges certain inherent challenges in this approach as well. Most significantly, complete neutrality is frequently impossible because of the curricular choices that every teacher makes. As Simon explains, "...the inclusion or exclusion of curricular materials is replete with moral implications."[17] Specifically vis-à-vis World Religions, we also need to keep in mind a concern Simon raised with values clarification: Pedagogical neutrality in and of itself does not provide a theoretical framework for understanding religious diversity. Teachers can share their knowledge within the context of neutrality. However, students are not necessarily empowered with their own theoretical tools for continued engagement with religious plurality. Pedagogical neutrality is likely the most effective *traditio* for our purposes, but it needs to be supplemented with additional theoretical grounding.

Envisioning a New Pedagogy

The factors discussed above argue in favor of further rethinking how we teach World Religions at the high school level. It may be the case that a new pedagogy is warranted. I offer below one such possibility that reconfigures the curriculum with a foundational unit that addresses cultural and ethical relativism, as well as religious pluralism, and is followed by two units that focus on faith traditions and engaged research.

The Foundational Unit: Relativism and Pluralism

Comprising roughly one-quarter of the total course, our foundational unit (which addresses both relativism and pluralism) would allow us to arm our students with a conceptual framework for understanding the religious multiplicity encountered in today's world.

Addressing Ethical and Cultural Relativism

Our survey could begin with an introduction to the concept of ethical and cultural relativism, explicitly naming and addressing this topic as a natural and age-appropriate response to the encounter with "the Other." A logical starting point for such an examination would be Herodotus' famous conclusion that "custom is the king o'er all," which emerged from his encounter with the Persian and Indian civilizations.[18] Herodotus reconciled the existence of competing values and truth claims by understanding all truth as culturally dependent. What might be immoral in one culture is moral in another. Ruth Benedict, a more contemporary proponent of relativism, similarly argues in favor of the cultural dependency of all truth claims, admonishing that our society has "failed to understand the relativity of cultural habits."[19] Examining Native American and other cultures, Benedict arrives at the same conclusion as Herodotus. Such culturally based relativism (the notion that Truth exists but is different for different people) needs to be distinguished from what Diana Eck terms nihilistic relativism: the notion that "if all religions say different things, this only proves that all of them are false."[20] In this interpretation of relativism, the encounter with "the Other" leads the individual to the ethical conclusion that no Truth exists.

Relativism, as many in the fields of religion or philosophy understand it, is a highly problematic way of looking at the world: It calls into question religion, ethics, and in its extreme, all knowledge and understanding. It is therefore, important that we walk our students through the various secular and religious critiques of relativism. From a secular perspective, Louis Pojman leads us to the following insights: First, while cultural relativism is a fact, it does not mean that Truth is relative—Truth may be absolute despite the relativity of culture; second, relativism does not take into account the realities of the common human experience—we're all human beings; third, mediating conflicting truth claims through the critical use of reason is not blind ethnocentrism—it is possible to have rational, defensible criteria for judging conflicting truth claims; fourth, in its extreme, relativism boils down to anarchic individualism.[21] From a developmental standpoint, John Gibbs also notes that adolescent relativism is inherently unstable because in advocating the notion that "we should not impose our truth claims on others" one is, in fact, creating an absolutist moral rule: "never do X."[22]

From a religious perspective, Hans Kung dismisses as "equally untenable" what he calls arbitrary pluralism, the unwillingness to acknowledge falsehood, and indifferentism, exempting certain positions from critique. Such positions lead to what Kung describes as "cheap tolerance, to [the notion that] 'anything goes.'"[23] While relativism can in one sense be viewed as positive, in that it is not a confrontational response to religious diversity, John Cobb, contributing to Gillis' assessment of the paradigm model, suggests that we must move beyond this toward "a search for truth, a truth which may exist in pure form in the expression of neither tradition but which nevertheless abides within each tradition."[24] In positive terms, and in sharp contrast with relativism, John Hick elaborates such a vision of religious multiplicity as "different conceptions and perceptions of, and responses to, the Real from within the different cultural ways of being human."[25] The Real exists. Culture represents the different lenses through which we attempt to describe it.

Introducing a Religious Pluralism Framework

The second component to this introductory unit is the religious pluralism paradigm. Paul Knitter provides a superb overview of the responses to religious diversity in his book, *No Other Name*. In this work, Knitter first examines the popular responses to multiplicity, placing them in three categories:

- all religions are relative;
- all religions are essentially the same;
- all religions have a common psychic origin.

Each of these three positions is examined in-depth with Knitter offering serious critiques of each. Knitter adds his own critique to the notion that all religions are relative, noting that "all truth is experienced as having universal relevance...[therefore, i]f something is true for us, we want to let others know about it."[26] In reality, human beings do not experience truth as being as fungible as relativists would have it be. In response to the notion that all religions are the same, Knitter explains that "one cannot encounter and become truly aware of the universal common reality in all religion except through the mediation of some particular form or symbol. The universal is not simply there for the taking; it always makes itself present through some particular manifestation...[w]hat is too naively forgotten is that the external forms of religion do affect the way the Ultimate is experienced..."[27] The third popular response has its roots in the notion that "religious faith has its origins in the human psyche: all religions arise from (or as part of) a common psychological process within the individual..."[28] Knitter responds to this position by noting that it is overly individualistic and subjective. In order "[t]o be true, religion must foster not only individual but societal wholeness."[29] In addition, Knitter also questions whether this position adequately accounts for the role of history in shaping religious traditions. The lack of historicalness of the "common psychic origin" approach disregards the ability of religion to adapt to, and be molded by, historical developments that take place outside of any determinable common human psychic needs/desires.

Knitter next addresses the religious attitudes toward pluralism, which he categorizes as belief in:

- only one true religion;
- salvation only in Christ;
- many religious paths, but one norm;
- many religious paths to one center.

The notion that there is only one true religion has typically characterized the way most religions, particularly the Abrahamic religions, have viewed the existence of other religions. As Knitter notes, such an exclusivist view ignores the reality that there are "followers [of other religions who] recogniz[e] the reality of a Transcendent Being and liv[e] lives of love and justice..."[30] The second position, that salvation is only possible in Christ, affirms the existence of "general revelation," revelation that might be the basis for truth in other religions. However, it holds that other religions have corrupted or gone astray from this general revelation. From a Christian perspective, thus, salvation is only possible through Christianity, through the saving grace of Jesus Christ. (This position can be interpreted more broadly as one where any religion recognizes some truth in other religions, yet maintains salvation is only possible through its particular truth.) Knitter criticizes this as well, noting that it is in essence a slightly more open form of exclusivism.[31] The idea that there are many religious paths but one norm has also characterized the Christian encounter with other religions. This approach recognizes general revelation, and even the possibility of salvation via other religions. However, it affirms that salvation in actuality only occurs because my God is saving you: you can be saved via Hinduism or Buddhism, but it's really Christ (or my God) who is saving you. This inclusive position undermines the unique reality of other religions by attempting to co-opt whatever truth exists in them. It is a form of religious chauvinism.[32] Finally, Knitter outlines one last approach, what he refers to as a "theocentric model," the notion that there are many religious paths to one common center (the center being God). As noted theologian Raimundo Pannikar explains it:

> It is not simply that there are different ways leading to the peak, but that the summit itself would collapse if all the [unique] paths disappeared. The peak is in a certain sense the result of the slopes leading to it...It is not that this reality [the ultimate mystery] has many names as if there were a reality outside the name. This reality *is* the many names and each name is a new aspect.[33]

With God at the center of all religious understanding, we can view each religion as providing a distinct and valuable path toward one Truth. This approach is the one Knitter implicitly advocates.

Understanding more fully the popular and religious attitudes toward pluralism, we can next elaborate the pluralist approach to World Religions. Diana Eck provides us such a framework, outlining three essential building blocks. First, pluralism is not diversity. Eck notes that one can observe diversity without being a participant. Pluralism requires active engagement.[34] As Judith Simmer-Brown explains it, "...[p]luralism is a commitment to communicate with and relate to the larger world—with a very different neighbor, or a distant community."[35] Second, pluralism is not simply tolerance: "...[t]olerance alone does nothing to remove our ignorance of one another by building bridges of exchange and dialogue. It does not require us to know anything new..."[36] Third, pluralism is not relativism. Echoing the thesis of this paper, Eck notes that pluralism is not "...an indiscriminating twilight in which 'all cats are grey,' all perspectives equally viable, and as a result equally uncompelling."[37] Finally, Simmer-Brown supplements Eck's framework with one additional axiom that pluralism is not syncretism: "...[s]yncretism cannot tolerate difference, and so two traditions or truths get blended together...[t]his is an approach which avoids the challenges of diversity through homogenizing and blending difference...This is not pluralism...pluralism respects the differences which reside in the variety of religious traditions, without reconciling or integrating those differences..."[38] Eck's approach challenges us to actively engage in understanding new truths in a way that goes beyond mere tolerance, while honoring and not glazing over the distinctness of different religious paths.

The Faith Traditions Unit: Core Curriculum Recast

World Religions courses tend to be taught as if each religion were a stand-alone entity. In the interest of "fairness," most World Religions curricula allocate the five major religions roughly "equal" course time so each gets roughly one-fifth of the total course. In reality, there is great inter-relatedness between many of the great religions, and an equal division of course time does not capitalize on this. The Abrahamic Religions (Islam, Christianity, and Judaism) have great commonality in terms of their basic theological structure (monotheism, scriptural authority, eschatology, cosmology) as well as cultural and historical origins. The same is true for the Indic-origin religions. Given the great resonance and structural similarity of the Abrahamic religions, devoting the majority of any course (three-fifths or more) to these religions is an inefficient use of resources, unless a conscious decision has been made to pedagogically emphasize these faiths. In the absence of such a conscious decision, we need to recognize the deep interrelationship between many religions and teach them accordingly. Accepting such an approach does not mean discarding the unique aspects of each faith, but it does advocate consolidating and streamlining how we teach the connected material. For example, reframing our World Religions courses in such a manner might involve teaching Islam, Christianity, and Judaism as an "Abrahamic Faiths" unit, and Hinduism and Buddhism (possibly along with even Sikhism and Jainism) as an "Indic Religions" unit. Each of these two units could be allocated one-quarter of the total course time, for a combined total of one-half the course.

Reconfiguring the traditional core World Religions curriculum in such a way serves several purposes. First, rather than attempting to introduce students to very specific aspects of five complex, multifaceted religions, we whet their appetites by providing an overview of two very different theological and historical currents, the Abrahamic and the Indic. Mastery of the particular would not be the goal, rather an appreciation for the philosophical, theological, spiritual, and historical trends represented by these two great strands of religious thought. A primary goal would be to create solid foundations in each of these two strands so that the student could successfully conduct additional independent research on specific elements of the constituent religions and/or pursue future tradition-specific coursework at the collegiate level. This approach would also create space for the introduction of significant new course elements (in our final unit) that would help us in further addressing the challenges of relativism.

The Research-Based Unit:
Opening the Curriculum to Student "Commitments"

Following our foundational unit and the faith traditions unit, the final one-quarter of the course could be devoted to opening up the curriculum in a way that evokes the kind of personal commitment that Perry considers essential to moving students beyond the lenses of relativism. This final one-quarter of the course could offer our students the opportunity to engage in teacher-guided independent research and presentations. The inclusion of such a unit would in essence ask students to "commit" in some way to the course material by picking research topics of personal interest to them. They would then investigate these topics in greater detail and present their findings to their classmates. Depending on the total time available, one or two such research projects could be conducted by each student.

The critical ingredient here would be expanding the range of research options beyond the five major religions. We will be better able to foster true commitment and engagement by allowing our students to explore in greater detail what genuinely speaks to them. Toward this goal, we must be willing to let students research and study not only Islam, Christianity, Judaism, Hinduism, and Buddhism, but also non-traditional and non-institutional options such as Humanism, Native American Spirituality, Earth-centered Spiritualities, Confucianism, Taoism, Sikhism, Jainism, Ba'hai'ism, Mysticism, and/or the pagan Greek, Norse, or Egyptian religions. Commitment to the subject matter of World Religions does not necessarily mean commitment to, or engagement with, one of the five great, present-day institutional religions.

Those teaching at the high school level are well acquainted with the relativistic worldview that many of our students possess. While relativism is a developmentally age-appropriate stage for many of our students, the prevailing World Religions pedagogies have not been sufficiently examined for how methodology and course content directly and indirectly reinforce, rather than challenge, such thinking. I believe that as moral and spiritual guides, we must challenge our students by directly and systematically addressing the inherent flaws and inadequacies of relativism. Even more importantly, we as teachers must challenge relativism because it undermines the autonomy and uniqueness of the faith traditions we seek to illuminate. Rather than becoming institutional vehicles for promoting shallow tolerance, homogenizing syncretism, and moral subjectivity, we must proactively address the dangers inherent in the study of World Religions and provide our students conceptual frameworks for making sense of religious multiplicity. One such model has been offered here, but with the recognition that every school has different needs and circumstances. It is hoped that the ideas contained herein will stimulate further thinking and inspire teachers of secondary school World Religions to enter into dialogue with one another and revisit existing curricula. What we have to offer our students in terms of better understanding the religiously diverse world around them is great. Let us ensure, to the extent we can, that we do not unintentionally leave them affirmed in thinking that the existence of competing truth claims means that there is no Truth.

Notes

[1] Ronald Duska and M. Whelan, *Moral Development: A Guide to Piaget and Kohlberg* (New York: Paulist Press, 1975), 45–47.

[2] John C. Gibbs, *Moral Development and Reality: Beyond the Theories of Kohlberg and Hoffman* (Thousand Oaks: Sage, 2003), 65.

[3] Larry P. Nucci, *Education in the Moral Domain* (New York: Cambridge University Press, 2001), 92.

[4] Duska, 49.

[5] James W. Fowler, *Stages of Faith: The Psychology of Human Development and the Quest for Meaning* (New York: HarperCollins, 1981), 82.

[6] Duska, 103.

[7] Fowler, 50.

[8] Nucci, 92.

[9] Fowler, 81.

[10] Mary C. Boys, *Educating in Faith: Maps and Visions* (San Francisco: Harper & Row, 1989), 194.

[11] Charles M. Shelton, *Adolescent Spirituality: Pastoral Ministry for High School and College Youth* (Chicago, IL: Loyola University Press, 1983), 54–55.

[12] Ibid., 56.

[13] Ibid.,56.

[14] Katherine G. Simon, *Moral Questions in the Classroom: How to Get Kids to Think Deeply About Real Life and Their Schoolwork* (New Haven, CT: Yale University Press, 2001), 180.

[15] Ibid., 187.

[16] Ibid., 188–89.

[17] Ibid., 190.

[18] Herodotus, "Custom Is King," in *Ethical Relativism*, ed. John Ladd (Belmont: Wadsworth, 1973), 12.

[19] Ruth Benedict, *Patterns of Culture* (Boston: Houghton Mifflin Company, 1934), 11.

[20] Diana L. Eck, *Encountering God: A Spiritual Journey from Bozeman to Banaras* (Boston: Beacon Press, 1993), 194.

[21] Louis Pojman, *Ethics: Discovering Right and Wrong* (Belmont: Wadsworth, 1990).

[22] Gibbs, 65.

[23] Hans Kung, *Christianity and World Religions: Paths to Dialogue* (Maryknoll, NY: Orbis Books, 1999), xix.

[24] Chester Gillis, *Pluralism: A New Paradigm for Theology* (Louvain: Peeters Press, 1998), 57–58.

[25] John Hick, *An Interpretation of Religion: Human Responses to the Transcendent* (New Haven, CT: Yale University Press, 1989), 376.

[26] Paul F. Knitter, *No Other Name: A Critical Survey of Christian Attitudes Toward the World Religions* (Maryknoll, NY: Orbis Books, 1985), 36.

[27] Ibid., 52.

[28] Ibid., 55.

[29] Ibid., 70.

[30] Ibid., 94–95.

[31] Ibid., 100–1.

[32] Ibid., 128–29.

[33] Ibid., 153.

[34] Eck, 191.

[35] Judith Simmer-Brown, "Commitment and Openness: A Contemplative Approach to Pluralism," in *The Heart of Learning: Spirituality in Education,* ed. S. Glazer (New York: Penguin Putnam, 1999), 100.

[36] Eck, 193.

[37] Ibid. 193.

[38] Simmer-Brown, 101.

Works Consulted

Benedict, Ruth. *Patterns of Culture*. Boston, MA: Houghton Mifflin Company, 1934.

Boys, Mary C. *Educating in Faith: Maps and Visions*. San Francisco, CA: Harper & Row Publishers, 1989.

Duska, Ronald and M. Whelan. *Moral Development: A Guide to Piaget and Kohlberg*. New York: Paulist Press, 1975.

Eck, Diana L. *Encountering God: A Spiritual Journey from Bozeman to Banares*. Boston: Beacon Press, 1993.

Fowler, James W. *Stages of Faith: The Psychology of Human Development and the Quest for Meaning*. New York: HarperCollins, 1981.

Gibbs, John C. *Moral Development and Reality: Beyond the Theories of Kohlberg and Hoffman*. Thousand Oaks, CA: Sage, 2003.

Gillis, Chester. *Pluralism: A New Paradigm for Theology.* Louvain: Peeters Press, 1998.

Herodotus. "Custom Is King." In *Ethical Relativism,* ed. John Ladd. Belmont: Wadsworth, 1973.

Hick, John. *An Interpretation of Religion: Human Responses to the Transcendent.* New Haven: Yale University Press, 1989.

Knitter, Paul F. *No Other Name: A Critical Survey of Christian Attitudes Toward the World Religions.* Maryknoll, NY: Orbis Books, 1985.

Kung, Hans. *Christianity and the World Religions: Paths to Dialogue.* Maryknoll, NY: Orbis Books, 1999.

Ladd, John. *Ethical Relativism.* Belmont: Wadsworth Company, 1973.

Nucci, Larry P. *Education in the Moral Domain.* New York: Cambridge University Press, 2001.

Pojman, Louis. *Ethics: Discovering Right and Wrong.* Belmont, MA: Wadsworth, 1990.

Shelton, Charles M. *Adolescent Spirituality: Pastoral Ministry for High School and College Youth.* Chicago: Loyola University Press, 1983.

Simmer-Brown, Judith. "Commitment and Openness: A Contemplative Approach to Pluralism." *The Heart of Learning: Spirituality in Education.* New York: Penguin Putnam, 1999.

Simon, Katherine G. *Moral Questions in the Classroom: How to Get Kids to Think Deeply About Real Life and Their Schoolwork.* New Haven: Yale University Press, 2001.

Chapter 8

Pilgrims and Pilgrimage: A Thematic Introduction for Secondary School Students to the Study of Religion

Timothy L. Morehouse

Days and months are travelers of eternity. So are the years that pass by. Those who steer a boat across the sea, or drive a horse over the earth till they succumb to the weight of years, spend every minute of their lives traveling. There are a great number of ancients too, who died on the road. I myself have been tempted for a long time by the cloud-moving wind— filled with a strong desire to wander.
~Matsuo Basho, *The Narrow Road to the Deep North*

At my first job as a secondary school religion teacher, I was put in charge of a religion elective for juniors and seniors entitled, "The Inward Pilgrimage." That course gave students a basic introduction to religion and the psychology of human development. Having little training in psychology, when it came time for me to teach the class, I dropped the psychology component, took up a study of pilgrimage literature, and focused the attention of the course on the motivations, worldviews, and experiences of representative pilgrims from the religious traditions of the world. The course kept its original name, but "Pilgrims and Pilgrimage" is probably a better title for the class that I ended up teaching. This reconfigured course not only introduced students to religion and to the practice of pilgrimage, but also engaged them at a personal level in order to ask them some basic questions about meaning, purpose, and value in human life. It remains one of the most popular courses that I have ever taught.

In what follows, I share the basic content and pedagogical philosophy of this course, explain why it has succeeded, and use the course to make a case for why secondary school students will benefit from taking such a course, or in fact any introductory course in the study of religion.

Framing up the Course and Organizing the Reading

My real preparation for teaching "Pilgrims and Pilgrimage" began in graduate school with John Carman's seminar on "Teaching the Introductory Course in the Study of Religion."[1] We explored a number of useful ideas in that seminar, but the one that Dr. Carman stressed in particular was that an introductory course in the study of religion could be organized in more interesting ways than as a sequential survey of religious traditions (the "this is week three, so it must be Judaism" formula). The most prominent scheme among these was to organize the introductory course by a theme found in religious practice, so we looked at university courses that did this, and also designed thematically oriented courses of our own. Among others, we looked at the possibilities and limitations of courses on sacrifice, healing, and on the interpretation of sacred texts. The wonderful book *Tracing Common Themes: Comparative Courses in the Study of Religion* provided more examples, notably among them a course on pilgrimage taught by Richard R. Niebuhr, Diana Eck, and William Graham to undergraduates at Harvard.[2] The syllabus for the Harvard course and Richard Niebuhr's article about it inspired my own pilgrimage class.[3]

The content of my secondary school course has changed over the years, but a steady set of priorities has shaped the syllabus in each of its forms. The course always begins with a few basic articles and lectures on pilgrimage and religion so that students learn a basic vocabulary with which to discuss primary sources that follow. My favorite of these introductory articles is Richard R. Niebuhr's "Pilgrims and Pioneers."[4] I like to begin with this article in particular because Niebuhr treats pilgrimage both as an activity common to almost all human beings and as a religious practice. He describes pilgrims as "persons in motion—passing through territories not their own—seeking something we might call completion, or perhaps the word clarity will do as well, a goal to which only the spirit's compass points the way."[5] Following this definition, someone can be considered a pilgrim whether or not that person identifies wholly, partially, or not at all with a religious tradition. This is definitely a liberal and inclusive definition, but I use it for several reasons. First, I agree with it. Second, it allows both secular and religious students to approach the phenomenon of pilgrimage with the sort of open imagination that rarely accompanies the study of a strictly "religious" topic. Finally, the use of Niebuhr's broad definition eventually allows students to compare traditionally religious pilgrimage narratives (like Bunyan's *Pilgrim's Progress*) with less strictly religious accounts (such as Kerouac's *On the Road*), in order to ask their own questions about what sort of journey can rightfully be called a successful pilgrimage, or a pilgrimage at all.

From this broad definition, the course introduction moves to excerpts from anthropologist Victor Turner's "The Centre out There: Pilgrim's Goal"[6] that provide more examples of pilgrimage in a religious context. Turner is particularly helpful in explaining how pilgrimage reinforces basic elements of a religious worldview, and in doing so reinforces the broad picture given by Niebuhr. Finally, though it focuses on the spiritual journey of the mystic rather than on pilgrimage *per se*, Robert S. Elwood Jr.'s chapter, "The Mystic Path" in his *Mysticism and Religion* also gives students language to describe different "stages" or "moments" in the journeys of the pilgrims that we study.[7] This article allows students to make explicit the connection in any pilgrimage between external changes in physical surroundings and internal changes within the pilgrims themsleves.[8]

Having made an introduction, the course moves quickly to pilgrims and their stories. With each pilgrim or set of pilgrims comes an introduction to a new religious tradition. Normally, we begin with one or two of Matsuo Basho's travel diaries in *The Narrow Road to the Deep North and Other Travel Sketches*.[9] This unit provides an introduction to Buddhism, to Shinto, and because Basho is one of the finest Haiku writers in Japanese history, to the connection between artistic and spiritual discipline. After Basho, we generally look at Christianity and its pilgrims. The Gospel of Mark works well in this unit. Bunyan's *Pilgrim's Progress* can also be effective with strong instructional support,[10] and in a very different way, J. D. Salinger's *Franny and Zooey* has also been effective and enjoyable.[11]

For Islam, accounts of the Hajj are important, and in this vein students have appreciated looking at appropriate sections from *The Autobiography of Malcolm X*.[12] Contemporary videotaped accounts of the Hajj supplement and deepen students' understanding of the ways in which a Muslim pilgrim's itinerary connects the pilgrim not only to other Muslims but also to the religious career of the prophet Muhammad himself.[13] With Judaism, the journey of the Jews as a people features prominently. Biblical accounts of the journey out of Egypt work well, as in a very different way do stories of Holocaust survivors.[14]

With the religious traditions of South Asia, Gita Mehta's novel *A River Sutra* has been popular not only because it tells the tales of several pilgrims, but also because it raises important questions about the value and place of traditional religion in the contemporary world.[15] Finally, the course has also at times featured the tales of secular or quasi-religious pilgrims, and tried to place these accounts in relation to their religious counterparts. Kerouac's *On the Road* has worked well in this regard,[16] as have chapters from Annie Dillard's *Pilgrim at Tinker Creek*,[17] as well as the Bruce Springsteen CD, *The Ghost of Tom Joad*, which takes its listeners on a journey through the poverty and alienation of the American underclass.[18] In these cases and others, students find pilgrims who purposely or accidentally leave what Richard Niebuhr calls an "abiding place," who then follow the wisdom of religious (or quasi-religious) traditions across "a country not their own" in order to reach a new abiding place at their journey's end (or to use Turner's phrase, in order to find a new "center out there").

Even this quick survey comes with a few warnings. First of all, a single secondary school semester will not accommodate all of the traditions and all of the literature mentioned above. In any given term, one has to pick and choose, and the choices I have made are the ones mentioned above.[19] Second, this reading list reveals an emphasis in my course on the pilgrimage experience of individuals and their personal growth. This approach does not mean that communal experiences of pilgrimage, the effect of pilgrimage on communities, or the effect of communal journeys on individuals are left out altogether (as suggested in different ways by the work on Judaism and Springsteen), but it does mean that the backbone of the current course consists of longer accounts of pilgrimage, either fiction or nonfiction, that allow students to closely follow one or two pilgrims from each of the religious traditions that the course features in a given semester. I see this bias toward individual experience as permissible so long as communal experience is not left out completely. Finally and importantly, to introduce students to both traditional and contemporary religious narratives, I make sure that all versions of this class feature premodern as well as contemporary sources.

Pedagogical Philosophy and Implications for Teaching

As I imply above, I take it for granted that the identity of pilgrim may apply at one time or another to every human being and that my seniors in particular come to the pilgrimage class quite aware of their own imminent departure from the "abiding places" in which they have been raised. This means that the personal experience of students is important in my class and must be given its due. At the same time, if personal experience overwhelms the class, nobody learns much about religion or about the pilgrims on whose stories the class is based. For this reason, no matter how personal our discussion, we never leave our texts far behind. Additionally, I try not to forget that the class it-self makes a kind of passage together as a group, and that this passage must also be recognized, guided, and affirmed. With all this in mind, the pedagogical aim of the course resolves itself into the cultivation and maintenance of a provocative tension among journeys that happen in three different "worlds": in the worlds of the texts that we read, in the world of each individual student, and in the common world that we inhabit in the classroom every day.

My class assignments and evaluative tools reflect this plan. Generally I begin with the world of the text, and have students read an introductory section of a pilgrim's account. After discussing this account and thereby bringing the pilgrim's voice into our discussion, I do a lecture or two, or give a few readings on the basic elements of the pilgrim's religious worldview. If our text is nonfiction, biographical details may be covered at this point. If fiction, the biography of the author may be helpful. Journal entries follow that ask students to reflect on aspects of the pilgrim's journey or on aspects of their own lives that this journey evokes. Important differences and continuities are noted. Meanwhile in class, discussions take most of our time, focusing on journal questions and on the accounts of the pilgrims themselves. Quizzes are used to ensure that reading gets done and that important concepts are understood, and the major evaluation for each unit of the course comes in the form of a test, a short project, or simply in the accumulated grades for journal entries on a given text. In this way, each sort of assignment motivates and informs differently. Journals quickly refine an understanding of, and reactions to, the text in question. Quizzes ensure basic common knowledge and keep the class moving as a single group. Class discussions and other special projects bring broad and speculative student reflection into the common life of the class.

As far as assessment is concerned, while I want students to reflect on pilgrimage in "three worlds (in the world of the text, in their own world, and in the world of the classroom)," almost all of my grading focuses on the reflection that students do on the texts that we cover. This is so for several reasons. First of all, while I myself think that students' lives will be enriched if they are able to view them through the lens of pilgrimage, and that class discussions will be more interesting as a result, I refuse to penalize a student who does not want to do this, or one who does not want to show me evidence that he or she has done so. If a student wants to keep his or her own world shut to the world of the class, I affirm that right to privacy. Second, while I think that the movement of the class as a group is important, I am also unwilling to penalize the individual members of a class if the class never does work very well together. Our experience as a group will be impoverished if this is the case, but because there are many reasons for poor group dynamics in a class, I will not lower students' grades in the event that the group does not work particularly well together. This said, I do grade in part, as most secondary school teachers do, the level of investment that a student puts into the course. If journal entries are superficial or class participation (silent or verbal) is consistently lackluster, this lack of enthusiasm will probably show up not only in grades on obligatory tests, but also in grades for the journals themselves, and in my overall evaluation at the end of the term.

Finally, the mention of class participation and of students' private lives raises a general and important pedagogical concern for instructors in the study of religion at both secondary and university levels. This is the problem of the extent to which, and the manner in which, students should be urged to identify with the religious people whom they study. For while it is important for any scholar or student of religion to identify in some imaginative way with those whom they study, it is also not constitutionally permissible in public schools (or I would argue a simple proposition in multi-religious private ones) for instructors to encourage this identification in any way that urges students to participate in a specific religious tradition that is under study.[20] Many instructors in the study of religion (at secondary and university levels in both public and private schools) address this issue by steering clear of assignments and ways of speaking that encourage participation in a religious tradition. Under this strategy, the closest that one gets to religious participation is observing a place of worship on an optional field trip, or perhaps viewing a film. Public school courses both at the university and secondary level must operate this way, and many courses at private institutions do so as well.

That said, some religiously identified private schools and universities have a policy of allowing or encouraging students to participate in religious activities in conjunction with academic courses in religion. The idea behind such a policy is to encourage students not only to reflect on religion or their own religious identity, but also to explore this identity by standing on the threshold of religious experience as tentative participants. To help students do this, a course might draw on the religious experience of a school-sponsored worship service, or might use class time to introduce religious practices such as devotional writing, prayer or meditation. In the United States currently, this approach to teaching religion in secondary schools (mixing analysis of religion with some sort of practice) commonly takes two forms. In the first case, the school or university is anchored in and seeks to cultivate a single religious tradition (for example, Roman Catholicism, Judaism, or Islam), and instructors teach participation in quite explicit terms. In the second scenario, schools less intent on teaching participation in a single religious tradition may allow teachers from one tradition or another to encourage some participation among those students who want to do so. In these sorts of schools, "participation" may mean anything from joining a worship service on a field trip to voluntarily sampling a religious practice such as prayer or meditation. In either case, it is important to emphasize that the stated educational policy of the school or the unstated ethos of the school allows teachers who teach about religion to also teach participation in religion.

As a private school teacher who does not work under the constitutional prohibitions of teachers in public schools, I am not legally prohibited from urging participation in religious practice, but in fact I usually end up taking a position not so far from my public school colleagues. I do this first in response to the ethos of my school, a place with religious and nonreligious students from many traditions whose parents assume that they come to class to learn about, rather than participate in religious practice. A second more personal reason is that I want students of various religious affiliations, and of no affiliation at all, to feel equally welcome in my classroom, and I worry that even voluntary classroom participation in religion can become coercive. Finally, even if a group of students do want me to teach a religious practice in class, I do not want to introduce those students to a practice that I, in my role as a classroom teacher, am not able to help them nurture and support. This means that religious practices in my class are handled by means of intellectual reflection, and not by means of doing the practices themselves. I urge students to reflect on religious experience and will even sometimes reflect on my own, but I don't do more than that. At the end of the day my students may indeed be pilgrims, but my purpose as a classroom teacher at Trinity School is not to lead them on a series of religious pilgrimages. It is rather to show them how, and that such pilgrimages are possible.

Explaining the Success of the Pilgrimage Class

For reasons that I have hinted at so far, students really enjoy this class. To explain more directly why this is the case, it is best to start by pointing out again that our reading list is full of compelling stories. They show real people trying to work through real-life problems, and making pilgrimages in order to face and surmount these problems. Another reason is that juniors and seniors in secondary school feel themselves ready to honestly encounter the ways that different sorts of people wrestle with what makes a meaningful human life. Such students know that people hold a variety of religious and philosophical views, and are curious about why they do. Additionally, because people with religious views shape the course of world and national events, students naturally want to know as much as possible about what motivates them.

Beyond these reasons, students enjoy this course because (as Richard Niebuhr points out) the practice of pilgrimage is a basic human activity, and seems to them at some level as fitting a rite of passage as the ones given to them by American popular culture (to earn a driver's license, to use drugs and alcohol, or to have a piercing done, or a tattoo made). In fact, it seems to me that my students respect the journeys about which they read and the transformations that accompany them. Finally, students like this course because they themselves are preparing to leave home soon for college, and therefore take seriously the idea that a significant journey awaits them. Their career in secondary school has given them an impressive array of intellectual skills, and they want to apply these skills to an examination of, and preparation for, their own incipient departures from home. They want their trip to adult life to be worthy, enjoyable, and meaningful, and this class on pilgrimage allows them to read about others who have shared these desires, and in one way or another succeeded in fulfilling them. Of course, they know that their own religious or philosophical commitments will probably differ from those whom they study, but equally important are the similarities that they find. These resemblances let them know that they are not the first humans to make difficult journeys in search of themselves, their God, and their place in the world.

The Introductory Course in the Study of Religion and the Secondary School Curriculum

After all this, an essential question remains: why take the time and trouble to include a course on pilgrimage (or any other course that introduces the study of religion) in a secondary school curriculum? The simple answer to this is that secondary school students benefit enormously and uniquely from taking such a course. I will finish explaining how this is so, but before I do, it is important to understand

why many American high school students are not currently introduced to any study of religion at all.

This omission is most easily understood in historical terms.
Throughout the nineteenth and part of the twentieth centuries a sort
of protestant Christian hegemony ruled over American public schools.
Students might pray in school, or before athletic events. Graduation
ceremonies would include Baccalaureate services. In many areas, it
was tacitly assumed that students were Christian, so that students
definitely learned about religion, but through a protestant Christian
lens. This way of handling religion in schools has been called "The Sacred Public School." By the 1950s in some communities, and by the
1970s in most, this protestant hegemony was overturned in favor of
another model that came to be known as "The Naked Public School."
In this model, religion became a taboo topic, avoided for fear of law-
suits, political battles, and parental complaints. Teachers avoided discussion of religion altogether because they did not want to appear to
advocate for its practice. The positive contribution of this "Naked Public School" was that teachers became aware of constitutional prohibitions against asking students to participate in religious activities.
Schools became more sensitive to the religious and philosophical diversity in their student and parent bodies. The cost of this "Naked
Public School" was that basic religious literacy was lost during a period of time when the religious landscapes of the United States and
the world were becoming more, not less, complex.

In a number of private schools that had been founded by religious
communities, similar evolutions took place for a variety of reasons.
Some schools grew away from the need to teach religion as they became financially independent and no longer needed the support of the
religious communities that had founded them. Others, quite often
protestant Christian schools, felt that teaching religion classes sup-
ported a religious identity that their increasingly diverse populations
would no longer support. Many schools simply found it less important
to be religiously identified as the ambient culture became increasingly

accepting of private schools that taught no religion. With pressure for college admission often driving enrollment, it is also true that many private schools wrestled with the need for religion requirements. Could not such requirements be dropped to make room for other courses that were more attractive to college admissions officers? Finally, it must be admitted that religion classes in a number of institutions lacked the academic rigor of their competitors and were simply swept away in favor of more reliable options. In truth, a number of these forces were often at work in any given school, and the result was roughly the same: As the twentieth century moved forward, schools that were more loosely affiliated with religious institutions minimized the study of religion in their curricula, or dropped it altogether.

Still, many private schools did continue to teach about religion, and it is in such a context that I came to understand the reasons why an introduction to the study of religion is so valuable for high school students. I hope that a case to support this claim has been implied in the course of this essay, but keeping the pilgrimage class in mind as a model, it is possible to generalize three basic arguments in favor of such an introduction that make it even more explicit. Because none of these arguments suggests that it is necessary to have students do anything but learn about religion, they all should hold equally well for public or private schools.

The first argument for introducing students to the study of religion is that they gain a basic religious literacy. This sort of literacy is important for several reasons, the first of which is that it makes possible a high level of competency in other academic disciplines such as history, geography, civics, and the study of literature. Religious references and questions in these fields are often minimized or overlooked by teachers who feel unprepared or disinclined to explore them fully. (How exactly was Martin Luther King, Jr. influenced by African American Christianity? Was Holden Caufield a Christ figure or not? To what extent is J. D. Salinger's work influenced by the Buddhist teachings that flooded New York City in the 1950s?) With an introduction to the study of religion under their belts, students will feel comfortable searching out the sources of religious references themselves, in secondary school and in college as well. To this way of thinking, an introduction to religion becomes one important component of a liberal arts education.

Basic religious literacy and a basic respect for religious difference are also critical if liberally educated students are to assume responsible positions as citizens of a world in which religion shapes both national and global events. Not so long ago, commentators in the West predicted that secularization would make religion irrelevant as a force in human life. The chaotic aftermath of Yugoslavia's dismemberment, the events of September 11, 2001, the Afghan war, the Iraq war, and the spread of "world" religions in the United States completely disprove this prediction. How now can students evaluate and respond to such events? How will they decide for themselves to what extent, and how, religious impulses have shaped the world and nation in which they live? They cannot do so very well without an introduction to religion that does not dismiss or reduce it. Some understanding of the topic is required if they are to become well-informed citizens of their nation, and of the world.

A final argument for the study of religion in high school has to do with a school's responsibility to prepare students who can think in sophisticated terms about ethical and philosophical or theological questions. Public school teachers and their counterparts from different sorts of private schools will think about this task in different ways, but most teachers will that agree that part of their job is to encourage students to reflect carefully about what is good, and about the human condition in the world. This encouragement can, and should be, given in every class. History and English classes have long been popular locations for this sort of encouragement, but courses that study religion are perhaps even better suited for it. This is so for several reasons, the most striking of which is that any comparative study of religion introduces students to a variety of worldviews that are accompanied by a corresponding variety of ethical systems. As students compare the ways that various thinkers construe the world and the nature of human goodness in it, they will naturally have to ask themselves where they stand as well. So long as the teacher does not advocate any single point of view but rather introduces several, the product will be a student who can live in a complex world, and think for herself about the nature of that world, of humans, and of the good.

Notes

[1] John Carman is the Parkman Professor of Divinity and Professor Emeritus of Comparative Religion at Harvard University.

[2] *Tracing Common Themes: Comparative Courses in the Study of Religion,* John B. Carman and Steven P. Hopkins (Atlanta, GA: Scholar's Press, 1991), is out of print, but a good place to find other ideas for thematically structured courses in the study of religion is at the American Academy of Religion syllabus project: www.aarweb.org.

[3] Richard R. Niebuhr, "Pilgrimage as a Thematic Introduction to the Comparative Study of Religion," in *Tracing Common Themes: Comparative Courses in the Study of Religion,* John B. Carman and Steven P. Hopkins, eds., (Atlanta, GA: Scholar's Press, 1991), 51–64.

[4] Richard R. Niebuhr, "Pilgrims and Pioneers," *Parabola* 9.3 (1984): 6–13.

[5] Richard R. Niebuhr, "Pilgrims and Pioneers," 7.

[6] Victor Turner, "The Centre Out There: Pilgrim's Goal," *History of Religions* 12 (1973): 191–230.

[7] Robert S. Elwood, Jr., *Mysticism and Religion* (Englewood Cliffs, NJ: Prentice-Hall, 1980), 167–84.

[8] Different religious, scholarly, and psychological traditions use varied schemes to describe both external and internal change. Because each pilgrimage account also suggests its own scheme of progress, I feel comfortable using only one or two of these generalized conceptual models to begin with. I use Niebuhr and Ellwood, but other models (such as the ox herding drawings of Zen Buddhism) could also be introduced as the class progresses.

[9] "The Records of a Travel Worn Satchel," and sometimes "The Narrow Road to the Deep North," in Matsuo Basho, *The Narrow Road to the Deep North and Other Travel Sketches* (New York: Penguin Books, 1966), 71–90 and 97–143.

[10] John Bunyan, *The Pilgrim's Progress* (New York: Oxford University Press, 1998).

[11] J. D. Salinger, *Franny and Zooey* (Boston: Little, Brown and Company, 1961).

[12] Malcolm X, as told to Alex Haley, *The Autobiography of Malcolm X* (Random House, 1975); and Spike Lee, *Malcolm X* (Warner Home Video, 1992).

[13] Particularly good is *Hajj: The Pilgrimage* (Princeton, NJ: Films for the Humanities and Sciences, 2000).

[14] See for example, Elie Wiesel, *Night* (New York: Bantam Doubleday Dell, 1982).

[15] Gita Mehta, *A River Sutra* (New York: Random House, 1994).

[16] Jack Kerouac, *On the Road* (New York: Penguin Classics, 1991).

[17] Annie Dillard, *Pilgrim at Tinker Creek* (New York: HarperCollins, 1998).

[18] Bruce Springsteen, *The Ghost of Tom Joad* (New York: Sony, CD #67484, r.d. November 21, 1995).

[19] I have not yet dealt with Native American traditions or much with religion in China or Sub-Saharan Africa, but hope to do so in future versions of the course.

[20] I do not mean to imply here that the First Amendment of the United States Constitution prohibits public school teachers from teaching *about* religion. To the contrary, the constitution clearly supports instruction *about* religion so long as such instruction is not coercive in favor of one tradition or another. In fact, I hope that this article suggests that a course on pilgrimage can be offered to seniors in the context of a public school English or history department.

Works Consulted

Basho, Matsuo. *The Narrow Road to the Deep North and Other Travel Sketches.* New York: Penguin Books, 1966.

Bunyan, John. *The Pilgrim's Progress.* New York: Oxford University Press, 1998.

Carman, John B., and Steven P. Hopkins, eds. *Tracing Common Themes: Comparative Courses in the Study of Religion.* Atlanta, GA: Scholar's Press, 1991.

Dillard, Annie. *Pilgrim at Tinker Creek.* New York: HarperCollins, 1998.

Elwood, Robert S., Jr. *Mysticism and Religion.* Englewood Cliffs, NJ: Prentice-Hall, 1980.

Kerouac, Jack. *On the Road.* New York: Penguin Classics, 1991.

Malcolm X, as told to Alex Haley. *The Autobiography of Malcolm X.* New York: Random House, 1975.

Mehta, Gita. *A River Sutra.* New York: Random House, 1994.

Niebuhr, Richard. "Pilgrims and Pioneers." *Parabola: Myth, Tradition & The Search for Meaning* 9.3 (1984): 6–13.

Salinger, J. D. *Franny and Zooey.* Boston, MA: Little, Brown and Company, 1961.

Springsteen, Bruce. November 21, 1995. *The Ghost of Tom Joad.* New York: Sony CD #67484.

Wiesel, Elie. *Night.* New York: Bantam Doubleday Dell, 1982.

Chapter 9

In Our End Is Our Beginning

Mark Rigg

The other night I was out to dinner with my family. As we munched our meals and tried to keep our young children happy, a high school girl and her parents came in and sat in the booth behind us. Because the girl's voice was loud and often strident, we learned a great deal about her and her life at school. At one point the girl, whom I shall call Sarah, started complaining that a conversation about religion had emerged in a history class. Apparently several of the students in the room had even begun to express convictions of some kind. When her parents showed no surprise at this turn of events, she explained to them that the Constitution forbade this kind of conversation in school and that "Christians can't tell Buddhists they're wrong! Buddhists can't tell Muslims they're wrong! Muslims can't tell Jews they're wrong!" Her parents put up a few feeble attempts to talk about people's rights to self-expression, but it was clear that Sarah was having none of it.

What I am not looking to draw from this little story is a lament about how Americans are ignorant of the Constitution or about young people's intolerance for the supposed failures of tolerance in organized religion. These may well be issues worth lamenting, but this is too small a story for that much grief; and, frankly, it seems to me unkind to ask the young woman to bear the burden of such large social issues. Rather, I would like to point out the way in which Sarah got something right—at the level of subtext at least. What she got right was the sense on the part of many, many people in education that religion is a private matter. That she misunderstood the constitutional separation of religion and state as actually forbidding students the expression of religious conviction is an unsurprising consequence of the kind of educational system we have in the vast majority of secondary schools, both public and private. I am sure none of her teachers ever told her that religion is a private matter; in fact, I would be surprised if her teachers had said anything at all about religion. I cannot recall, in my dozen years of public education, a single classroom conversation about a genuinely religious topic. These two approaches amount to the same thing, though. In both cases the message is clear: Religion is a forbidden topic. It is private in the same way that family squabbles are and sex used to be: Everyone knows what is going on "out there," but polite, tolerant people do not talk about it.

The inadequacy of such an approach has become clear to me through the course of my own education. My high school years at a solid though not exceptional public school gave me a sense of the importance of mastering traditional subjects (except, of course, theology), a desire to succeed in some sort of intellectual environment, and an unreflective assurance that religion or a life concerned with the spirit is nonessential. Simply put, I came to understand that human history can be adequately and even fully understood without an understanding of the numinous and the various beliefs surrounding it.

My four years at a fine New England liberal arts college mostly reinforced and intensified these beliefs. Except that once in a while it became clear how helpful it would be to have a better understanding of the major world religions or at least of the major western religions. I signed up for a course in seventeenth-century poetry and discovered that some of the most useful background material at my disposal was what I had learned fifteen years earlier in Sunday School: Donne, Herbert, Milton, and others all assumed that the reader knew the biblical stories and the history of God in the West and shared their sense of the contemporary value of such stories. Courses in Latin and Greek produced a similar experience: These ancient people actually believed in the numinous! Furthermore, I had comparable experiences with history, foreign languages, and architecture. Probably all that kept me from falling into a clear sympathy for a life of faith was my unexamined belief that the history of the West and perhaps of the world is one of progress, progress on the spiritual as well as the material level. In short, the fact that these authors were in the past automatically made their opinions suspect.

By the end of college, then, though I could not have articulated it, I was becoming conscious of, and therefore skeptical of, the idea that the human story can be understood separate from its religious elements and also of the belief that the fundamental engine that drives the world—or the western world at least—is progress. The final push that exposed both of these assumptions came from an unlikely source: a gentle Episcopal priest who had been a private school chaplain and whose faith life seemed as tolerant and conventional as could be. Then in a brief, passing conversation she mentioned, "I don't believe in rights." She could not have surprised me more if she had said that she did not believe in the sun or in peace or in roses. When I pushed her, she elaborated just a bit: "I don't believe we have a right to this or that. I believe we have gifts; and I believe in gratitude." In many ways, that two-sentence elucidation set the curriculum for the next four or five years of my life. What could it mean that a person of her erudition, a priest and a teacher and an American, did not believe that rights existed? I had never heard anybody seriously contemplate such a thing. If statements about rights could be claims of faith and not of fact, i.e., a set of beliefs that some trust and others do not but that cannot be proven in the lab or on the blackboard or through argument, then what else might be up for grabs? Moreover, if, instead of the language of rights, she employed—without translation into some modern idiom—the biblical language of covenant and gift, of grace and gratitude, was this not confirmation of my earlier suspicion that the past was more than a series of rough drafts in preparation for the glories of the present? Finally, if the past could be as relevant as the

present, then the whole materialist philosophy of progress was suspect.

My path to an educational philosophy, then, has been shaped by
contrasting much of the philosophy of education in the schools where
I was taught with the understanding of learning that appeared again
and again in the actual authors that I read.[1] I had learned in high
school that scholars do not place a high value on religion. I had
learned that the past was primarily of interest in an archaeological
way: We might dig it up or mine it for insights into how people
thought and acted "back then," and we might occasionally in a play or
a poem find useful insights into the human psyche; but we should
never suspect the ancients of knowing much about theology or science
or the like that could still be useful to us. When I went back and read
the pre-moderns, though, I discovered the opposite of both of these
claims: I discovered that the vast majority of scholars throughout time
had placed a very high premium indeed on spiritual insight. In addition, I discovered in a more experiential way that their insights—their
poetry and drama, their myths, and their theology—were deeply
meaningful and helpful to me and to others who took them seriously.
The language of the recent past, the Enlightenment vocabulary of progress and freedom from the past, came to seem not an emancipation
or a revolution but rather an aberration, a failure to keep the baby
while throwing out the bath water of the past (or perhaps of confusing
the baby with the bath water!), and an inability to recognize in itself
the element of faith in its claims.

The result of all this has been for me a redefining of faith that is
more in line with thinkers of the first or thirteenth century C.E. than
with those of the eighteenth or twenty-first. In contemporary usage
faith is often little more than a synonym for religion. Faith-based op-
erations are funded by a particular church or religious group. The
term "person of faith" is roughly equal to "religious person." All of
this, again, is the result of a modern desire to place religion in its own
container, preferably airtight. Were we to take a more ancient and

broader definition of faith as "assurance of things not seen" we could begin to be honest about the pervasiveness of faith in education: the faith of English teachers in the beauty and meaningfulness of literature; the faith of math and science teachers of the value of learning formulae and theorems that most of their students will not use again later in life; the faith of art and music teachers that using a paint brush or playing an instrument or loving jazz expands the richness of a person's life. Were that to happen, were we to use faith as a way of denoting trust in endeavors that enrich us, we could then be more honest about the value of a specifically religious faith among the other faiths that we have.

Right now I am imagining objections to what little I have written so far. One is pragmatic and comes from someone who fears that I am seeking, under the rubric of "faith in education," to introduce a particular religion into public schools with the ultimate goal of catechetical education and the conversion of people considered unbelievers. Nothing could be farther from the truth. As will, I hope, become clear, I am deeply suspicious of the desire of educators to impose large answers on large groups of people. That kind of universalism is, in my reading of intellectual history, as much a tenet of the Enlightenment as of any kind of theism, and I eschew it.

Am I, though, critiquing public education while praising the private? Yes and no. Yes, there is no question that I see a real shortcoming in the lack of religious dialogue in public secondary schools. No, I am not offering private schools as a panacea. On the contrary, I do not see most of our finest private schools behaving much differently from the public schools. They may have a bit of scripture as their motto; they may meet in a chapel instead of in an auditorium and have services instead of assemblies; but the goals and assumptions are much the same. In other words, they may have a history of theism, and the trappings may still be in place; but I do not see many of them making a serious effort to confront the secular materialism that the students see in the media and in the public lives of so many Americans.

A similar but more philosophical objection comes from one who is a proponent of a progressive, secular agenda; and it concerns my use of the word faith. This objection suspects that I have defined faith as broadly as I have not because I believe it a better use of the term but merely in order to allay the fears of rationalists and secularists. My real motive is understood to be covert evangelism: "He will say that everything is faith, and before you know it, Christianity and French literature and chemistry will all be on an equal footing because their respective teachers 'have faith' in the value of the material." The tendentious side of me points out that this kind of suspicion of religion and religious thinkers is an Enlightenment begging of the question. It assumes that evangelism and religious faith are superstitious errors and therefore views all attempts to bring them into the conversation as an effort in bad faith (no pun intended). Of course, if they are right about religion, that is, if they are right that there is no God or at least none worth attending to, then bringing religion into the public debate is almost certainly a bad idea (though I suppose it may still be done with honorable intentions). However, the opposite is equally true: If there is such a divine being, then leaving the Divine out of the conversation is a big mistake.

The other part of me is more sympathetic and acknowledges that I would be very uncomfortable indeed if someone were to use a general argument for faithfulness of one kind or another as a pretext for establishing a particular religion as the official voice of the state. My defense against an accusation of harboring covert designs, then, must be a further clarification of my use of the word faith. As I hope will become clear, what I advocate is faith not in God or gods but in the theological enterprise itself; or, to put it another way, faith in the value of asking spiritual questions. Just as a math teacher knows that her job is not to make all of her students professional mathematicians, so a teacher who raises spiritual or theological questions knows that his job is not to make his students priests or even churchgoers. On the contrary, the theology teacher and the math teacher have a similar task: to present students with information that other human beings have found useful. Here the parallel between theology and other disciplines is clearer: Because the chemistry teacher believes that the structure of the universe matters, he teaches chemistry; because another believes that the French have a beautiful language and a history of fine authors, she teaches French literature. Because another believes that questions of origin and meaning matter, she teaches the theological enterprise: the questions it asks and the range of possible answers, including theism, atheism, secularism, polytheism, and so on.

Does the question arise of what to teach? Which religion gets more airtime, what books are to be read? Sure, but teachers in other disciplines encounter the same kind of questions all the time. History teachers cannot teach all of history; English teachers cannot teach all the good books. Do these teachers conclude that the subject should not be taught because they are unable to teach all of it? No. I will come later to some practical suggestions about what a school serious about theological education might consider, but must turn now to what I believe to be the strongest argument of all in favor of addressing somehow, at some conscious and intentional level, the kinds of issues raised by the study of theology.

I have so far offered stories about the high price people pay who believe that religion is either *de jure* or *de facto* a forbidden topic in American education, and I have offered some personal reflections on the gains available to someone who can set history and literature and the like in their religious contexts. I have high hopes that a reader might be moved by these to reevaluate the paucity of theological reflection in American education. However, as valuable as these stories and insights may or may not be, it is simple logic that the strongest argument is one that rests not on persuasion but on proof. If an argument ends on the hard rock of knowledge, if it ends with a conclusive QED, then one may point to the argument and say, "There, if anywhere, truth is to be found." In the case of education, if one could prove that there is a field of learning about which it is impossible not to teach, that education by definition offers lessons in this particular field, then who could argue but that the best thing is to teach it well? If one has no choice but rather must do something, of course one should do it well. I propose that all humans have faith, and that all education, whether it wishes to or not, teaches faith.

The argument can be made complex, but the simplest form is this: The human condition is one that is based neither entirely on trust nor entirely on knowledge. We do not simply follow instinct or some inner voice, but neither are we simply biological machines, calculating and acting in accordance with our calculations. We are, I think, too smart for the first option and too ignorant for the second. We possess some knowledge; we strive for more. It is the nature of being human, however, not to have verifiable knowledge about some of the largest questions we face: "Where do we come from? Why are we here? What constitutes a 'good life'?" Each of us comes to some kind of answers to these questions and then acts in accordance with what we believe to be true. This trust is just as well called faith. Can someone who believes in many gods prove it to us? Is the atheist any more able to prove that there are no such gods? I think not. As many before me have pointed out, it is the glory and the shackle of humanity that we are *homines religiosi*—people of faith. That faith or trust, grounded as it is in our ignorance, must be applied to the widest variety of worldviews: theistic, deistic, secular, humanist. No one is exempt from acting in the world with faith. To believe is to believe; not to believe is to believe.

If these claims are true, then the question does not become "Do we teach faith?" but "What do we teach about faith?" The only path that is obviously misguided in such a case is to say, "Let's teach nothing about it at all and let the students learn whatever they happen to learn." No coach, no teacher, no counselor would ever take such an approach with anything he thought important. Indeed, to do so would be to forsake one's calling to be a coach or a teacher or a counselor.

We do not want our students to learn whatever they happen to learn wherever they happen to learn it about American literature or how to play a sport or whether to use drugs. If we did, we would be content to let them acquire this information from the latest movie or TV show or ESPN broadcast. I do not think I am very far out on a limb to suggest that, if we have reached that point, it is time to turn in our chalk and grade book, our cleats and whistles, and go home. The educator who does not value education needs to call it quits.

How should educators respond to the insight that teaching about faith is inevitable? A helpful analogy might be found in the teaching of a subject that came to be considered vital if not exactly inevitable. I am thinking of the introduction into most public and private schools in the second half of the twentieth century of sex education. Though the issue is, of course, complex, it seems relatively uncontroversial to point out that due to a variety of influences such as the media, suburbanization, the various radical movements and counter-movements of the sixties, to name just a few, educators began to see the need to educate children on sex. There was dispute about what to teach, largely because it was understood that it was impossible to talk about sex without acknowledging that there were deep moral issues involved. In the end, however, the vast majority of Americans came to believe that basic knowledge of human anatomy, sexual health, and sexually transmitted diseases were important to the growth and welfare of our children.

Such an example might be seen to undermine sympathy for my basic argument. Those who have favored sex education and those who have favored religious education in schools have not always seen eye to eye. However, I maintain that the analogy between sexual and theological education is a good one: In each case the temptation is to say nothing, to declare the topic private and out of bounds; however, in each case to say nothing is to allow our children to learn about basic human issues through resources largely outside our control, resources co-opted by the media and other interests happy to use these issues in the pursuit of profit.

Once we have acknowledged the fundamental nature of the theological pursuit—the human-ness of asking questions of origin, meaning, happiness and the like—the awesome issue that follows is "What do we teach?" How can we select among the myriad opinions, insights, and worldviews that are available for our consideration? One kind of answer is practical: It involves identifying key concerns such as good and evil, the existence or non-existence of the divine, the nature of happiness; making some reasonable divisions among representatives of the various traditions such as western monotheism, eastern polytheism, secular humanism, philosophical agnosticism, and so on; it also involves finding or creating textbooks that seek to lay these materials out in an even-handed way.

The practical consideration, however, is guided by another that must precede it: the teleological consideration. In short, all good teaching begins with a clear, well-defined understanding of the *telos*, the goal, at which one is aiming. A teacher makes certain fundamental decisions about what he or she wants the students to know at the end of the course. Let us take history as an example. A teacher cannot teach just history: She has somewhere between 150 and 180 days in this full-year course, and that is surely not enough to cover all of history, even if we understand that to mean no more than "all of human history." So she limits it to United States history; then she decides that such a course will essentially be a political investigation of history; and so on. While the syllabus indicates that the students will move from concrete to abstract, from events to their meaning, the teacher has worked in the other direction: Beginning with all of history, she has made a series of educational decisions that begin by looking at the knowledge of the student at the end of the course. In fact, if she is especially farsighted, she may look even farther than that: She may write her course taking into account the kind of citizen her course will help to mold or the kind of political participant her course may assist in creating.

Not teaching theology has meant, in effect, that we have ignored the obvious truth that all people think and act based at least partly on their religious worldview. Starting with the important tenet that we do not want to teach one particular religion, we have failed to realize the legitimate goal of helping our children to make their theological decisions in a context of basic knowledge. Again the analogy to sexual education is apt. For many years we taught nothing or virtually nothing about sex, trusting the mores of the culture and the family to sustain people's sexual health. However, it became clear that such a system was no longer adequate, if it ever had been in the first place. The same principle applies to theology. In a culturally less diverse time, in a time when theological education was happening routinely in most people's lives in a church or synagogue or meeting hall, it was possible to assume that children were facing the fundamental spiritual issues that people everywhere have faced in all times. Further, it could be assumed that the ethical insights largely shared among the major religious traditions were being inculcated and were largely shared by the community. It seems to me patently obvious that such a situation no longer obtains. My own experience and the stories I hear from colleagues across the country are that a great many of our students come from homes where virtually none of the great human issues are being addressed; further, our students come from an ever-increasing range of families and communities. We can choose to ignore education in the life of the spirit, I suppose, just as educators of the previous generation could have avoided sexual education. However, we should not, then, be surprised that our students make poor ethical and spiritual decisions based on inadequate information.

To facilitate a conversation about this complex subject, I propose now to offer four basic models of religious education and to critique their capacities and their appropriateness in the world of private and public schools. They are arranged along a spectrum that might be understood in terms of doctrinal specificity; however, as with so many spectra, the far edges meet.

The first model is the catechetical model. Though the word *catechetical* is primarily a Christian term, I mean here nothing more or less than schools which are explicit about their faith affiliation and who teach that faith as an integral part of their curriculum: Roman Catholic parochial schools and Jewish yeshivas would be examples. A school grounded in this model is unlikely to suffer from teleological blindness because its religious goals are integral to its mission. While there is the danger of what we often call without thinking a "parochial" outlook, my own limited experience is that students who come out of good schools of this type are often more versed in religious traditions other than their own than those from more liberal or "open-minded" schools. Such schools typically teach world religions and ethics in addition to studying their own scripture and tradition. As a pattern for schools of no tradition or of a variety of traditions, however, the catechetical model is clearly of limited use.

Of vastly more use to others as a pattern is the second model: the theological model. This model is grounded in the understanding of faith that I proposed above: faith as the conviction of the value or meaningfulness of something. More particularly in this case, faith is trust in the value of theological questions and in looking at such questions from a theistic, as compared to a secular, point of view. While the theological model does not expound a particular creed, it recognizes that a full grasp of the human story includes weighing the various roles and claims of theological worldviews. It is unapologetically open to and even inclined to theistic answers. It cannot help but point out, for example, the roles of the numinous in human history and the wide range of fields such as literature where religion has played a central role. Unlike secular education it is not, of course, married *prima facie* either to cultural apathy about religion or to the myth of progress so central to our society.

There are, it seems to me, at least three advantages to an education that engages the theological model. The first is that the vast majority of the curriculum would look very much like that of any other school; students at such a school would find themselves as prepared for college and careers as students of other schools. While a theological curriculum would be in place, its purpose would not be to intrude on the other disciplines but to augment, even as now the various departments of knowledge augment each other.

The other two advantages to this model are in the form of challenges. First, the theological model challenges the materialistic worldview that pervades the popular culture. Virtually every human religion that we might want our students to study, from contemporary Buddhism to ancient Greek polytheism, offers a critique of the view that matter is all that exists and that material goals are sufficient to fulfill us. Even more, the theological model, while not advocating a particular religion or denomination, is unapologetically theistic and asserts that a worldview that incorporates a god-picture (or gods-picture) is more likely to get us to the true nature of things than a materialist worldview. Such an advocacy is a challenge to our students to look beyond the mall or the successful career for sources of meaning.

From my own teaching I conclude that such an alternative would be deeply welcome. My students tend to fall into one of two camps: Some genuinely believe that stuff will make them happy, that the right gadgets and car and college and career will produce an earthly but abiding happiness. Frankly, the young lives of such students produce in me sadness akin to watching a car accident: While I know that there will be a crash coming, in this case an epiphany about the limits of a life spent in quest of material happiness, I am largely incapable of preventing it. The second group of students, though, has intuited that stuff is unlikely to make or keep them happy but do not have especially clear ideas about what to put in its place; they tend either to embrace athletics and academics and other opportunities for success in a kind of desperate alchemy, hoping that the right combination of achievements will make them happy; or they reject all these avenues, believing that the world and its pleasures are a charade.

Perhaps most striking is what these students have in common, both with each other and with most of the adults around them: They express their perspective economically, that is, through what they purchase. In other words, they and we have been so conditioned by our consumer culture that all perspectives, even those antithetical to this culture, are now expressed through buying power. Do you value material gain? Great, here are the car and the elite college and the house you must buy. Do you disdain the material culture? Terrific, here are the CDs and the clothing catalogues and the organic food aisles at the grocery that will help you express these preferences. In light of this, a single course that challenged our students explicitly with a few different non-materialistic value systems could be a shock to their systems from which they might have the good fortune never to recover.

The second challenge the theological model offers comes fairly straightforwardly from presenting various forms of ancient wisdom and insight in a positive light. First, such a challenge would at least force students to examine the Enlightenment doctrine of progress explicitly; for if ancient cultures can speak words to us that are worthy of our time and reflection, then it cannot be a fact of observation like gravity that the human race is on a path of inevitable or at least historical progress. Further, this challenge would ask those who are ardent supporters of the modern doctrine of tolerance to live out their beliefs: If we are to be tolerant, then we must tolerate the existence and discussion of such old-fashioned beliefs as are found in Judaism or Christianity or Taoism.

The danger of this model is, of course, that it can become catechetical, that teaching from a theistic point of view can become a pretext for teaching a particular religion's doctrine about theism. Care must be taken; as in many fields of inquiry, an unscrupulous or uninformed teacher can do damage. However, my experience teaching American and British literature leads me to believe by analogy that this model can work. At the end of the year, I occasionally ask my students if, based on the work done in the classroom, they can tell which of the many literary and philosophical positions learned in the course are similar to my own beliefs and tastes. Usually they tell me that at first they thought I was a Calvinist because I spent so much time on the Puritans; but then our work on Jefferson led them to believe I was a Deist; then the high energy level in the classroom during Emerson left them certain I was some sort of Transcendentalist. The pattern continues with Romanticism, Naturalism, and Modernism. Why should theology teachers not be able to get to the end of the year with their students knowing that, while they advocated for the value of theological education and some sort of appreciation for the numinous, it is unclear whether their teachers were Buddhists or Jews or Unitarians or deists or humanists?

The third model is the religious studies model. At first glance this approach might appear little different from the theological model, and in practice the two certainly overlap: Each seeks to expose students to a variety of faith responses to what I have been calling the great questions of humanity. However, the fundamental assumptions regarding the purpose of religious education that undergirds them are quite different. Whereas the theological model presupposes the value of theism and of theological inquiry and is therefore teaching this material for its own sake, the religious studies model presupposes the value of religious knowledge separate from explicit assertion of its truthfulness and is therefore more likely to be teaching from a sociological or psychological or historical perspective. In other words, one teaches Buddha's Four Noble Truths or Jesus' Sermon on the Mount not because it might be true but because so many human beings have considered the issues being addressed to be fundamentally important, because our society and our psyches and the history of our peoples bear the stamp of this or that religion.

This worldview shares to a large extent the first of the advantages of the theological model: It too offers the opportunity to examine, if less of a justification to critique, secular materialism. It is less useful in offering a counterbalance to the myth of progress that pervades our culture. This probably should not surprise us, for both the myth of progress and the religious studies model are deeply influenced by the Enlightenment. The former imagines that it occupies a position that stands largely outside the ebb and flow of human history and sees the past as something that has been escaped. The latter often seeks to critique the world's religions from a similar position, one of imagined disinterest: the value of each religion's contribution to the human story is adjudicated by a figure who knows the many religions but subscribes to no single one. To believe that one can be such an unmoved mover (or, more precisely, an unjudged judge) is, as I hope is immediately obvious, a faith claim and one that is certainly not open to factual verification.

Indeed, the central philosophical problem and practical danger of the religious studies model is that there is no clear mechanism for determining what gets taught. If religion is to be taught not for itself but because of the broad effect it has on culture and history and the like, then how does one decide in principle what to teach? Once it is granted that all people have worldviews and that all worldviews have faith claims as some of their foundational pillars, how does one go about choosing? I am afraid that the answer is that one is at the mercy of the interests and perspectives of the teacher or whoever sets the curriculum.

It is of course quite possible that one would get a teacher with the ability to teach both the familiar and the unfamiliar, someone with the sense to introduce students to a broad range of religious and philosophical traditions. However, if a teacher has a particular ax to grind, the material taught may well be fairly exotic. Alternatively, if a teacher is antagonistic to organized religion, the students may well get some heavy doses of gnosticism or radical Jesus studies or even New Age materials. In such cases it is hard to see how one could form a significant philosophical objection: These are forms of religion that the students may well encounter in their own lives. In short, the religious studies model elevates the importance of deciding who teaches the course; for that teacher's sense of what constitutes important religious information will have to fill the philosophical vacuum created by the very nature of the worldview itself. (There is, I think, a practical way of making these kinds of curricular decisions, and I will come to it.)

Finally, there is the unitarian model. I use this term, though my readers (and the part of my computer that capitalizes words it believes to be proper nouns!) are probably tempted to make the mistake of equating this position with the Unitarian faith. There is certainly overlap with some versions of Unitarianism, but I really mean no more than the following: This position is unitarian in the sense that it believes that all religions are finally one, that they are all ultimately making the same claims. In short, this position is summed up visually by the wall of The Hard Rock Café in Manhattan: Images from the major world religions—crosses, the symbol for Om, an image of the Buddha, and others—surround the words "All is one." Such a position obviously goes further than the religious studies model; it says not just that it can judge among the religions but that it can, as it were, see through them, that it can pierce their shells of difference to their core of identity.

The first observation to make is that we have come full circle: The Unitarian worldview is every bit as much a faith as any espoused by those using the catechetical model. A school that explicitly taught this doctrine would be as catechizing as a parochial school or a yeshiva. This insight itself is not necessarily a problem, but it is important to recognize how vast is the theological claim that religions that believe themselves to be saying different things about the Divine are in fact agreeing. Such a claim becomes a problem if, in deference to a belief that tolerance requires it or politeness demands it, we pretend that it is not the faith claim that it is. For while the catechetical model is also certain to preach, no one is in danger of missing that fact.

While in theory a school might ground its religious education in such a worldview, in my view there are two related reasons to avoid such an approach. I believe that such an approach is both patronizing and intellectually untenable: It requires the advocate to make the claim that the vast majority of explicitly religious people are ignorant of the true nature of their own faith. It requires, for example, telling Muslims that their understanding of Paradise as a reward for fidelity to Allah is really the same reward as that which awaits Buddhists who have striven for nirvana; it requires telling Jews that, at some level, disobedience to the LORD involves the same mistake as the failure of an Emersonian transcendentalist to listen to the inner echo of the Over-soul. This approach emerges, I think, largely from the belief that religious folk are superstitious and probably not especially bright: What they need is someone who can stand above the fray and tell them what it all really means. If the price for this reconciliation is both disrespect for the individual and corporate beliefs of billions of people, together with the dubious claim to have seen identity in opposing positions, then—apparently—so be it. Not only is this patronizing and intellectually problematic: It is intolerant and is precisely the kind of judgment that public schools must and most private schools want to avoid.

Where does all of this leave us? Is there a way forward that puts the life of the spirit into the conversation without proselytizing and without scorn? Regarding this most central of human matters, is there a way to be disinterested without being uninterested?

The answer, I believe, is Yes, though how that Yes is played out will vary from school to school. For simplicity let me offer two kinds of encouragement, one for private schools and one for public.

The encouragement for private schools (other than perhaps those already engaged in the catechetical model) is that they consider seriously the theological model. One of the genuine blessings of a private school is that one can talk about religious issues without immediately worrying about the legality or the appropriateness of such conversation. Perhaps even more beneficial are the ways that the theological model enhances the mission that most private schools have already. The theological perspective is countercultural and augments the other ways a school calls its students to stand apart from much of what the culture offers. It provides the opportunity for richer conversation than is possible when the ground rules require that only secular philosophies can play. It offers insight into a wide diversity of scholastic fields: Theology has affected art, architecture, science, literature, and on and on. Finally, when taken seriously it offers a platform for critiquing what most people want to identify as evil worldviews: Nazism, violent fundamentalism, fascism, and others. In short, when genuine theism is allowed a seat at the table, greater articulation is possible on a wide front.

Public schools are obviously in a different position. However, they too have the duty to intellectual honesty to realize that spiritual issues can be ignored but not avoided. Human beings are not omniscient, and hence they all exist in faith; they believe this or that; they trust this or that. To teach nothing is to pretend that we do not share such fundamental issues, and it means allowing our children to learn about spiritual issues from the parts of our culture that are happy to exploit them. It also means abetting the view that all of human history can be understood separate from the spiritual beliefs of the humans who lived it.

I propose that public schools consider seriously the religious studies model. The lack of a mechanism for deciding what gets taught that should so bedevil a private school can actually be turned to advantage in the public school setting. Because the very nature of public education in America precludes a religious answer to the question of what gets taught, the decision can be made much as the decision is made to teach United States history rather than, say, French or Japanese history—that is, on practical grounds. For surely United States history is taught in America for the simple reason that it is appropriate that American students learn their own history. Why not decide religious education on similar grounds: What religious information is likely to be most valuable to the students?

I can almost hear the skeptic cringe! He is sure that my next move will be to point out that the vast majority of Americans are at least nominally Christian and that therefore Judeo-Christian religious information should take pride of place. *Au contraire*! While I do believe that analyzing proportions could be a helpful mechanism for reflecting on what to teach, I would cast my net far wider than the three or four religions with the largest representative populations among students and parents. Indeed, I would agree wholeheartedly with my imagined critic that such an approach becomes nothing more than state-sponsored religion. Rather, I would engage in two steps designed to ensure that my students are gaining helpful religious information.

First, I would define worldviews broadly. For example, just about all of my students, regardless of religious background, are influenced by secularism and materialism: These are in many ways the spiritual *lingua franca* of the culture. Such faith perspectives, as well as those that are affecting the world scene in obvious ways, should be discussed. Second, I would be sure to juxtapose different worldviews with the explicit aim of avoiding the dangers of proselytizing: If we teach theism, we teach humanism and atheism; if we teach polytheism, we teach monotheism. If we look at religious fundamentalists, we also look at pacifists or materialist fundamentalists. If we study Christianity, we take the time to compare it to Judaism on the one hand and Deism on the other. Every student needs to understand that what is being provided is information for the journey; the measures of success would be on the one hand that such information is of use in life and on the other that the students do not know at the end of the course what particular faith claims the teacher herself espouses.

I began with a short story about Sarah and her belief that religion was *verboten*, a private affair and one that it was illegal and probably immoral to share. While I used that story as a device for opening an argument about the state of spiritual education, it is time to come clean: I also told that story as a way of exorcising some of the pain I felt while listening. It is a pain on her behalf, a pain that she should know so little and yet be so antagonistic to the rich field of inquiry and insight that is theology and religious study. At a personal level I wanted to tell Sarah that I believe God cherishes her; at a pedagogical level I wanted to tell her to go read the Constitution; as one who reflects on the state of religious education, I wanted to ask the question the Professor asks in C. S. Lewis's *The Lion, the Witch and the Wardrobe*: "Bless me, what *do* they teach them at these schools?" My hope is that someday we will teach them how to think about the great questions of religion and meaning just as today we teach them to think about the great questions of calculus and literature and history.

Note

[1] It occurs to me that a reader might infer a troubling ingratitude on my part toward the many teachers from whom I have had the honor of learning. Nothing could be farther from the truth. In fact, it was these very teachers who often clarified the distinction I am attempting to elucidate and who have inspired my thinking about the four models. Isn't that the experience of many of us—that our teachers are often at odds with the school or system within which they work; that they are often both more passionately radical and more passionately traditional than any contemporary philosophy of education could ever be? So, at least, it has been for me.

Chapter 10

Walking the Talk:
The Classroom as Spirituality Workshop

John J. Roberts

What would a class be like that took spirituality and education seriously? I will suggest some possible answers to that question, by way of sharing a few of my own experiences over more than two decades teaching a course intended to bring spirituality and education into proximity. In drawing on personal experience, I am mindful of Dag Hammarskjold's advice in one of his gnomic "markings," "Never, 'for the sake of peace and quiet,' deny your own experience or convictions."[1] However, we will commence with another bit of wisdom, this time from C. S. Lewis in his little book *Miracles*: "What we learn from experience depends on the kind of philosophy we bring to experience. It is therefore useless to appeal to experience before we have settled, as well as we can, the philosophical question."[2] Just as the foundation of a building is generally out of sight, so our apparently simple topic rests on several hidden philosophical assumptions, and our first task is to settle these, or at least bring them to light.

"Begin by defining your terms," one of my philosophy professors was fond of declaring. It is sound advice for our present inquiry, because one word in the title is particularly slippery: "spirituality" can mean everything or nothing. For some, spirituality has specific religious referents; for others, spirituality is simply synonymous with ethics; and for yet others, the concept is nugatory and the word an empty signifier. When the same word can be invoked by a Christian fundamentalist and by a secular humanist, we may well recall T. S. Eliot's warning in "Burnt Norton" about how easily words "strain, / Crack and sometimes break, under the burden, / Under the tension, slip, slide, perish."[3] Now, I hope every reader, even our friends the religious sectarian and the secular humanist above, will be able to find something of value in the experiment I will relate in the second part of this essay, but I feel obligated to make clear now where the biases lie. We live in our stories, and my own story is Christian and ecumenical rather than narrowly sectarian. The Christian cross is for me such a splendid symbol because in my reading the vertical stroke represents relationship with God while the horizontal bar represents social relationships, and the theological line and the ethical line must inevitably intersect. When asked about the heart of torah, Jesus famously replied, "Love God, and love your neighbor,"[4] and for me the latter is fully grounded in the former. We humans, like other creatures, have infinite value because of the Creator, and our attitude should properly be reverential appreciation, even awe, toward the mystery of the creation as well as toward what Rudolph Otto called the *mysterium tremendum* behind the creation.[5]

So that is my story, just as every reader lives in his or her own story. Nevertheless, all human stories do have their conjunctions, and I suspect and hope that our varying definitions of "spirituality" all partake of some of the same fundamental values, however we might articulate them. For example, in *The Good Life*, Peter Gomes points to the four cardinal virtues of the classical tradition (prudence, justice, temperance, and fortitude) and the three theological virtues of the Pauline tradition (faith, hope, and love).[6] Honesty, trust, fairness, respect, and responsibility are the fundamental values emphasized by the Center for Academic Integrity at the Kenan Institute for Ethics at Duke University.[7] Thomas Lickona, one of the best-known advocates of the character-education movement, calls respect and responsibility "the fourth and fifth Rs," but he goes on to identify a cluster of attendant moral values including fairness, tolerance, prudence, courtesy, honesty, helpfulness, compassion, cooperation, courage, kindness, and self-control.[8] Ernest Boyer recommends seven "core virtues": honesty, respect, responsibility, compassion, self-discipline, perseverance, and giving.[9] The Character Counts! Coalition suggests a focus on its "six pillars of character": trustworthiness, respect, responsibility, fairness, caring, and citizenship.[10] The most recent list to come across my desk is even longer, at eighteen virtues—Margaret D. Walding builds the CSEE elementary school virtues curriculum around goodness, compassion, thankfulness, faith, courage, charity, patience, truthfulness, hope, tolerance, forgiveness, humility, reverence, justice, loyalty, perseverance, stewardship, and peacefulness.[11] The degree of overlap among such lists is remarkable and usefully reminds us of the common ground we share, but which we all too easily forget in our arguments over such flashpoints as the alleged relativism of values-clarification exercises or the advisability of posting the Ten Commandments in public places.

Having just written such an irenic sentence as that, I feel almost guilty for now taking up the cudgels of controversy. However, any proposal at this time to address both education and spirituality is certain to generate a specific kind of opposition, and it will not do to pretend otherwise. Readers of a certain age will recall Sgt. Joe Friday on the old *Dragnet* show, who always wanted the facts, ma'am, just the facts. Well, Joe Friday has spawned a huge progeny. We have today our own version of the old back-to-basics movement, in the testing frenzy that is sweeping our schools. From the highest government levels in Washington on down to local school boards, calls for accountability in education have seized upon objective testing as the panacea: How students perform on batteries of high-stakes tests increasingly determines whether students are promoted or held back, whether teachers receive bonuses or pink slips, whether schools are celebrated or shuttered. Students and teachers already staggering under the burden of alphabet soup like SAT and ACT, NAEP and AP, now face the prospect of even more hurdles in everything from reading to math, with ungainly bureaucratic monikers like "Criterion Referenced Competency Tests" that do not even make acronyms. Instead of measuring the curriculum, the tests become themselves a substitute curriculum; class time must be devoted to test-taking drills instead of biology or history, teachers must degenerate into mere testing coaches, and the reductiveness of numbers extends its tyranny. To put the matter another way, we might change the metaphor from television to philosophy, from Sgt. Friday to A. J. Ayre. Philosophically, it is as if the logical positivists are in control. Facts, the logical positivists asserted, have an objective basis, an objective authority, whereas values are nothing more than emotive projections of the subjective self-conscious. Thus, the accountability juggernaut rumbles across the land, confidently armored in its objectivity, its facts, its numbers. The claims of spirituality are drowned out by that rumbling.

The irony is that this comfortable world of objective facts can be misleading. Newtonian physics has long since succumbed to Heisenberg's uncertainty principle: We now understand that we cannot be objective observers of an experiment, for the very act of observing alters the outcome. Today we find risible the rationalism of the Enlightenment, as when Spinoza dreamed that a universal and necessarily true philosophy might be built on rational pillars the way Euclid constructed an entire geometrical system upon five pristine axioms. "How can we know the dancer from the dance?" asked Yeats,[12] and the answer seems to be that we cannot. With mordant wit the Polish poet Zbigniew Herbert drives home the same point:

> so is blurred
> so is blurred
> in me
> what white-haired gentlemen
> separated once and for all
> and said
> this is the subject
> and this is the object....[13]

In departments of philosophy, logical positivism has followed the mechanistic Newtonian model into the musty museum of discarded paradigms. Contemporary epistemology—theories of knowing, of how we know—assures us that if there is such a thing as Reality, we cannot know it directly but only indirectly, through our models of it. The thing itself, the *Ding an sich*, forever eludes us, filtering through our screens more or less distorted. The author of Exodus 33:20 simply practices good epistemology in having God warn Moses that no human can look full upon God and live. To be sure, some postmodernists have concluded that the only option is deconstructionist nihilism, but there are seminal thinkers who demur. Michael Polanyi is one. Moving beyond the subjective-versus-objective juxtaposition, Polanyi has argued that all knowledge is in fact "personal knowledge." The familiar dichotomy between scholarly detachment and active engagement turns out, Polanyi demonstrates, to be one more instance of the either-or proposition. Polanyi avers that we can know more than we can tell, and we can tell nothing without relying on our awareness of things we may not be able to tell. For instance, "We know a person's face, and can recognize it among a thousand, indeed among a million. Yet we usually cannot tell how we recognize a face we know. So most of this knowledge cannot be put into words."[14] Another example: nothing could be clearer than the difference in "touch" between a child practicing five-finger exercises and a concert virtuoso at the piano, but accounting for the difference is notoriously vexatious.[15] To cite a third illustration from Polanyi, children riding bicycles are actually engaged in an incredibly difficult feat, but if they understood the principle involved in keeping their balance—"for a given angle of unbalance the curvature of each winding [along a series of appropriate curvatures] is inversely proportional to the square of the speed at which the cyclist is proceeding"—and tried consciously to adhere to it, in very short order skinned elbows and barked knees would result.[16] I am reminded that James Boswell once asked Samuel Johnson for a definition of poetry, and Dr. Johnson replied, "Why, Sir, it is much easier to say what it is not. We all *know* what light is; but it is not easy to *tell* what it is."[17]

Nonetheless, the assumption of objectivity constitutes the subtext for much of the contemporary political debate over reforming education in this country. The febrile accountability movement assumes that what cannot be measured must not be real, or at least not important. Spirituality is subjective and therefore suspect; values may possibly have a place in the home, but certainly not in the classroom. Surely we know better! It was not that many decades ago that the most highly cultivated nation in the entire world gave us Nazis like Ilse Koch, "the bitch of Buchenwald," notorious for her lampshades made from the skin of camp inmates. To cite George Steiner's justly famous reflection on the Holocaust: "We know now that a man can read Goethe or Rilke in the evening, that he can play Bach and Schubert, and go to his day's work at Auschwitz in the morning."[18] To us, one of the strangest notions current among the ancient Greeks was the conviction that salvation comes through knowledge, that knowing what is right will of course lead to doing what is right. Instead, for us, the relationship between what we know and what we do, between knowledge and virtue, is excruciatingly problematical. "The harsh truth," notes Ernest Boyer, "is that knowledge unguided by an ethical compass is potentially more dangerous than ignorance itself."[19] The tragedy of Socrates is that he had students like Alcibiades and Critias; Nero might have been less a monster had he not honed his gifts at the feet of Seneca. The point could not be put with more admirable brevity than halfway through "The American Scholar," when Emerson declares: "Character is higher than intellect."[20]

Any effort to separate intellect from character is finally doomed to frustration, although report cards sometimes make an artificial attempt by stipulating one grade for behavior and another for, say, Spanish. While most people would probably assume that the B or A in Honors Algebra I represents an assessment of the student's math work, in my experience teachers themselves generally blur the line, even instinctively. In a recent faculty meeting I heard a colleague say, "I teach children, not biology." It is a familiar nostrum. Back in 1944, near the beginning of *Teacher in America,* Jacques Barzun cited "a man with a warm heart" who raised the rhetorical question, "Should we teach subjects or boys and girls?" Barzun responded: "This play on words confuses the whole issue. The only way to teach somebody is obviously to teach him something."[21] Given the date of publication, we can overlook Barzun's masculine pronoun, but we should not overlook his argument, which is valid as far as it goes. Grammatically, his warmhearted interlocutor and my contemporary colleague are both dealing in a kind of nonsense: Their witticism ignores the distinction between direct and indirect objects. One teaches (direct object) some-*thing,* such as biology, (indirect object) *to* children.

However, if we pursue the matter beyond syntax, we must recognize that Barzun's position has its limitations. There is a saying so familiar I have no idea who first uttered it: "Education consists in what remains after we have forgotten everything we learned in school." For verification, I simply appeal to the reader's own memories. Most of what we consciously recall from our school days is not academic at all; we have vivid recollections of certain teachers and classmates, perhaps, or certain traumatic and triumphant events. If we try to dredge up specific academic memories, what comes to mind is astonishingly minuscule. In my own case, I remember a few German conjugations, a couple of physics formulas, a clutch of history dates...but most of the data that populated the foreground of my attention in school has long since gone the way of the periodic table or the partitive construction in French. Who can tell where all past years are, wondered John Donne; where are the snows of yesteryear, asked François Villon. Well, I would dearly love to know where all that information I memorized for quizzes and tests and exams throughout all those years of schooling went.

However, I now know very well what has taken the place of all the trivial data. All those years of pre-school, elementary school, junior high school, high school, college, and graduate school have congealed into a set of attitudes and convictions and assumptions that now operate at the core of my being. A deep respect for the life of the mind, a sense of history, and an understanding of logical inquiry anchor the educated person, while others are doomed to float moment by moment like flotsam on the surface swells of life. All those myriad specifics from the years and years of schooling slowly percolate and finally settle into meaningful abstractions, gut-level instincts, foundational principles. Few of my friends from my school years remain, for example, but I now know what friendship is; my athletic jacket with its patches has long since gone to some Goodwill store, but I now appreciate what sportsmanship is; the copious notes prepared for my dissertation defense have long since disappeared, but I now understand scholarship. I now sometimes forget the dates for Browning's life (1812–1889, by the way), but I trust I will carry with me always the sensitivity to esthetic beauty his poems indirectly taught me.

So children learn spiritual values, such as the love of friendship or sportsmanship or esthetic beauty, obliquely rather than directly. Values cannot be transferred the way a quarterback hands off a football. The pedagogical truth is that as soon as we try to inculcate things like ethics directly, we pervert education into indoctrination. The study of word origins is sometimes a dead end—I am still trying to figure out what satire has to do with "medley" or even "a dish of mixed fruits offered to the god," or what an almanac has to do with (according to some accounts) the Arabic for the place where camels are quartered overnight—but upon occasion etymology can be enlightening. The first-conjugation Latin verb *educo/educare* means "to bring up, rear, educate," according to the books, but beyond that the word is related to "draw out, lead out." We need perhaps look no further than the prefixes—*ex-* in the Latin *educare* means "out" (thus I fancy *educare* to imply "to lead out of ignorance") whereas *en-* in the Middle French *endoctriner* means "in" (I would suggest as in "to dump dogma into the passive student receptacle")—to see that the enterprise of education is inevitably set at loggerheads with that of indoctrination. God is surely on the side of education: As Milton reminds us, God gave Adam and Eve free will because God understood that moral automatons could not be moral creatures at all.[22]

Schooling without spirituality is ersatz education; moreover, it is not even possible. Although "spirituality education" cannot happen directly, "spirituality and education" is inevitable. Quite simply, no human undertaking is or can be values-free. Whether or not we like it or are even aware of it, we teachers and students are constantly shaping or reinforcing or undermining our individual and collective value systems. Robert Coles persuasively argues that teachers in fact teach mostly by example, and unconscious example at that. "What do we really want our awake and aware children or students to believe in, to learn from what we say and, yes, most powerfully, influentially, from what we all the time do?" Coles asks in *The Moral Intelligence of Children*. "In point of fact, we are constantly answering that portentous question by indirection, and not rarely, unbeknownst to ourselves, through the conduct we offer to our witnessing children."[23] As the twig is bent, so grows the tree; as moral philosophers from Aristotle to Bellah have noted, we somehow form habits of the heart or ingrained orientations that, if all goes well, are virtuous habits. Gomes observes in *The Good Life* that

> proficiency in virtue, like proficiency on the piano, requires practice. Virtue is both an art and a discipline, but the art is compromised if the discipline is not made perfect in practice. One does not save the virtues for an extraordinary moment of need: in order for them to be available when they are truly needed, they must be practiced when it would seem that one could be doing something else.[24]

Not surprisingly then, the fervent if sometimes despairing hope of every parent and teacher is caught by the compiler of Proverbs: "Train children in the right way, and when old, they will not stray."[25]

What, then, would a class be like that took spirituality and education seriously, and did so in ways both legitimate and efficacious?

How can we now put the theoretical into practice, how do we give flesh and bone to the abstruse, the esoteric? How do we address the chasm that all too easily yawns between classroom study and personal relevance? How can teachers structure a class so that, regardless of the title in the course catalog, the environment is conducive to spiritual growth?

For the past quarter of a century, the issue has been more than merely hypothetical for me. I am blessed to work in an independent school that lets me teach one or two sections annually of the required two-semester senior survey of New Testament, in addition to my regular smorgasbord of English classes. I have found some approaches that work, some that do not work, some that work one year but not the next; I have found some things that will bear transfer to my English classes and other things too fragile to survive outside an avowedly "religious" classroom. Much would seem appropriate for a Muslim school or a Jewish school, not just a Christian school; the sacred text in my course is the Christian Bible, but in many respects it could just as well be the Qur'an or for that matter a physics book. Some things would be equally applicable to a public school setting while others are less portable. In short, some of what I will describe can be exported intact, other pieces can be easily adapted, and certainly everything can be improved upon.

The initial class meeting is crucial for the entire year, because in distributing and explaining the written course description, I try to bring the students into the experiment with full cognizance, full collaboration; there are occasions when teachers quite properly have designs upon students of which they are unaware, but this is not one of those times. Our class, I say, will be a workshop, a kind of laboratory for experiments in bringing spirituality and education together. We will not merely memorize Bible verses such as "In everything do to others as you would have them do to you" (Matthew 7:12); we will strive to live out the precepts. We will try to move the lessons we study from our heads into our hearts. The following excerpt from my course description indicates the tone:

> I believe we have a vocation here: you are called to learn, as I am called to teach. But it's not a sharp distinction, because I expect to learn from you and I expect you to teach each other. I expect you to contribute insights and questions during our discussions, I expect you to listen attentively to each other, I expect you to prepare for our classes just as I myself am expected to prepare. We must develop our class into a little community, and community always entails mutual obligations. But best of all, since God designed humans to be social creatures, community is our end and our purpose and our joy.

The range of reactions as we discuss the course syllabus in those first days each fall has become predictable. Some students do not at first "get it"; they have no idea what the rest of the class and I are talking about. Little in their previous experience has prepared them for such a seemingly off-beat approach. As long as they are open and curious, time will likely bring them around. Other students are charmed by the proposal and seem eager to explore it. Still other students are young cynics: They just want to figure out what the "prof" wants so they can give it to him and pocket their A. Still other students are skeptical or at least suspicious; they want to know, for instance, exactly how the grade will be determined. Their pragmatic concern about that bottom line gives us a natural transition now to sketch out some aspects of the course, and we might as well begin with the grade book, fraught as it is with emotional baggage.

Grades

Grades are the unfortunate but inevitable currency of schooling, and nobody knows it better than high school seniors. While it helps that many—perhaps most—universities could not care less how a student does in a religion course (indeed, many colleges routinely recalculate the GPA of applicants to exclude "minor" coursework in areas like religion), still a grade is a grade is a grade. My own course is a rigorous academic program, not an exercise in "Sunday school" piety: I introduce students to the scholarly discipline of New Testament studies; we use a college-level text[26] as well as a Bible; we do formal exegeses (library research papers); we have tests on the technical vocabulary of the field; we write book reports and polish oral presentations, and so forth. Consequently, students are rightly concerned to find that part of their grade will be determined by whether they seem to be trying to implement in their interpersonal dealings what they learn.

To quote again from the syllabus:

> I retain rights to a personal fudge factor; I'm convinced there is something called professional judgment, which is grounded on knowledge and experience and thus differs from mere opinion. Numbers are useful, as far as they go, but the truly important things in life elude quantification; besides, the perfect quiz, test, or grading rubric has yet to be invented. In the education racket, what I'm subscribing to here is called "holistic grading."

The report cards my doting mother kept from my childhood assure me that it used to be customary to give grades in "deportment" or "citizenship" as well as in English and the other subject areas. Most teachers would probably concede that we do still include those social imponderables, even in our course calculations. It is not unusual for "class participation" or some similar euphemism to be listed on course descriptions as worth a certain portion, five percent or even ten percent, of the final grade, nor is it unusual for teachers to incline toward compassion rather than standards when considering whether to pass or fail a struggling student who has worked conscientiously all term. The truth is that only a Scantron machine does its grading work while impervious to the awareness that this student enters the class cheerfully and that one morosely, that this student always volunteers to help a sick classmate catch up while that other student wallows in self-absorption. No doubt there are good reasons why teachers are reluctant to discuss this "fudge factor" more forthrightly. "The teacher just doesn't like me" becomes an all-too-handy explanation for any disappointing grade. Furthermore, even if the student is receptive, parents often are not. I sometimes wish my school would stop billing itself as "a college preparatory school" (a life-prep school would be better), or that we could issue along with the letter of acceptance we mail to applicants a notarized transcript with columns of A's and B's already inscribed. Maybe then we could focus on the business of learning and avoid the hysteria over country-club bragging rights and the college-admissions marketing games. However, I might as well wish for the right lottery numbers.

There are other reasons as well for the ubiquitous notion that grades should be objective, not subjective. Perhaps because parents, students, and teachers have little acquaintance with epistemologists such as Polanyi, it is widely assumed that a grade based on the "facts" will have more validity and reliability than a holistic professional judgment. I have actually had some colleagues, and not just in the math department, who thought a 79 on a test meant precisely a 79. These concrete thinkers seem oblivious to the reality that no evaluation instrument this side of the Pearly Gates is perfect. Angels presumably communicate via extrasensory perception, but we mere mortals must embody our communication—and our human attempts at incarnation are never immaculate. My students and I know very well that if I compose a test on which they are to identify the speakers for fifty quotations from *Hamlet*, their raw scores will not be the same as if I had picked a different fifty quotes. The evaluation instrument itself is irremediably intrusive: This student is naturally more proficient on essay tests than he is at matching column formats, that student does poorly on multiple-choice formats because she is smarter than the teachers who compose the items and thus second-guesses her way straight into wrong answers, a third student suffers panic attacks that mask her meticulous preparation, and so on. We inevitably test things other than what we intend to test. The perceptive teacher will be attuned to patterns (e.g., does this student score better on memory work than on creative assignments, or perform well on everything except time-pressure tasks?) and will make adjustments in the final grade for any anomalies. The good teacher must also exercise professional judgment with an acute sense of humility, knowing that God alone looks on the heart. No wonder the temptation to hide behind the "objective" number crunching of a calculator or a computer grade book program is so enticing.

Grades are metaphors; numbers are symbols. At my school, seventies are C's and eighties are B's, so a 79 might represent several different things: It might be encouragement, a metaphorical way of saying, "You have struggled mightily and although you did not break free of the C range I am giving you the highest possible C"; on the other hand, it might be chastisement, a metaphorical way of saying, "You just were not willing to put forth the extra bit of effort that would have earned a B." Grades mean nothing ripped out of context. A teacher who records a 79 simply because that was the objective, factual, literal figure that appeared in the calculator window is a numerical fundamentalist, a logical-positivist parody. However, because there are a few such teachers around, and more than a few students who share the same assumptions, I have become resigned to taking more lecture time than I would like early in the course for a reconsideration of psychometrics. One useful lever: It helps that students are familiar with the pedagogical practice of subtracting penalty points for work that misses the deadline. A modicum of class discussion will lead most students to recognize that the resulting grade generally does not reflect mastery of the particular subject so much as extraneous considerations like calendar-handling skills or even character traits such as procrastination. Once students have granted that concession, the dominoes can begin toppling.

Another approach that has proven helpful is to involve the students in determining their own grades. Prior to each of our reporting periods, I generally ask my students to write a self-evaluation that includes a grade, and then I try to incorporate as much of their viewpoint into my own official assessment as I can. To some of my colleagues, this practice smacks of heresy; aside from their spot in the faculty parking lot, no prerogative is more inviolable to them than their sovereign right to assign grades. However, our students are, after all, experts in the field: They often know our schools better than we do; they generally know how much work different courses entail; they know which teachers are hard graders or easy touches; and they certainly know how dutifully they have actually labored for us and how well they have assimilated the material. I have found that when I ask students to share their honest self-perceptions with me, most respect the invitation and respond conscientiously. As for the others, they are easily identified.

Honor Code

I work at a school that does have an institutional honor code, but even in its absence we could devise an honor system within our class community. In some ways, a class-generated code might be all the more effective for not being part of the background noise, part of the taken-for-granted institutional setting. Of course, considerable time can be expended in discussing personal and corporate integrity, proposing specific phrasing of the code, hammering out procedures, and reaching consensus on norms—time that might be devoted instead to another chapter in the textbook, to an additional essay assignment, to more of the nuts and bolts of academic coursework. I am convinced the time is well invested.

The resulting "honor code" should not be left on the shelf as something passive; the classroom must become, in John Keats's felicitous phrase, a "vale of soul making."[27] Thus, for example, I make a point of leaving the room occasionally during tests; I have students grade their own quizzes; I let them make up missed tests and quizzes on their honor, giving them the paper in a sealed envelope, making sure they know the expectations (how many minutes, open or closed book, and so on), and telling them to bring the work back to me at their earliest convenience. Naturally, I would do less of this with younger children, but generally my juniors and seniors seem appreciative and respond honorably. Sometimes even the exceptions are to be celebrated: One girl stayed after class this past spring to confess that she had changed two wrong answers while grading her own quiz, and I am convinced she grew more in moral stature from that momentary failure and its acknowledgment than if she had never known temptation. As Milton memorably puts it in "Areopagitica": "I cannot praise a fugitive and cloistered virtue, unexercised and unbreathed, that never sallies out and sees her adversary, but slinks out of the race where that immortal garland is to be run for, not without dust and heat."[28] In short, the teacher who affirms an honor code but then puts the desks three feet apart and prowls the room while students take the test is a hypocrite.

Buddy System

Early in the fall, I ask students to pair off as "buddies." The syllabus lays out a practical justification:

> We do not cancel class in the event of someone's individual absence. Since you are responsible for what you've missed out on, you should arrange to have a "buddy" to make careful class notes, take an extra handout, give you a phone call, etc., in case you are gone.

The buddy system obviously emphasizes personal responsibility, but it also fosters interpersonal nurturing, serving as a kind of classroom adaptation of the parable of the good Samaritan. As the year progresses, as the students become more comfortable, as the group bonds more cohesively, we experiment with permutations of the system, such as expanding the number of buddies in each set to three, or even four. I fondly (in the archaic sense of "foolishly," no doubt, as well as in the other, modern sense) dream of the day when I am able to end the year with a class in which everyone has become part of the same buddy group.

Group Projects

The buddy system also lends itself to various kinds of collaborative learning. Buddies already paired might be assigned a joint research project, to culminate in a joint essay or a joint presentation to the class. Several pairs of buddies might be temporarily glued together in larger units for peer review of each other's papers or as vocabulary-review study groups. Sometimes existing buddy pairings might intentionally be disrupted for the sake of new associations. One year I had two quite distinct cliques in a class so I found myself occasionally forcing Montagues and Capulets to dance with each other. Sometimes collaborative work results in shared grades for the group members, but not always; we humans are vicious competitors as well as social creatures, and competition for grade book recognition can quickly poison otherwise fruitful collaborative projects.

The Service Component

We all know of schools that provide community-service programs or even require a certain number of service hours for graduation. My own school sponsors a thriving if voluntary community-service program. I have tried various ways of bringing service under the course umbrella, not because I am displeased with the school's own plan but rather because I am convinced that any gospel worthy of the name must have feet under it. It is one thing to study Jesus' precepts about the disadvantaged, and a very different thing to implement them. The logistics of arranging class field trips can be daunting, and the hassle of, say, taking the class to a nearby St. Vincent de Paul center to sort clothing can all too easily engender discouragement rather than invigoration. Instead, the approach I have settled upon is to tell students that they must come up with a proposal for my review: at some point during the semester, I expect each student to participate in a soup kitchen, tutor in a remedial program, participate in a charity walk-a-thon, assist with a Habitat house, or something similar. The experience should result in a reflection paper or oral report or some other way of achieving closure.

Classroom Clean-Up

At the end of *The Moral Intelligence of Children*, Robert Coles refers to "a moral curriculum," which he says might include activities such as serving snacks in a nursing home or reading to the blind or cleaning up a playground.[29] At my school this past year, we experimented with taking the last minute or two of the last class of each day for classroom clean-up. As with anything that becomes institutionalized and routine, the results were mixed. I remain convinced that a few moments every week or two for teacher and students to help each other straighten up the chairs and desks, pick up trash from the floor, erase the boards, and bid each other farewell can be well worth cutting that last sentence from the day's lecture. "Ecology," after all, may be a new word but it is fabricated from ancient Greek components. For that matter, one of Adam's first epiphanies must have been the realization that we should not foul our own nests. Students who help clean up their classrooms just might some day turn into citizens who pay attention to their vehicles' gas mileage or the destination of their cast-off trash.

"Outside the Safety Zone"

This omnibus category is comprised of those infinite ways teachers find to help students venture beyond their comfort zones. For instance, I urge my New Testament students to visit places of worship beyond their own turf: A Jewish student might attend a Kingdom Hall, a Roman Catholic might go to an AME service. A student who customarily uses the term "homophobia" probably does not share the same world view as a student who refers to "the homosexual lifestyle," so asking the two students to research the question of ordaining gay clergy *from a viewpoint not their own* and then present a class report can be illuminating, in rare instances even life-altering. A few years ago one of my students whose home and church had taught her that women should not be in positions of ecclesiastical authority undertook videotaped interviews with half a dozen women of the cloth in our city, and the result was not just a good class presentation: The last I heard, she was contemplating the ministry herself. Another innovative if less literal way to relocate the class walls occurred to me in 1997 when Robert Duvall's *The Apostle* hit the theaters: Because there are few Pentecostal students at my school, I began to set aside a couple of periods each year for a class viewing of Duvall's tribute to an often-overlooked branch of Christianity. Still another option is the use of guest speakers; visitors in my New Testament course have included an imam from a local mosque, a rabbi from an orthodox synagogue, a theologian from the Presbyterian seminary nearby. Fair game is "Anything, everything tricky, risky, nonchalant, /Anything under the sun to outwit the prosy," as Robert Francis puts it in his poem "Catch."[30]

Enough. The handful of suggestions above will be sufficient stimulus. I have not said anything about Quaker communitarian practices, such as students and teachers calling each other by first names or setting due dates for papers by consensus decision, but readers will have already thought of adding such ideas to the mix. Throughout my career I have been perpetually impressed with the creativity and common sense of dedicated teachers.

Before concluding, one objection must be acknowledged. The course components I have explored have in common the liability of being time-intensive. Like others in our harried society, students and teachers constantly hear "Time's wingéd chariot hurrying near"[31]— which is extraordinarily ironic considering that in its etymological origins our word "school" has to do with "leisure." In part, the problem is that schools have become shrines for the worship of the god Coverage, and because the knowledge base continuously expands, we face an ever more hopeless task. Another significant part of the problem is the testing mania I criticized earlier: One colleague recently lamented that she could not pause for interesting but irrelevant student questions because the course was Advanced Placement Biology and the time was already insufficient for finishing the textbook and preparing for the AP exam. One of my former headmasters now retired, Donn Gaebelein, was fond of the term "postholing": Our students would be better educated, he opined, if schools did more in-depth work on fewer topics, rather than skating superficially over everything. Perhaps educators should hijack Mies van der Rohe's dictum "Less is more" as the banner for a revolution. However, until the revolution comes, teachers who find themselves stepping into a canned course or a "teacher-proof" curriculum might have no alternative but to restrict themselves to just one or two of my admittedly time-intensive suggestions. I can proffer this solace: It is my distinct impression that classes move more quickly and more successfully through their academic lessons once quality time has been invested in foundational matters such as an honor code or a buddy system. Moreover, it might serve as consolation if I also admit that I myself do not try to do everything simultaneously; one year I might emphasize the honor code and minimize the buddy system, then reverse those priorities the next year.

Attentive readers will have noticed one other common trait among the components above: They are hardly candidates for newspaper headlines. Most courses, after all, include guest speakers, group projects, and so on. Perhaps the difference, or at least for the teacher the conscious and intentional difference, lies in the context for the activities rather than in the activities themselves. The teacher concerned with spirituality and education will introduce a guest speaker from an area Hindu temple not just directly to enhance cognitive knowledge; such a teacher will be aware not only of the next day's quiz on Hinduism but also will understand that seeds are being sown which might not germinate for a long, long time. The point bears reiteration: In a culture obsessed with instant gratification and short-term return on investment, what teachers do is a great curiosity, a fierce anomaly—we plant seeds that will not come to fruition in the lives of our students for many years, even decades. As James Fowler eloquently demonstrates in his classic *Stages of Faith*, spiritual maturation is a slow and painful process, and when we adults contemplate our own faltering, recursive progress along its trajectory, we must perforce have greater patience with the adolescents and children in our classrooms.[32]

Notes

[1] Dag Hammarskjold, *Markings*, trans. Leif Sjoberg and W. H. Auden (New York: Alfred Knopf, 1971), 84.

[2] C. S. Lewis, *Miracles* (New York: Macmillan, 1947), 11.

[3] T. S. Eliot, *The Complete Poems and Plays, 1909–1950* (New York: Harcourt, Brace and World, 1962), 121.

[4] With more elegance and nuance than my bald summary; see especially the saying preserved in Luke 10:25ff.

[5] Rudolf Otto, *The Idea of the Holy*, trans. John W. Harvey (1917; reprint, London: Penguin, 1959), 26 et passim.

[6] Peter Gomes, *The Good Life: Truths That Last in Times of Need* (New York: HarperCollins, 2002).

[7] "Fundamental Values Project," Center for Academic Integrity, Oct. 1999, http://academicintegrity.org/values.asp

[8] Among Lickona's writings, see especially *Educating for Character: How Our Schools Can Teach Respect and Responsibility* (New York: Bantam, 1991).

[9] Ernest Boyer, *The Basic School: A Community for Learning* (Princeton: Carnegie Foundation for the Advancement of Teaching /Jossey-Bass, 1995), 183–85.

[10] The Character Counts! Coalition is a project of the Josephson Institute of Ethics; see the Web site at http://www.charactercounts.org.

[11] Margaret D. Walding, *Creating Classrooms and Homes of Virtue* (Atlanta: Council for Spiritual and Ethical Education, 2002).

[12] "Among School Children," l. 64, in *The Poems of W. B. Yeats,* ed. Richard J. Finneran (New York: Macmillan, 1983), 217.

[13] From "I Would Like to Describe," in Zbigniew Herbert, *Selected Poems*, trans. Czeslaw Milosz and Peter Dale Scott (Baltimore: Penguin, 1968), 39.

[14] Michael Polanyi, *The Tacit Dimension* (Garden City, NY: Doubleday, 1966), 4.

[15] Michael Polanyi, *Personal Knowledge: Towards a Post-Critical Philosophy* (1958; reprint, New York: Harper and Row, 1964), 50–51.

[16] Polanyi, *Personal*, 50.

[17] James Boswell, *The Life of Samuel Johnson* (New York: Modern Library, n.d.), 634.

[18] George Steiner, *Language and Silence: Essays on Language, Literature, and the Inhuman* (New York: Atheneum, 1967), ix-x.

[19] Boyer, 176.

[20]Ralph Waldo Emerson, *The Selected Writings of Ralph Waldo Emerson,* ed. Brooks Atkinson (New York: Modern Library, 1950), 54.

[21] Jacques Barzun, *Teacher in America* (Boston: Little, Brown, 1945), 32.

[22] E.g., *Paradise Lost* 3.99–134.

[23] Robert Coles, *The Moral Intelligence of Children* (New York: Penguin Putnam Plume, 1997), 132.

[24] Gomes, 211. Robert N. Bellah et al., *Habits of the Heart: Individualism and Commitment in American Life,* updated ed. (Berkeley: U of California P, 1996). Bellah acknowledges (e.g., 312) that the phrase "habits of the heart" is actually Tocqueville's; see Alexis de Tocqueville, *Democracy in America,* ed. J. P. Mayer and trans. George Lawrence (New York: Doubleday, Anchor Books, 1969), 287.

[25] Bruce M. Metzger and Roland E. Murphy, eds., *The New Oxford Annotated Bible,* (New York: Oxford University Press, 1991), Proverbs 22:6.

[26] Currently Bart Ehrman's *The New Testament: A Historical Introduction to the Early Christian Writings,* 3rd ed. (Oxford: Oxford University Press, 2003).

[27] In the famous letter of April 21, 1819, to his brother and sister, George and Georgiana: "Call the world if you please 'the vale of soul making.' Then you will find out the use of the world"; see *The Complete Poetical Works of Keats,* ed. Horace E. Scudder (Boston: Houghton Mifflin Co., 1899), 369.

[28] John Milton, "Areopagitica," *John Milton: Complete Poems and Major Prose,* ed. Merritt Y. Hughes (New York: Odyssey, 1957), 728.

[29] Coles, 199.

[30] Robert Francis, *The Orb Weaver: Poems* (Middletown, CT: Wesleyan University Press, 1960), 6.

[31] The familiar words come from Andrew Marvell's poem "To His Coy Mistress," widely available, e.g., R. F. Brinkley, ed., *English Poetry of the XVII Century* (New York: Norton, 1936), 516–17.

[32] James W. Fowler, *Stages of Faith: The Psychology of Human Development and the Quest for Meaning* (1981; reprint, New York: HarperCollins, 1995), esp. Ch. 23, 269–91.

Works Consulted

Barzun, Jacques. *Teacher in America.* Boston: Little Brown, 1945.

Bellah, Robert N. *Habits of the Heart: Individualism and Commitment in American Life.* Berkeley: University of California Press, 1996.

Bennett, William J. *The Book of Virtues: A Treasury of Great Moral Stories.* New York: Simon and Schuster, 1993.

Boswell, James. *The Life of Samuel Johnson.* New York: Modern Library. N.d.

Boyer, Ernest. *The Basic School: A Community for Learning.* Princeton: Carnegie Foundation for the Advancement of Teaching/Jossey-Bass, 1995.

Brinkley, R. F., ed. *English Poetry of the XVII Century.* New York: Norton, 1936.

Coles, Robert. *The Moral Intelligence of Children.* New York: Penguin Putnam Plume, 1997.

Ehrman, Bart. *The New Testament: A Historical Introduction to the Early Christian Writings.* 3rd ed. Oxford: Oxford University Press, 2003.

Eliot, T. S. *The Complete Poems and Plays, 1909–1950.* New York: Harcourt, Brace, and World, 1962.

Emerson, Ralph Waldo. *The Selected Works of Ralph Waldo Emerson,* ed. Brooks Atkinson. New York: Modern Library, 1950.

Finneran, Richard J., ed. *The Poems of W. B. Yeats.* New York: Macmillan, 1983.

Fowler, James W. *Stages of Faith: The Psychology of Human Development and the Quest for Meaning.* New York: HarperCollins, 1995.

Francis, Robert. *The Orb Weaver: Poems.* Middletown, CT: Wesleyan University Press, 1960.

Gomes, Peter. *The Good Life: Truths That Last in Times of Need.* New York: Harper - Collins, 2002.

Hammarskjold, Dag. *Markings.* Trans. L. Sjoberg and W. H. Auden. New York: Alfred Knopf, 1971.

Herbert, Zbigniew. *Selected Poems.* Trans. C. Milosz and P. D. Scott. Baltimore, MD: Penguin, 1968.

Hughes, Merritt Y., ed. *John Milton: Complete Poems and Major Prose.* New York: Odyssey, 1957.

Lewis, C. S. *Miracles.* New York: Macmillan, 1947.

Lickona, Thomas. *Educating for Character: How Our Schools Can Teach Respect and Responsibility.* New York: Bantam, 1991.

Metzger, Bruce M. and Roland E. Murphy, eds. *The New Oxford Annotated Bible.* New York: Oxford University Press, 1991.

Otto, Rudolf. *The Idea of the Holy.* Trans. John W. Harvey. 1917. London: Penguin, 1959.

Polyani, Michael. *Personal Knowledge: Towards a Post-Critical Philosophy.* 1958. New York: Harper and Row, 1964.

———. *The Tacit Dimension.* Garden City, NY: Doubleday, 1966.

Scudder, Horace E., ed. *The Complete Poetical Works of Keats.* Boston: Houghton Mifflin Company, 1899.

Steiner, George. *Language and Silence: Essays on Language, Literature, and the Inhuman.* New York: Atheneum, 1967.

Walding, Margaret D. *Creating Classrooms and Homes of Virtue.* Atlanta, GA: Council for Spiritual and Ethical Education, 2002.

Chapter 11

Religion, Spirituality, and Education in a (Not Entirely) Secular Culture

Warren A. Nord

Once upon a time it was the task of schools in America to nurture the spiritual dimension of children's lives. So, for example, the most commonly used schoolbook in the American colonies in the eighteenth century—the *New England Primer*—taught the alphabet as follows:

> **A** wise son makes a glad Father, but a foolish son is the heaviness of his mother.
> **B** etter is little with the fear of the Lord, than great treasure and trouble therewith.
> **C** ome unto CHRIST all ye that labour and are heavy laden, and He will give you rest.

After the alphabet came "The Dutiful Child's Promises" ("I Will fear GOD, and honour the KING"), the Lord's Prayer, the Apostle's Creed, the Ten Commandments, the "Duty of Children Towards Their Parents," and a list of the books of the Bible. A list of numerals is prefaced by the claim that they will "serve for the ready finding of any Chapter, Psalm, and Verse in the Bible." The *Primer* concludes with the Westminster Assembly's Shorter Catechism (which at forty pages is not so short): "What is the chief end of Man?" Answer: "Man's chief end is to glorify God, and to enjoy him forever." Question: "What rule hath God given to direct us how we may glorify and enjoy him?" Answer: "The Word of God which is contained in the Scriptures of the

Old and New Testament is the only rule to direct us how we may glorify and enjoy him."[1]

Arguably, the primary purpose of schooling in the American colonies was to make good Christians. This was in the days before public schools, although public schools too had a religious dimension in the beginning. Indeed, public schools were Protestant schools in some important ways for a century or more. It was widely believed, for example, that morality required religious foundations, hence the need for devotional Bible-reading in the Protestant Bible. No doubt a good deal of religious rhetoric and ceremony was also incorporated into the school year.

Still, public schooling had largely, if not quite entirely, shed its religious purposes and content by the end of the nineteenth century. One can chart this transition neatly by noting the decline of biblical and religious material in successive editions of the McGuffey Readers over the course of that century. How, therefore, did American education come to be secular education?[2] The answer is not that public schools were secularized by the Supreme Court, which did not address the role of religion in public education until 1948, or by ideological secularists. Rather, schools inevitably reflected the changing ideas and values that were shaping American culture more generally. As America became more religiously diverse, religion became a source of conflict so, in time, it was "disestablished" in public schools, which would instead teach the unifying "religion" of Americanism. As the hearts and minds of Americans were increasingly devoted to economic advancement and the consumer goods of this life, salvation and the spiritual goods of life paled by comparison. By the end of the nineteenth century, education was increasingly practical. Scientists and their colleagues in the social sciences and professions found that they could do physics and biology, medicine and psychology, without any reference to God, so there was no need to keep Him in the science textbooks. Our culture became increasingly secular.

Even so, it did not become entirely secular. Surveys consistently show that about ninety percent of Americans claim to believe in God. No doubt much of this is nominal belief, but much of it is sincere. Conservative churches are growing, and on the more liberal side of the aisle there is considerable evidence of a new spirituality in our culture. We continue to give much more money to organized religion than to any secular cause. Religious voices are prominent in our culture wars, in battles over abortion and homosexuality, capital punishment and social justice, and schooling. Even the old sharp lines of demarcation between science and religion appear to be blurring. Interdisciplinary discussions in cosmology, the life sciences, ecology, and the health sciences now often include theologians. As secular as our culture has become—and it has become very secular—there continues to be a fairly strong religious counterculture.

How is it, then, that on Friday evening or Sunday morning we can affirm the sovereignty of God over all of life, but on Monday morning there are no implications for what we say in the classroom? For it would seem, as the theologian Max Stackhouse once put it, that any God worth worshipping will have implications for what we think about the world and how we live our lives.[3] Indeed, in the western religious traditions it has been held that God created the world and that nature is the handiwork of God; that we have souls and there is an afterlife; that we are obligated in our actions to serve God, doing justice to humankind; that history has a divine purpose and that truth is revealed in Scripture as well as in moral and religious experiences.

We don't all agree about whether God exists or what the implications are if God does exist. But unless we assume that God doesn't exist it would seem that the momentous consequences of God's existence for how we understand the world and how we live our lives would warrant some consideration in the curriculum. However, the rule of American education, both higher and lower, is that whatever the significance of religion in ancient times and far away places, God is irrelevant to understanding our world in the here and now. No doubt there are religious academies and private schools of various kinds that continue to take religion and the spiritual dimension of life seriously, but public schools and many private schools don't. In fact, education may be the most secular domain of American culture. Given the vitality of religion and spirituality in America this is something of a scandal.

I believe that public schools, indeed, all schools, should take religion and the spiritual dimension of reality seriously. What this means will require some explanation. I will begin by describing how public and, no doubt, much private schooling marginalizes religion. I will say why this is a problem and offer, in response, three secular arguments for taking religion seriously. I will also say something about how schools might do this, before concluding with my assessment of the prospects for such a project. First, however, terminology.

The terms "religion" and "spirituality" have different meanings, and those differences are important, especially nowadays. Casting his glance back at the history of Catholicism, Richard McBrien claims that to be spiritual means "to know, and to live according to the knowledge, that God is present to us in grace as the principle of personal, interpersonal, social and even cosmic transformation."[4] In his book on spirituality in contemporary America, Robert Wuthnow broadens the definition somewhat in writing that "spirituality consists of all the beliefs and activities by which individuals attempt to relate their lives to God or to a divine being or some other conception of a transcendent reality."[5] The philosopher of religion David Ray Griffin distances spirituality even more from God and religion in his book *Spirituality and Society* by using it "to refer to the ultimate values and meanings in terms of which we live, whether they be otherworldly or very worldly ones."[6] In light of such differences, Eugene Peterson has helpfully noted that the current usefulness of the term "spirituality" lies "not in its precision but rather in the way it names something indefinable yet quite recognizable: transcendence vaguely intermingled with intimacy."[7] I rather like Peterson's definition but that is not the point; the point is that spirituality means somewhat different things (though not entirely different things) to different people, and in different traditions.

One characteristic of the new spirituality in America is that it refuses to be confined within the institutional structures of traditional religion, which is often viewed as stifling, bureaucratic and authoritarian; it is, instead, deeply individualistic.[8] It is also profoundly eclectic, drawing on a wide range of both religious and secular resources in seeking new forms of meaning: Eastern religions, myth, meditation, humanistic and Jungian psychology and various kinds of therapy, holistic healing, new developments in cosmology, deep ecology, left-right brain research, feminism and goddess religion, the self-help movement, and, on its ill-defined borders, shamanism, astrology, channeling, reincarnation, witchcraft, and neopaganism.

Because the new spirituality is so eclectic and diffuse, so individualistic and so anti-institutional, there is no way to count its adherents. What is clear is that the language of spirituality has become increasingly common, infiltrating and influencing most domains of contemporary culture. I suppose that we shouldn't be surprised that spirituality in America is changing as we move from being a nation of communities to a nation of commuters: increasingly, faith is no longer something people inherit but something they seek.[9]

Having said all of this, I will continue to use the terms *spirituality* and *religion* more or less interchangeably. While there has always been more to organized religion than spirituality, the great religions have always had a spiritual core. Moreover, while in some of its guises the new spirituality takes on an almost secular cast, it more often shares with traditional religions an understanding of reality with God (or the Transcendent by whatever name) at its center.

Standards and Textbooks

Over the last decade I have reviewed eighty-two high school textbooks in subjects such as history, economics, home economics, literature, health, and the sciences for their treatment of religion. I have also read the national K-12 content standards that have been developed by thousands of scholars, teachers, and representatives of professional organizations. Does God measure up to American standards? How seriously do textbooks take religion?[10] I will comment on texts and standards in history, economics, and the sciences, but the problems we find here cut across the curriculum. My comments are offered with the awareness that there are many good teachers who teach more than the texts and enrich their students' learning.

History

Even though history textbooks and the national history standards pay a great deal of attention to religion they do not take religion as seriously as they should.

First, we should keep in mind that unless students come to history classes knowing a good deal about religion, they are not likely to learn enough to actually make much sense of it. High school world history texts typically devote about three pages to explaining the origins, basic teachings, and early development of each of the great world religions. American history texts may provide a few mystifying paragraphs on Native American religions, and then jump into the Puritans as if students knew what Protestant Christianity was all about (even though many will never have had that course in world history that would have exposed them to the Protestant Reformation).

Given the amount of material that must be covered in the 800 to 1,000 pages of a history text it is, perhaps, inevitable that not enough pages can be devoted to religion to make much sense of it. I am less forgiving of the fact that both the standards and the textbooks badly understate the influence and importance of religion in the modern world. Religion virtually disappears as we page past the eighteenth century in the world history texts, and the Civil War in the American histories. The world histories devote about one percent of their space to religion after 1750. The American histories devote even less space to religion in their accounts of post-Civil War America. Indeed, if we exclude discussions of the Holocaust, each of the texts I reviewed gave more space to the Watergate Scandal than to all of religion since the Civil War. Most texts devote more space to railroads than they do to religion. The national history standards are only marginally better.[11] Susan Douglass's study of state history standards reveals essentially the same picture.[12]

One of the reasons that religion disappears as we approach the present is that modern civilization has become much less religious; but, as I have suggested, we have not become totally secular—though that might be a reasonable conclusion for a student to draw from the texts. More importantly, the standards and the texts are virtually silent regarding theology and the intellectual development of religion over the last several centuries. This is relevant, for religion, after all, is not a static set of beliefs and institutions; it has changed profoundly in response to modernity, but, again, neither the texts nor the standards take such intellectual developments seriously. Instead, they tend to freeze the intellectual development of Christianity in the Reformation, while most other religions are frozen much earlier in their classical shapes. As a result, students are given virtually no sense of how religious traditions have responded intellectually to modernity and, inevitably, they appear to be fossilized remnants of the past. It is true that there are, typically, brief discussions of the conflict over Darwin in the world histories, and the Scopes Trial in the American histories; in both cases the point is to show how resistant conservative religion is to modernity.

Almost always it is religious conservatives who criticize textbooks, so it is worth noting that the texts ignore liberal religion all but completely. While the American histories typically give the Social Gospel a couple of paragraphs, neither the American nor the world histories mention the development of modern biblical scholarship or the development of liberal theology (Jewish or Christian) in the nineteenth and twentieth centuries. The Second Vatican Council, probably the most significant Christian theological event of the last four hundred years, is briefly mentioned in only two of the eight texts I reviewed most recently and is not mentioned in the 250 pages of the national history standards. When religion is mentioned in recent times it is almost always in the context of wars and fundamentalism.

Most importantly, while the great western religions have held that God is revealed in the events and shape of history, none of the texts discusses religious interpretations of history. For example, half the world history texts I have reviewed in recent years do not bother to explain what B.C. and A.D. (or, B.C.E. and C.E.) mean. The other half typically explain what the abbreviations stand for in a sentence or two, mentioning that the birth of Jesus was traditionally ascribed to the year 1, but that's it.

So what is the significance of this? For Christians, Jesus is God incarnate. Indeed, God's incarnation into this world is the turning point in the unfolding drama of human history. Interestingly, none of the world histories that I have reviewed mention this claim about Jesus, for example, the Christian belief that he was God. Nor does the birth of Jesus make any difference at all in the way the texts divide history up into periods. If one looks at the omnipresent time lines in texts one sees that the joints of history are to be found in the break between ancient and classical history, Greek and Roman history, Roman and medieval history, but not between B.C./B.C.E. and A.D./C.E. That is, students are taught to conceive of the shape of history in secular rather than sacred categories. One could make parallel arguments regarding the calendars of Judaism and Islam.

If it is widely acknowledged that students must learn something about religion in the course of studying history, we typically take this to mean that some mention of religious leaders, movements, and institutions should be incorporated into our historical narratives. However, those narratives must be secular narratives. Indeed, our standards of historical evidence, our conceptions of historical causation, our interpretations of the meaning of history, are, like historical periodization, entirely secular. That is, while students will learn a little about religion in the course of studying history, we teach them how to think about religion in secular historical terms; we do not teach them how to think about history religiously.

In sum, then, if students take a course in world history, they will learn a great deal about religion in premodern history, though far less than what they need to know to actually make sense of it (and it is worth keeping in mind that many states do not require high school students to take world history.) Students will learn next to nothing about religion over the last two centuries in any history course—and they will learn nothing at all about theology. Perhaps most importantly, they will learn uncritically to interpret history in secular categories.

Economics

The scriptures in all religious traditions address the economic domain of life—matters of wealth and poverty, work and stewardship, justice and human nature. There is also a vast theological literature of the last century dealing with economics. Within Christianity, for example, this literature ranges from Pope Leo XIII's seminal 1891 encyclical *Rerum Novarum*, through the Protestant Social Gospel, to Reinhold Niebuhr's Christian Realism, liberation theology, and Pope John Paul II's recent encyclical *Centismus Annus*. Most mainline Christian denominations and ecumenical organizations have official statements addressing economic issues.

Central to scripture and this recent theological literature is the claim that we must employ moral and religious categories to understand the economic domain of life. As the American Catholic Bishops put it in their 1986 statement on the economy, we must guard against a "tragic separation" between religion and our economic life. People cannot "immerse [them]selves in earthly activities as if [they] were utterly foreign to religion, and religion were nothing more than the fulfillment of acts of worship and the observance of a few moral obligations." Indeed, economists, like all of us, must realize that "human dignity, realized in community with others and with the whole of God's creation, is the norm against which every social institution is measured."[13]

How seriously do economics texts take religion? In the 4,400 pages of the ten economics texts I reviewed, all of the references to religion add up to two pages and pertain to distant history. With the sole exception of one reference to religious organizations as nonprofit organizations, there are no references to religion in the forty-seven pages of the new *Voluntary National Content Standards in Economics*.

Neither the texts nor the *Voluntary Standards* address poverty as a moral or spiritual problem. They are silent about the relationship of the First World to the Third World. They ignore the effect of economics and technology on the environment. They are oblivious to the moral problems of a consumer culture. They ask no questions about dehumanizing work. They emphasize the importance of the profit motive and competition while saying nothing about the possibility of excess profits or the possible costs of competition. They never appeal to the dignity of people, the sacredness of nature, or obligations to any larger community or to God.

The problem is not just what is left out; it is also what is included. The texts and national standards teach neoclassical economic theory. Economics is a "value-free" science and the economic world can be defined in terms of the competition of self-interested individuals with unlimited wants for scarce resources. Values are subjective, personal preferences. Decisions should be made according to cost-benefit analyses that maximize whatever it is that we value and that leave no room in the equation for duties, the Sacred, or those dimensions of life that are not quantifiable. Economics is one thing, religion, quite clearly, is another.

What happens when we divorce economics and religion? The sociologist Robert Wuthnow reports that when "asked if their religious beliefs had influenced their choice of a career, most of the people I have interviewed in recent years—Christians and non-Christians alike—said no. Asked if they thought of their work as a calling, most said no. Asked if they understood the concept of stewardship, most said no. Asked how religion did influence their work lives or thoughts about money, most said the two were completely separate."[14]

There can be little doubt but that the way we teach economics contributes to the growing secularization and de-moralization of our economic life. Indeed, it is virtually impossible to reconcile the understanding of human nature, values, and economics found in the texts and the *Voluntary National Standards* with that of any religious tradition.

So should we teach students about alternatives to neoclassical theory? The *Standards* provide a clear answer: Students should be taught only the "majority paradigm" or "neoclassical model" of economic behavior, for to include "strongly held minority views of economic processes risks confusing and frustrating teachers and students who are then left with the responsibility of sorting the qualifications and alternatives without a sufficient foundation to do so."[15] We certainly do not want to confuse teachers or students with alternatives.

Science

The continuing controversy over evolution and creationism provides a good example of how the politics of our culture wars simplify and distort a rich cultural conversation. As it is usually portrayed, the conflict is one between fundamentalists (who read Genesis 1 to mean that God created humankind, and perhaps all of nature, in six days) and all the rest of us reasonable folk who accept evolution. However, it is not so simple.

Yes, religious liberals have accepted evolution pretty much from the beginning (that is to say, from Darwin on), but many of them have wanted to hang on to the idea that evolution is purposeful and that nature has a spiritual dimension to it. The biology texts do not teach that evolution has a purpose. Instead, they teach the "neo-Darwinian" synthesis of modern genetics with Darwinism, according to which evolution is the product of natural selection acting on the random mutation and recombination of genes.

It is tremendously important to understand that the radical thrust of Darwin's theory in his own day, and of neo-Darwinism in ours, is not just that they conflict with a literal reading of Genesis, but that they stand in tension with all religious conceptions of design and purpose in nature. Darwin was himself clear that evolution is not purposeful: There is no more design to be found in nature, he wrote in his *Autobiography*, than in the course which the wind blows.[16]

Now what are the religious responses to all of this? There are fundamentalists who deny that evolution happened at all. Some liberals argue for the "two worlds" view in which science and religion are about different and incommensurable domains of reality; they are conceptual apples and oranges. Science is about mechanics; religion is about meaning, and we should not confuse them. Other liberals have tried to integrate science and religion, evolution and theology. Some argue that neo-Darwinism provides only a partial explanation of origins; there is purpose in evolution, it is just that scientific method is too restrictive to allow scientists to consider all the relevant evidence. Catholic theology sees a providential God behind the "secondary" causes of evolution, and insists that science cannot account for the development of animals into persons (with souls). Process theologians and some feminist theologians argue for an immanent or incarnate God embodied in the workings of nature, who directs evolution from within. Moreover, there are some scientists who argue for "intelligent design theory," holding that God—or at least a cosmic designer—is the best scientific explanation for complex interrelated developments in evolution—in cellular biology, or in the origins of DNA, for example.

That is, not all opposition to neo-Darwinism comes from fundamentalists. Some of it comes from mainline and liberal theologians and dissident scientists. Of course, the biology texts and the National

Science Education Standards ignore not only fundamentalist creationism; they also ignore these more liberal religious ways of interpreting biological evolution.

There is also considerable speculation among scientists, theologians, and philosophers about cosmic evolution. There now appears to be evidence that the universe was fine-tuned to produce life. Life is extraordinarily complicated and improbable, and if the Big Bang had been different in only the smallest degree—and I mean the *very* smallest degree—the universe would have been lifeless. Yet there is life. Arguably, this outcome was, in some way, programmed from the beginning, and God seems the most reasonable explanation. The physics texts and the Science Standards are silent.

There is also a truly vast religious literature on the environment that cuts across theological traditions and the spirituality movement. Some of this literature argues for the virtue of stewardship, often on biblical grounds. However, much eco-theology, process theology, and creation spirituality goes further, claiming that modern science misconceives nature as inert matter, and theology misconceives God as wholly transcendent. Instead, God acts in and through the processes of nature, which are reconceived as sacred or spiritual. In this regard, Eastern and Native American religions have been particularly influential in shaping a more spiritual view of nature. Neither the science texts nor the standards address religious interpretations of nature or the environmental crisis.

There are other points of intersection between science and religion regarding spirituality and healing; genetic engineering; chaos theory and divine causality; quantum mechanics and free will; evolutionary psychology and morality; the origins of life; conceptions of sexuality, and so on. That is, there is a lively, ongoing discussion among intellectuals in our culture about the relationship of science and religion. The nature of this relationship was not settled with the Scopes Trial. *Time, Newsweek, U.S. News and World Report,* and *The New Republic* have all run recent cover stories on science and religion, each exploring a growing sense among intellectuals that nature may be open to, or require, religious interpretation. Theologians quite properly use scientific insight to shape their theological convictions about nature, and scientists—at least those working at the level of basic theory—are at least sometimes drawn into theological reflection.

What can we conclude? The standards and the texts ignore one of the most momentous questions of modern intellectual and cultural history. The implicit message is that science is fully adequate for giving a complete account of nature. God clearly does not measure up to scientific standards, and religious interpretations of nature are, in effect, condemned to irrelevance.[17]

Then there is the rest of the curriculum. Health and sex education and home economics texts and curricula avoid any discussion of religious ways of thinking about sexuality, marriage, abortion, and homosexuality. While some literature anthologies are organized chronologically and include historical religious literature, most literature anthologies include only recent secular literature. Civics textbooks discuss government and law and rights and justice without any discussion of religion. The growing character education movement in public education bends over backwards to avoid any reference to religion in nurturing virtues and moral values. What is the problem with all of this?

The Problem

There are a variety of ways of making sense of the world. Many of us accept one or another religious interpretation; others of us accept one or another *secular* interpretation. We don't agree—and the differences among us often cut deep. Even so, public schools—and many private schools—systematically teach students to think about the world in secular ways only. They do not even bother to inform them that there are religious alternatives—apart from distant history.

To be sure, educators are not explicitly hostile to religion; they do not overtly attack religious practices or theology. However, in some ways ignoring religion is worse than explicit hostility, for students remain unaware of the fact that there may be tensions and conflicts between their religious traditions and what they are taught about science, economics, morality, sexuality, psychology, and history. By eliminating the awareness of religious possibilities, education makes religious accounts of the world seem implausible, even inconceivable.

No doubt much of what students learn in their secular studies is compatible with religion. The problem lies less with the particulars, with the facts they are taught, than with the philosophical assumptions, the governing worldview, that they are taught to use to interpret the various subjects of the curriculum.

In fact, it is misleading to talk about the subjects of the curriculum. Students do not learn about subjects, which are open to contending interpretations. Rather, they are taught disciplines, particular—always secular—ways of thinking about their various "subjects," and this is always done uncritically. It is assumed that secular ways of interpreting a subject are adequate for getting at the truth and meaning of it.

The problem, then, is not just that religious ways of interpreting the world are ignored; it is that the secular disciplines make sense of the world using very different categories from those of religions. For example, under the influence of modern science we have come to accept and uncritically convey to students a fact-value distinction according to which reality is understood in terms of morally neutral, quantifiable, "objective" facts. While values are "subjective" and personal, reality can be known only through sense experience rather than through moral and religious experience. In teaching economics and the sciences (and often in teaching history) we assume that the truth about these domains can be adequately conveyed in such naturalistic or objectivist categories. It has traditionally been held, however, that from a spiritual or religious vantage point we can know dimensions of reality through personal encounters, moral and religious experience; reality is, consequently, richer than it is on a naturalistic account; it is experienced (and may be understood) as personal, purposeful, value-laden, spiritual.

The cumulative effect of teaching students to think about everything they study in secular categories is that public education nurtures in them a secular mentality.

It is important to realize that the problem isn't merely intellectual, it is also moral and spiritual. We shape our lives—our self-understanding of who we are and how we should live our lives—against a background understanding of reality that is acquired, in large part, though certainly not exclusively, from formal education. No doubt most students will continue to believe in God (as an abstract proposition), but God is apt to have little to do with how they live their lives for, after all, nothing they learn about history, literature, sexuality, morality, nature, psychology, or economics hinges on God. Education drains the world of its spiritual meaning.

Three Arguments

My question now is this: What obligation do educators have to include religious voices in the curricular conversation, not just as cultural artifacts in the study of history, but because religion should be taken seriously by students in thinking about how to make sense of the world and how to live their lives here and now?

First, a liberal education requires it. Let me suggest two aspects of a liberal education that are relevant. A liberal education is a broad education; it cannot be narrow, vocational, or specialized. It should introduce students to the major alternative ways in which humankind makes sense of the world—and some of those ways are religious. It should initiate students into an ongoing conversation in which representatives of various communities and traditions are allowed to contend with each other about how to make sense of the world and how to live their lives. It is, by its nature, comparative and critical.

A liberal education is also existentially deep rather than superficial; it cannot ride the surface of life but must address questions of good and evil, the meaning(s) of life and how we should live. Religions have traditionally addressed (and answered) the deepest questions of meaning. A liberal education is required if one is to live an examined life.

If contemporary religious voices did no more than echo faintly the writers and thinkers of long dead traditions there would be no obligation to listen to them—other, perhaps, than in the study of history. However, that is not the case; contemporary education fails to reflect anything of the intellectually lively conversations in our culture now about religion and the various subjects of the curriculum. Unlike our cultural marketplace, the educational marketplace of ideas is an illiberal, tightly regulated marketplace.

It might be argued in response that educators have an obligation to guide the thinking of students and that modern secular scholarship yields the truth. The problem is that we disagree about this. We disagree deeply about how to acquire the truth about sexuality and politics and economics and the origins of the world. If the dominant paradigms are secular, there continue to be religious alternatives.

In fact, what appears to be a secular consensus among scholars is artificial and misleading. It is artificial in that theologians cannot vote; they are not allowed into the main quad of the academy or of public schools but are exiled to divinity schools and seminaries. Their votes are not counted when we decide what frameworks of interpretation to teach our students. The truth of the matter is that we disagree deeply about the truth, and the only way we can get a consensus is by excluding the dissenters.

Does modern secular scholarship provide us with great insight into how the world works? Yes. Does it provide us with the truth? Perhaps. However, an educated judgment regarding the truth about nature, morality, history, economics, or psychology can only be made after listening to religious as well as secular voices. Our educational system does not nurture such conversations; it silences them. Modern education is deeply illiberal, and students should be liberally educated.

Then there is the question of justice. Consider an analogy. Until the last several decades textbooks and curricula routinely ignored women's history and minority literature. We are now almost all sensitive to the fact that this was not a benign neglect, but a form of discrimination, of educational disenfranchisement. Of course, the problem was not just that minority and women's history and literature were ignored; it was that sometimes conflicting, distinctively male, white, and western ways of thinking and acting were taught, and uncritically at that.

There are good educational reasons for including multicultural voices in the curriculum, but there are also reasons of justice—particularly (but certainly not exclusively) with regard to public education. As a civic society we ought to treat each other with a measure of respect, and this means that we must take each other, with our various ideas and ideals, traditions and subcultures, seriously.

Education has gone a long way toward including multicultural voices in the curriculum but, unfortunately, the multicultural movement has virtually ignored religion.[18] Even so, few subcultures are so educationally disenfranchised now as are religious subcultures. There is a fundamental question of justice and oppression here.

Now it may come as a surprise to many, but we are also constitutionally required to include religious voices in public schools. It is, of course, uncontroversial that it is constitutionally permissible to teach about religion, when done properly. No Supreme Court justice has ever held otherwise. However there is a stronger argument to be made.

The Court has been clear that public education must be neutral in matters of religion in two senses. It must be neutral among religions (it cannot favor Protestants over Catholics, or Christians over Jews or Buddhists); and it must be neutral between religion and non-religion.

Public schools cannot promote religion; they cannot proselytize; they cannot conduct religious exercises.

However, neutrality is a two-edged sword. Just as public education cannot favor religion over non-religion, neither can it favor non-religion over religion. As Justice Hugo Black put it in the seminal 1947 *Everson* ruling, "State power is no more to be used so as to handicap religions than it is to favor them."[19] Similarly, in his majority opinion in *Abington v. Schempp* (1963), Justice Tom Clark wrote for the Court that public schools cannot favor "those who believe in no religion over those who do believe."[20] In a concurring opinion, Justice Goldberg warned that an "untutored devotion to the concept of neutrality" can lead to a "pervasive devotion to the secular and a passive, or even active, hostility to the religious."[21] This is just what has happened. An "untutored" and naïve conception of neutrality has led to the prohibition of explicit hostility to religion, when the usual hostility has been philosophically rather more subtle—though no less substantial for that.[22]

There is no such thing as a neutral view. The only way to be neutral when we disagree is to be fair to the alternatives. That is, given the Court's longstanding interpretation of the Establishment Clause, it is mandatory in public education to require the study of religion if students are required to study disciplines that cumulatively lead to a "pervasive devotion to the secular"—as they do. Students must learn about a variety of religions; neutrality also means that public schools cannot promote or privilege a particular religion over others.

A cautionary note might be important here. It is sometimes held that public schools can promote spirituality even if they cannot promote religion; after all, Supreme Court decisions have been phrased in terms of religion, not spirituality, and some kinds of "spiritual" exercises such as meditation practices look much more secular than they do religious. I have noted that the new spirituality is an eclectic movement, but it certainly draws on religious ways of making sense of persons and reality, even while remaining non-doctrinal. No doubt context counts for a great deal; to the extent that spiritual practices are enmeshed with more traditionally religious ways of making sense of the world, constitutional considerations must come into play.

There are profoundly spiritual reasons for taking religion seriously in schooling. In fact, it is often assumed that anyone who wants to make room for religious voices in the academy must have religious motives. I want to be clear. I have argued for including religion in the curriculum not on religious grounds, but because of entirely secular arguments regarding liberal education, justice, and the First Amendment. Whatever you or I believe about God is irrelevant. The point is that because many people do believe in God, and because there are live, religious traditions of considerable intellectual and cultural vitality, a truly liberal education requires that religious voices be included in the conversation. So does justice, and in public schools, so does constitutional neutrality.

Taking Religion Seriously

How can we be neutral or fair? What would a truly liberal education look like? How do we take religion seriously in a secular age? Obviously, a great deal depends on the age of students. In elementary schools students should learn something of the relatively uncontroversial aspects of different religions—their traditions, holidays, symbols, and histories. I want to say just a little about how, as students grow older and more mature, they should be initiated into that sometimes unsettling conversation that constitutes a good liberal education.

Contemporary Religion

When we teach about religion only in the context of history we inevitably give the impression that religion is a thing of the past. We take religion seriously only when we present it to students as a live option for making sense of the world and their lives in the here and now. No doubt contemporary religions are grounded in historical revelations, narratives, and traditions, but if the religion is not dead, then it will continue to interact with, respond to, and shape contemporary life and thought, and students must appreciate this. That is, students must learn not just about the classic forms of the great religions, but about the developing forms of contemporary religions.

Conversation

The curriculum must provide more than parallel disciplinary monologues; it must nurture a conversation in which advocates of different perspectives contend with each other. Teachers and textbooks must make it clear that there are religious alternatives to secular ways of thinking about the various subjects of the curriculum. Students should appreciate the deeply controversial nature of claims in their texts and courses about the origins of the world, the meaning of history, the requirements of justice, and the nature of sexuality and homosexuality.

Obviously textbooks will—and should—continue to be written from the dominant perspective of scholars in the respective disciplines, but they are not free to ignore alternative views. A minimal fairness would require that a chapter in textbooks, and several sessions in courses, include some discussion of religious ways of thinking about the subject at hand.

Unfortunately, because teachers are trained to teach disciplines rather than subjects, they are not likely to be prepared to explain religious ways of approaching their "subjects." Furthermore, the very idea of such conversations is often explicitly rejected. The major scientific organizations have made it clear, for example, that there is no room for religious perspectives in science courses. My own view is that there should be a curricular conversation that mirrors the controversy and vitality of our ongoing cultural conversation.

Religion from the Inside

It is often enlightening to use the resources of modern secular scholarship in the humanities and social sciences to put religious texts and traditions into explanatory contexts (from the outside, as it were), but I want to emphasize here the importance of trying to understand different religious traditions from within. To understand people and texts and cultures we must hear what they say and see what they do in the context of their beliefs about the world, their philosophical assumptions, their reasoning, and their motives. People live within structures of meaning that define their lives, and if we miss this, then we miss them.

How do we do this? We do it through what Ninian Smart, the eminent scholar of world religions, calls "informed empathy" or that immersion of ourselves in the symbols and narratives, the experiences and worldviews of the people we are studying—that is, through using primary sources.[23] If we are concerned with fairness, we must let people and cultures speak for themselves. John Stuart Mill argued that it is not enough for students to hear the arguments of adversaries from their own teachers. If justice is to be done, Mill claimed, students must hear the arguments "from persons who actually believe them...in their most plausible and persuasive form.... Ninety-nine in a hundred of what are called educated men...have never thrown themselves into the mental position of those who think differently from them...and consequently they do not, in any proper sense of the word, know the doctrine which they themselves profane."[24] Fairness requires us to take people seriously on their own terms just as we would want them to take us. We might call this the "Golden Rule" of scholarship.

However, fairness is primarily an intellectual virtue. If we are not to prejudge where the truth lies, we must expose students to the alternatives fairly, as advocates of different positions articulate them. Let me add that people can be primary sources. It is always helpful to talk with people from different traditions; they might be guest speakers in a class or they might be part of the community whose members are being interviewed.

The Many Dimensions of Religion

History textbooks typically describe religions in terms of their "basic teachings," an approach that is congenial to Christians, for many of whom religion is primarily about belief and doctrine. Because many teachers are Christian, it is important that they recognize that other religious traditions are often unlike their own in placing much less emphasis on belief and doctrine and rather more emphasis on ritual or tradition or community or art or, perhaps, on spirituality. Moreover, we should not forget that religious experience is often claimed to be "ineffable," impossible to put into language. Because of this, religions often function symbolically; their natural language is poetry and symbol and metaphor, which point to or imaginatively convey truths that cannot be said literally. Indeed, to understand any religion—Christianity included—involves much more than knowing the basic beliefs and teachings.[25]

Consider an analogy: In educating children about music we are not content to have them read about the beliefs and compositions of composers and musicians; nor is it sufficient to scan sheets of musical notation; nor do we get at music by studying acoustics. It is only in listening to music—or better yet, in performing it—that an adequate understanding (from the "inside" as it were) is possible. Similarly, it is often argued that it is only in doing science, in performing experiments, that students learn what science really is.

While textbooks can provide a great deal of important factual information about religion, they inevitably fall short of conveying what it means to experience the world religiously. We cannot require students to practice a religion or spiritual exercises, but we can provide some imaginative sense of religion by way of literature and autobiographies, drama, film, and art.

Sufficient Time

As I have already noted, given the amount of material that must be crammed into a history textbook, religion will never be taken seriously enough for students to actually make sense of it. The variety of religious traditions and the complexity of religious language, symbolism, and theology render religion even more difficult for the oftentimes religiously illiterate student than those secular disciplines on which we lavish much more time and resources. It is not easy to think our way into the hearts or minds of people in a culture or tradition different from our own, even with the help of good primary sources.

If religion is to be taken seriously, if the importance and complexity of religion are to be acknowledged, then we need to carve space out of the curriculum for courses in religion—or "religious studies," the current term of choice in higher education. In addition, just as we require science teachers to be certified in science, so religious studies should become a certifiable field for teachers of religion. Some schools do offer courses in religion—typically in the Bible or world religions— but these courses are inevitably electives, which are taken by a small minority of students. Our cultural priorities being what they are, this is not likely to change, though we might justifiably wonder why it is more important for a college-bound student to take twelve years of mathematics and no religion rather than eleven years of math and one year of religious studies.

The Humanities

Finally, a more general point of education needs to be made. No one has argued as forcefully as Parker Palmer that education is not about information—about discrete facts, known objectively as it were. (Multiple choice tests are a kind of *reductio-ad-absurdum* of education—for those who have eyes to see.) Education, Palmer argues, is about healing, wholeness, empowerment, liberation, transformation, and transcendence. In education properly conceived "we come to know the world not simply as an objectified system of empirical objects in logical connection with each other, but as an organic body of personal relations and responses, a living and evolving community of creativity and compassion."[26] This, Palmer suggests, is the conception of education to be found in our spiritual traditions.

Something of Palmer's spiritual education lives on in the disciplines of the humanities which, at their best, are concerned with locating us in webs of meaning—historically, in terms of ongoing conversations with writers and thinkers who have shaped our world, and in community with people of our own as well as different cultures. The humanities are more attuned to our passions, to the lived texture of life, than the sciences and social sciences, which thrive on abstractions such as the reduction of individuals to self-interested utility-maximizers. The humanities take seriously the metaphors and myths that reveal to us what cannot be said literally. In studying the humanities, we learn stories that awaken our imaginations and nurture the empathy we need to think and feel ourselves in the hearts and minds of people unlike us. So, often, compassion is born. That is, the humanities nurture ways of thinking and feeling about persons and the world that are congenial to spirituality.

The humanities are not in good health, however. They suffer from their own naturalistic and postmodern demons. As our culture has become increasingly materialistic, the old idea of a classical education, grounded in the humanities, has largely given way to a utilitarian conception of education grounded in science, technology, and those basic skills that fuel our economic system. No doubt we continue to pay lip service to the humanities, but what we serve students is a very watered-down soup. The study of literature is often submerged in the welter of goals that can be found under the umbrella of "communication skills" or "language arts." History may be de-emphasized in a "social studies" curriculum that focuses largely on the present day and is rooted in the social sciences more than in the humanities. Courses in philosophy and ethics are virtually unknown, and courses in religious

studies are rare. Indeed, the idea of the humanities as a way of organizing or conceptualizing the curriculum is foreign to K-12 schooling.

Good News, Bad News

So, what are the prospects that religion will be taken seriously in
the foreseeable future? First, the good news; next, the bad news.

There has come to be, since the late 1980s, what might be called a
"New Consensus" about the role of religion in public education. This
consensus has been formally endorsed in a series of "common
ground" statements by a variety of religious, educational, and civil lib-
erties groups at the national level. The gist of it is:

- that it is constitutional to teach students about religion
  in public schools;
- that religion must be approached neutrally since public
  schools cannot promote or proselytize particular religious beliefs;
- that it is important for students to learn about religion.[27]

This is helpful, very helpful. Of course, word of this consensus at
the national level has not reached everyone in the trenches where our
culture wars are often fought. If there is agreement in principle on the
legitimacy and importance of studying religion, in practice religion
continues to be relegated almost entirely to the study of history, and,
as I have argued, that is not nearly good enough.

Well, that is the good news. What is the bad news? It will be an
uphill battle all the way.

First, while some educators agree that religion should be taken seriously, they argue that teachers are not prepared to do it right, and if
it cannot be done right it is dangerous to try. This response is shared
by many members of minority religious traditions, who fear that talk
of taking religion seriously simply opens the door to subtle, if not

overt, proselytizing by teachers who, no matter how well intentioned, will inevitably convey to students their prejudices and ignorance of religious traditions other than their own.

This is a legitimate concern; hence the need for major reforms in teacher education. Unfortunately, those reforms are not on the agenda of schools of education or departments of religious studies.

Second, many educators, particularly in public schools, find the whole idea of taking religion seriously to be much too controversial—though I think that they are shortsighted if they do. It is important to remember that it is also controversial to leave religion out of the curriculum. Indeed, because public schools do not take religion seriously, many religious parents have deserted them and with the Supreme Court's recent voucher decision, there will be more pressure for vouchers and the exodus may well prove much greater. In the long run, the least controversial position is the one that takes everyone seriously. If public schools are to survive our culture wars, they must be built on common ground. However, there can be no common ground when religious voices are left out of the curricular conversation.

Third, a greater problem is that no matter how religious they happen to be personally, most educators have little appreciation of the relevance of religion to the curriculum outside of history. This is in part, no doubt, because they themselves have been illiberally educated. They have been taught to compartmentalize their religious beliefs and values.

Fourth, there is no respectable constituency for change. Consider an analogy referred to earlier. Several decades ago textbooks and curricula said little about women and minority cultures. Educators then were naïve about the need to include multicultural voices in the curriculum, and, of course, multiculturalism has also proven controversial. Still, multicultural education is now commonplace. Things do change, with a little enlightenment and a strong enough lobby for change, and one might find hope in this.

Unlike multicultural education, however, there is no constituency pressing for the inclusion of religious voices in the curriculum, apart from the Religious Right, that is. While the Religious Right may not appear to want a fair and neutral consideration of different religious traditions, my sense of the situation is that many on the Right would—so long as they too have a place at the table. In fact, our cultural wars have led to tactical alliances between religious and secular liberals who wish to present a united front against those on the Right who would make America into a Christian country and our schools into Christian schools. As noted by James Davison Hunter, the most important battle lines in our contemporary culture wars separate liberals from conservatives, not religious from secular folk.[28] Given the Protestant heritage of our schools, it is not surprising that liberals are wary of all talk of religion in the schools; too often, however, liberals have uncritically accepted "religion-free" schools as the only alternative to religious schools.

Fifth, and most importantly, for all that I have said about the vitality of contemporary religion, it remains the case that science, technology, and capitalism are in the cultural saddle, riding humankind. Spirituality and religion are largely countercultural movements. If postmodernism has deflated the pretensions of science among many intellectuals in the academy, its influence outside the academy pales before the power of the master narratives of modern science and global capitalism. In such a world the educational agenda will almost inevitably be weighted in favor of basic skills, testing, computers, technology, and economics—and there will be all too little time for religion (or the humanities more generally).

None of this is to say there is no hope, of course. Indeed, religion has a good deal to teach us about hope. Moreover, no doubt, much can be accomplished locally, even if revisions in the master narratives of our time will continue to elude us for the foreseeable future. At the very least, we must keep in mind what the ideal is—and how far short of it we fall.

Notes

1 All of the quotations are from Paul Leicester Ford, ed., *The New England Primer* (1727; reprint, New York: Teachers College Press, 1962).

2 I have told the story of the secularization of American education in chapter 2 of my *Religion and American Education: Rethinking a National Dilemma* (Chapel Hill: University of North Carolina Press, 1995).

3 Max Stackhouse, *Public Theology and Political Economy* (Grand Rapids: Eerdmans, 1987), x.

4 Richard P. McBrien, *Catholicism: Study Edition* (Minneapolis: Winston Press, 1981), 1,058.

5 Robert Wuthnow, *After Heaven: Spirituality in America Since the 1950s* (Berkeley: University of California Press, 1998), viii.

6 David Ray Griffin, *Spirituality and Society: Postmodern Visions* (Albany: SUNY Press, 1988), 1.

7 Eugene H. Peterson, "Missing Ingredient," *Christian Century*, March 22, 2003: 30.

8 Robert Wuthnow writes that "public opinion polls reveal that most Americans think you should come up with your own definition of spirituality, rather than following the dictates of any religious institutions. Indeed, many of the people I have interviewed in various research projects describe a negative trade-off between spirituality and religious institutions. The latter, they say, are too formal and bureaucratic, even hypocritical, always raising money and running programs; spirituality, they say, cannot be forced into a model, for it is too ephemeral, emotional, intuitive, impulsive. Who defines spirituality—the institutions that certify what it means—are independent writers, again the artist and activists, but also mystics, secular saints, and just ordinary people in our neighborhoods. *Christianity in the 21st Century: Reflections on the Challenges Ahead* (New York: Oxford University Press, 1993), 45.

9 See Wuthnow, *After Heaven*, chapter 1.

10 For a more thorough discussion of the role of religion in the texts and standards see Warren A. Nord and Charles C. Haynes, *Taking Religion Seriously Across the Curriculum* (Alexandria, VA: ASCD Press, 1998), passim.

11 For example, there are 14 world history standards that deal with the four years of World War I, while only 13 deal with any aspect of religion in the period from 1750 to the present and, of these, only six deal primarily with religion. While 15 of the U.S. standards deal with Progressivism in the forty-year period from 1890 to 1930, only 14 standards deal with religion in any way in the period from the Civil War to the present, and of these only eight deal primarily with religion.

12 In her thorough study of state history and social studies standards Susan L. Douglass concludes that "with some exceptions, very little content on religion is written

into state world history standards for the period after 1800 in European history, and after 1500 in non-Western cultures. All students will have been exposed to information about the role of religion in American history before 1800, but they will receive little additional information during their studies of 19th and 20th century US history." *Teaching About Religion in National and State Social Studies Standards* (Fountain Valley, CA: Council on Islamic Education, and Nashville, TN: the First Amendment Center), 88.

[13] National Conference on Catholic Bishops, *Economic Justice For All* (Washington, DC: United States Catholic Conference, 1986), vi-vii, 12.

[14] Robert Wuthnow, *Christianity in the 21st Century*, 200.

[15] National Council on Economic Education, *Voluntary National Content Standards in Economics* (New York: NCEE, 1997), viii. For a more thorough discussion of religion, economics, and education (and bibliographical references) see *Taking Religion Seriously*, 105–16.

[16] Charles Darwin, *The Autobiography of Charles Darwin and Selected Letters*, ed. Francis Darwin (New York: Dover, 1958), 63. Cf. the "Statement on Teaching Evolution" of the National Association of Biology Teachers at www.nabt.org/oldsite/evolution.html.

[17] For a more complete discussion of the relation of science, religion, and education see *Taking Religion Seriously*, 134–63.

[18] For a corrective, see Warren A. Nord, "Multiculturalism and Religion," in *Multiculturalism and Bilingual Education: Students and Teachers Caught in the Crossfire*, ed. Carlos J. Ovando and Peter McLaren (Boston: McGraw-Hill, 2001), 62–81.

[19] *Everson v. Board of Education*, 300 U.S. 1, 18.

[20] *Abington Township v. Schempp*, 374 U.S. 203, 205.

[21] *Abington Township v. Schempp*, 374 U.S. 203, 306.

[22] The purpose of the Establishment Clause should be to require what the legal scholar Douglas Laycock has called "substantive neutrality." Such neutrality requires government "to minimize the extent to which it either encourages or discourages religious belief or disbelief, practice or nonpractice, observance or nonobservance." Religion "should proceed as unaffected by government as possible." ["Formal, Substantive, and Disaggregated Neutrality Toward Religion," *DePaul Law Review* 39 (1990): 1001–2.] In regard to the curriculum, "government must be scrupulously even handed, treating the range of religious and nonreligious views as neutrally as possible." ["Religious Liberty and Liberty," in *The Journal of Contemporary Legal Issues* 7 (1996): 348.]

[23] Ninian Smart, *Religion and the Western Mind* (New York: Macmillan, 1987), ch. 1.

[24] John Stuart Mill, *On Liberty*, in *The Essential Works of John Stuart Mill*, ed. Max Lerner (1859; reprint, New York: Bantam Books, 1985), 287.

[25] Here I again follow Ninian Smart who has distinguished seven "dimensions" of religion: doctrines (e.g., the Trinity, reincarnation); sacred narratives (e.g., the story

of Buddha, the story of the Exodus); ethical/legal teachings (e.g., the Torah, the Shari'a, the Sermon on the Mount); ritual (e.g., the Mass, daily Muslim prayer, meditation); religious experience (e.g., conversion experiences, mystical experiences); social institutions (e.g., monastic orders, the Temple in Jerusalem); and material culture (e.g., pagodas and cathedrals, idols, and icons). See *The Religious Experience of Mankind* (New York: Charles Scribner's Sons, 1976), ch. 1.

26 Parker Palmer, *To Know as We Are Known: A Spirituality of Education* (San Francisco: Harper & Row, 1983), 14.

27 A very helpful collection of the new consensus documents with commentary can be found in *Finding Common Ground: A First Amendment Guide to Religion and Public Education*, ed. Charles C. Haynes and Oliver Thomas, published by the Freedom Forum First Amendment Center at Vanderbilt University, Nashville, TN.

28 See James Davison Hunter, *Culture Wars: The Struggle to Define America* (New York: Basic Books, 1991).

Works Consulted

Abington Township v. Schempp, 374 U.S. 203 (1963).

Darwin, F., ed. (1958). *The Autobiography of Charles Darwin and Selected Letters.* New York: Dover.

Douglass, Susan. *Teaching about Religion in National and State Social Studies Standards.* Fountain Valley, CA: Council on Islamic Education and Nashville, TN: First Amendment Center, 2000.

Everson v. Board of Education, 300 U.S. 1 (1947).

Ford, Paul L., ed. *The New England Primer.* 1727. Reprint. New York: Teachers College Press, 1962.

Griffin, David R. *Spirituality and Society: Postmodern Visions.* Albany: State University of New York Press, 1988.

Haynes, Charles C., and Oliver Thomas. *Finding Common Ground: A First Amendment Guide to Religion and Public Education.* Nashville, TN: First Amendment Center, 1998.

Hunter, James D. *Culture Wars: The Struggle to Define America.* New York: Basic Books, 1991.

Laycock, Douglas. "Formal, Substantive, and Disaggregated Neutrality Toward Religion." *DePaul Law Review* 39 (1990): 1001–2.

———. "Religious Liberty and Liberty." *The Journal of Contemporary Legal Issues* 7 (1996): 348.

Lerner, Max, ed. *The Essential Works of John Stuart Mill.* New York: Bantam Books, 1985.

McBrien, Richard P. *Catholicism: Study Edition.* Minneapolis: Winston Press, 1981.

National Conference on Catholic Bishops. *Economic Justice for All.* Washington, D.C.: United States Catholic Conference, 1986.

National Council on Economic Education. *Voluntary National Content Standards in Economics.* New York: NCEE, 1997.

Nord, Warren A. *Religion and American Education: Rethinking a National Dilemma.* Chapel Hill: University of North Carolina Press, 1995.

Nord, Warren A., and Charles Haynes. *Taking Religion Seriously Across the Curriculum.* Alexandria, VA: ACSD, 1998.

Ovando, Carlos J., and Peter McLaren, eds. *Multiculturalism and Bilingual Education: Students and Teachers Caught in the Crossfire.* Boston: McGraw-Hill, 2001.

Palmer, Parker. *To Know As We Are Known: A Spirituality of Education.* San Francisco, CA: Harper & Row, 1983.

Peterson, Eugene H. Missing Ingredient. *Christian Century,* March 2003.

Smart, Ninian. *Religion and the Western Mind.* New York: Macmillan, 1987.

———. *The Religious Experience of Mankind.* New York: Charles Scribner's Sons, 1976.

Stackhouse, Max. *Public Theology and Political Economy.* Grand Rapids, MI: Eerdmans, 1987.

Wuthnow, Robert. *After Heaven: Spirituality in America Since the 1950's.* Berkeley, CA: University of California Press, 1998.

———. *Christianity in the 21st Century: Reflections on the Challenges Ahead.* New York: Oxford University Press, 1993.

Chapter 12

Freedom for Narcissus, Too: Liberating the Spiritual Dimension of the Religious Student

Matthew Hicks

Let me begin by applauding the progress and promise of including religious studies and religious viewpoints in American education. Educators, civic and religious leaders, and most lawmakers have made great strides in carving out an appropriate role for the study of religion in our schools. Currently, most state and national social studies standards give significant mention to religion and, hence, most states mandate that schools teach about religion.[1] A host of consensus documents have been created, owing to two decades of unwavering diligence and negotiation by Dr. Charles Haynes of the First Amendment Center, to advance the widely held notion that American students should be exposed to the academic study of religion.[2] Unlike forces influencing public education from the 1850s to the 1960s, today, relatively few people or organizations openly advocate that schools promote or denigrate any single religious or non-religious position. Because of universally required courses on multicultural awareness, most teachers leave colleges and universities with an understanding that their students will bring a variety of religious beliefs and practices to the classroom. In short, America's schools have begun to reflect the pledge and wisdom summarized in founding documents like Rhode Island's 1663 charter: "to hold forth a lively experiment, that a most flourishing civil state may stand and best be maintained...with a full liberty in religious concernments."[3]

A fair and accurate discussion of the current place of religion and spirituality in K–12 education, however, requires that I temper this optimistic appraisal of the "lively experiment." A number of hurdles persistently thwart the presence of religion and religious thought in America's classrooms. For example, textbooks continue to treat perfunctorily the place of religion in world history, not to mention its specific impact on American society and thought.[4] Furthermore, very few scholars (in either religious studies or education) study or acknowledge the relationship between religion and K–12 education. Because courses in religious studies usually do not count toward degree completion, teachers take to the classroom, at best, a cursory knowledge of the world's major religious traditions. Much needed pedagogical strategies for teaching this difficult subject are almost nonexistent. Consequently, most educators remain reticent to discuss religion in their classroom.

Some faculty members have tried to overcome these obstacles through the use of the mediating word, "about." This seemingly magic word has often functioned to distinguish between coercing students in matters of faith—teaching religion—and educating students in matters of faith traditions—teaching about religion. While it has served, since the 1960s, as a useful qualifier for thinking through the purpose of a course in religion, one word alone cannot eliminate the problems associated with including religion in the curriculum. In some sense, agreement that we should teach about religion only increases the ambiguity of how educators ought to treat this complicated subject. The following quote from a 1972 conference on religion and education should clarify the point:

> Teaching *about* (emphasis in the original) religion is not necessarily an answer to the problem. You may have seen, as I did, a couple of weeks ago, television debate between Bill Buckley and Madelyn Murray O'Hare, the well-known atheist. It was a screaming match for the most part. The one thing they agreed on was that public schools should teach *about* religion. Buckley undoubtedly envisioned a course magnifying the place of Christianity in American culture. Mrs. O'Hare plainly envisioned a course in the cor-

ruptions and perversions of the church. The issue is, of course, who establishes the syllabus, and who teaches it. The same material as taught by Mr. Buckley would produce a completely different attitude toward religion than if taught by Mrs. O'Hare. We might not like either one.[5]

How might educators maintain the forward momentum of creating places for the spiritual to occur during students' schooldays, while remaining sensitive to the perspectives and concerns of both the Mr. Buckleys and the Mrs. O'Hares of the world? The question is neither rhetorical nor hypothetical: An answer is demanded if we are to offer a complete, neutral (i.e., fair) and constitutionally permissible curriculum.

In this essay I propose that those interested in K-12 spirituality expand the conceptions of why we must include religious studies in the curriculum and reconsider the direction that our methodology, the how, is taking us. In the first case, I want to argue that fostering existential discussions in K–12 education that include more traditional religious viewpoints simply allows most students to be human beings. By our very nature we constantly engage questions of meaning and, for many of us, we filter these questions through the teachings of a specific religious tradition. In the second section, I postulate that transporting a university-like approach to a K–12 setting is philosophically and developmentally inappropriate. My hope in both discussions is to add wind to the sails already propelling the rapidly moving ship called "religion and education," as well as to suggest a more carefully navigated course so that our vessel does not capsize.

The Case for Human Beings

In 1930, fifty-three-year-old German-born author Hermann Hesse penned *Narcissus and Goldmund*. In this fascinating account of two medieval priests, Hesse beautifully articulates the human search for meaning. Hesse juxtaposes two main characters to illustrate two approaches to life: First, there is Goldmund leading a sybaritic, self-indulgent lifestyle; and then there is Narcissus, whose existence is mendicant and cloistered. Goldmund roams aimlessly, sleeping in forests, relentlessly hounding every female he encounters, eventually finding solace in his work as an artist; Narcissus devotes his life to his studies, his students, and his vows, finding peace and meaning in the monastery.

Hesse does not condemn either pursuit; in fact, he appears to condone both as possible ways to expose life's mysteries. The constant pairing of characters and frequent expression of two opposing per-spectives reinforces the dichotomy used by Hesse to reveal his idea of two potential paths to truth. A clear example of Hesse's thesis is seen in the book's ordering: Ten of the book's twenty chapters are devoted to the monastery and ten to the world. Hesse gave credence to both worldviews.

By drawing from *Narcissus and Goldmund*, I am not suggesting that there are only two possibilities for seeking Truth, and I am not suggesting a relativistic pluralism that holds that all truth claims are equally valid. Rather, I am claiming that all humans, like Narcissus and Goldmund, seek meaning, connection, purpose, and transcen-dence in their lives. Furthermore, many (perhaps most) students lo-cate their answers to these existential/spiritual/religious[6] questions in a way reminiscent of the character Narcissus: based in large measure on the teachings of a religious tradition. Of course, many students—whether or not they belong to a religious tradition—order their lives like the character Goldmund. These Goldmund-like students locate their spirituality in art, nature, or sport, and many of them accept and adopt a worldview grounded in materialism.[7] The rub, unfortunately, is that contemporary education tends to be more comfortable with Goldmund than with Narcissus. In today's classrooms, those students who, like Narcissus, define their lives in terms of, and seek meaning within, a specific religious tradition are stifled, if not shut out com-pletely.

Our present discomfort with making room for religious voices has historical antecedents. Early American education was seen as a way to transmit common values and religious convictions from one generation to the next. In fact, the common school, some have argued, was meant to replace the common church.[8] During the periods of the *McGuffey's Readers*, the Scopes trial, and for a decade beyond the 1963 *Abington v. Schempp* ruling, American education sought to symbolically preserve and pass on the faith of the majority.

Battling against this early understanding of public education, John Dewey, in 1934, offered a different interpretation of the educational mission in *A Common Faith*. According to Dewey, education had to cease imposing Christian beliefs onto students and assert a method and commitment to finding truth that was common to all citizens, not just Christians. For Dewey, the shared path to truth was found in the scientific method: "The mind of man is being habituated to a new method and ideal: There is but one sure road of access to truth—the road of patient, cooperative inquiry operating by means of observation, experiment, record and controlled reflection."[9] Dewey's stern rebuke of religious (particularly Christian) viewpoints was a reaction to the forced inclusion of Christianity in the public schools of his day.

There is, however, a fundamental problem with both the early model and Dewey's position: The concept of a common church, religion, faith, or spirituality is anathema to the very idea of America. We are not all committed to the idea that ultimate truth can be discovered through the scientific method any more than we are all convinced that Jesus is the Messiah. The roads taken to find truth are many, and if educators try to force every student onto the same road, collisions will occur.

In more recent times, many postulate that the solution to the diversity question lies in the philosophy of pluralism. I disagree. Pluralism is a perspective, and, in many ways, it is an exclusive position.[10] The idea that all religions contain beauty and truth is an idea subscribed to by many people. However, many students will come to the classroom committed to religious traditions that do not support this claim. Furthermore, why should educators try to move students away from the doctrines of their individual faith traditions? The Atheist, Buddhist, Christian, Hindu, Jain, Muslim, and any adherent to any other form of religious expression have a right to live and participate in our society in ways consistent with their individual traditions and allegiances. The religious liberty clauses celebrate and expect a religiously diverse body politic. The only thing that needs to be common about our students is their commitment to a set of civic principles: principles that allow everyone to seek meaning and connection according to the dictates of their conscience.

American education has moved, then, from an institution designed, in part, to pass on Christian teachings, to one in which primacy was granted to science and religious worldviews were silenced, to one in which we frequently hear calls to establish pluralism as our new common faith. All of these models, I wish to argue, view students as objects that need transformation. They remain committed to the melting pot rather than the mosaic. They are all a form of objectivism, telling "...the world what it is rather than listening to what it says about itself."[11] They continue to see students as vessels in need of filling, rather than as souls in need of liberation. Instead of trying to change our students, perhaps we might consider how our students, using all of the baggage that they bring from home, including traditional religious viewpoints, just might transform our schools and the world. To treat fairly all students—the Narcissuses and the Goldmunds—we must create a space for existential discussions and allow for religious interpretations of the same. In doing so, we are simply allowing our students to be themselves, to be human.

Of course, there are several other reasons to include the study of religion in the curriculum. For example, there is the argument for cultural literacy (à la E. D. Hirsch). Certainly, as many scholars have noted, students living in the most religiously diverse nation in the world need to have some knowledge of the religious traditions that they will encounter. A position statement adopted in 1984 by the National Council for the Social Studies summarizes this argument:

> Knowledge about religions is not only characteristic of an educated person but is also absolutely necessary for understanding and living in a world of diversity.... Since the purpose of the social studies is to provide students with a knowledge of the world that has been, the world that is, and the world of the future, studying about religions should be an essential part of the social studies curriculum.

There is also an argument for democratic citizenship. To be a citizen in a democracy that champions the cause of religious freedom requires practice. John Dewey, for example, recognized the need to teach students democratic principles so that they might effectively participate in this form of government: "What is happening proves conclusively, I think, that unless democratic habits of thought and action are part of the moral fiber of a people, political democracy is insecure."[12] Another example of this position is found in a consensus document, as mentioned above, endorsed by 24 diverse organizations: "Public schools uphold the First Amendment when they protect the religious liberty rights of students of all faiths or none. Schools demonstrate fairness when they ensure that the curriculum includes study about religion, where appropriate, as an important part of a complete education."[13] Both of these reasons are valid and vitally important to the educational mission. However, by pointing to the mystical insights of Hermann Hesse, I hope to prompt those interested in K–12 spirituality to go further in conceiving why we must include the voices, the perspectives of religiously oriented people in the curriculum.

In *Narcisuss and Goldmund*, Hesse writes about the divergent lives of two medieval confidants. One of them seeks spiritual knowledge through living in the world; the other finds comfort in the cloister. Both characters excavate their own souls as they struggle to unveil the meaning of life. All students have this existential drive. They want to discuss life's "big" questions such as, "Why am I here? Is there more to life than meets the empirical eye? Is there a God or gods? And what about angels and spirits? Why should we act as moral beings? Why do people suffer?" When we stimulate these conversations in secondary schools, slumberous eyes suddenly shine with an inquisitiveness and excitement rarely seen in most classrooms. Students' spirits are awakened as students begin to realize their existence as human beings.

Those students who, like Narcissus, find comfort, meaning, and answers to these question based on their own religious traditions will feel enlivened, perhaps liberated. Many of these students will, possibly for the first time in their educational lives, feel heard as educators move religious studies and religious viewpoints away from their relegated place in the "null" curriculum and into the conversational arena. The challenge is to have the courage to allow students to be who they are in terms of both being human and, for many of them, adherents to specific religious traditions. Finally, for those readers concerned with protecting religious freedom, I pose the following question: The First Amendment to the Constitution grants Goldmund the freedom to live, debate, and be expressive in the public square, including the American classroom. Should not there be freedom for Narcissus, too?

Religious Studies without Religion

A couple of summers ago, I attended a conference at Florida State University on teaching the Bible in Florida's public schools. I was researching at that time for a master's thesis on teaching about the Bible in public education and thought exposure to a state-sanctioned training session would prove beneficial. A dozen teachers, a few administrators, and a newspaper reporter attended the four-day conference. Dr. David Levenson, a New Testament scholar at FSU, and Dr. Corrine Patton, a professor of Hebrew Bible at the University of St. Thomas in Minnesota, guided the attendees through a somewhat rigorous course on the academic study of the Bible. Participants were provided sound methods and excellent resources for introducing students to the academic study of the Bible.

However, I departed from the training concerned that teachers were left believing that nothing should be said about traditional readings of this sacred text. In other words, they were taught to teach "The Bible—Without religion."[14] In fact, this is exactly how the reporter for the *St. Petersburg Times* newspaper section, *Floridian*, summarized the conference in her headline. This is a disturbing and, in my opinion, defective trend taking place in efforts to teach religious studies to K–12 students. I believe that allowing academic interpretations to usurp traditional religious perspectives in K–12 religious studies courses is philosophically and developmentally unsound.

Having read and interpreted the Bible in both secular and sectarian settings, I realized that the academic community and the devotional community begin their analyses from different starting points. Furthermore, I began to understand that the academic reading discounted, *a priori*, certain claims that many religious adherents accepted, *a priori* (e.g., miracles). Now, if one divorces the Bible from its miraculous claims, for example, then a vast majority of this religious epic becomes devoid of meaning—at least for the religious adherent. The criteria used to evaluate this sacred text differ from one community to the next. In other words, these different communities start from different places, pose different questions and, more often than not, draw different conclusions.

Belonging to both communities, I value both of these major approaches to the text and am not suggesting that academics are by definition anti-religious or that religious people are anti-intellectual. However, I understand when students who operate within only one of these worlds object to having the viewpoint of the other receive attention to the exclusion of their own interpretation. The solution, I suggest, is not to remove all traditional interpretations from the course, nor to suggest that any particular reading reveals the true meaning of the text, but to simply include as many interpretations as possible in the conversation. This does not mean that teachers ought to suggest that all readings are equally valid (see below), but rather, that in secondary classrooms all competing and conflicting worldviews and claims are welcomed, all voices are respected, and disagreements are allowed.

Occasionally, I hear three objections to this proposal. First, biblical scholars and other academics are reluctant to concede that the academic interpretation is just that: an interpretation. Many of these scholars have devoted their professional lives to the field of biblical or religious studies, subjected their work to the test of peer-reviewed journals and, therefore, aver that their conclusions are more accurate or complete than those produced by other communities. Second, I frequently hear educators and scholars remark that it is impossible to have the expertise to include all of the possible interpretations in a single course. How can a teacher be expected to know how Jews, Christians, Muslims, and academics (not to mention how scholars who happen to be Jewish, Christian, or Muslim or the vast array of intra-traditional approaches) interpret, for example, the creation account in Genesis? Third, I am sometimes reminded that the classroom is, after all, an academic setting and, therefore, should offer academic interpretations.

To the first protest I reply that the presence of other extant readings necessarily makes the academic interpretation an interpretation. When all other perspectives disappear, then that which is produced in the academy will become the sole, sacrosanct doctrine. Teaching through attribution remedies part of the second concern (e.g., some Jews believe X while some Christians believe Y, and so on). Also, teachers need not be experts to include several major interpretations in their discussions. Acknowledging that there are many ways to approach a sacred writing and including a few examples is enough to be fair to, and satisfy the intellectual curiosity of, most students. In the specific case of biblical studies, reviewing several commentaries will equip teachers with the requisite knowledge needed to introduce different readings. As for the third reproach, I suggest that we call K–12 classrooms "educational" settings—they are neither devotional nor academic settings, at least not in the university sense, where students function at cognitively and developmentally higher levels and act *in loco parentis*. An educational setting differs from these other two settings in that it does not force any particular interpretation onto students; it does not neglect academic or traditional voices; it does not superimpose one interpretation on top of the other; it does not necessarily evaluate one perspective through the lens of the other; it does not ask children and adolescents to question the logic of their faith system, whatever that system might be.

The last point—that educators should not ask students to question the logic of their faith system—rests not only on philosophical grounds, but acknowledges that children and adolescents understand their faith system in ways commensurate with their age. Just as there are age-appropriate ways to teach mathematics and science, so, too, are there age-appropriate methods for teaching religious studies. I want to make two claims based on this premise: First, adolescents are not likely to crumble and abandon their own system simply because they hear about other faith traditions; however, and second, this does not mean that educators should be insensitive to their students' traditions and/or superimpose an academic reading on top of traditional interpretations. Experiences from two more conferences will help illustrate.

A few years ago, I fielded questions at a Tennessee public forum on teaching about the Bible in public schools. Parents, civic and religious leaders and several teachers posed many challenging questions and made several helpful suggestions. As the crowd dispersed, one of the board members approached me and said, "No God, No Gandhi, that's the way I see it!" This board member has remained steadfast in his viewpoint, as he was later quoted in a Louisiana newspaper article stating, "If they don't want God in our schools, then we're not going to have Gandhi in our schools."[15]

After further conversation with this board member, and having listened carefully to others concerned with religious studies courses, I began to understand his worry as well as to understand how he understood the purpose of a course in religious studies. Foremost, he (and many, many others like him) believes that he does not have a voice in the school system. Why, he wonders, can we teach about Gandhi (apparently the representative of the Hindu tradition, in this board member's mind) and not talk about God (and here he specifically means the evangelical Christian's understandings of God)? In short, he, like many parents, simply wants some semblance of his faith tradition included in his child's education. This desire, in my opinion, is not altogether unreasonable.

His second concern stems from a belief that a course on world religions is designed to expose students to a smorgasbord of faith traditions from which they may select. Moreover, related angst derives from his feeling that exposure to these other faith systems might lead children away from their own traditions. These concerns, however, are unwarranted.

Courses on world religions are constructed to expose students to other ideas and belief systems. They are not, or should not be, designed to convert students or contrived to present religious traditions as options. Courses in world religions are structured to inform students about the history, beliefs, practices, and rituals of the world's major faith traditions.

In religious studies courses, conversations that occur among students who belong to different traditions will almost certainly stimulate students to reflect in a more profound and sophisticated way about their own spirituality. However, conversion among the very young and even adolescents as a result of learning about other traditions is not likely. K–12 students are not as easily persuaded to desert their tradition as one might initially think. Rather, as students learn about other faith systems, they become intrigued and perhaps even deepen their faith to their own tradition. William Damon, one of the leading thinkers on child and adolescent development, criticizes the idea that children will relinquish their beliefs, due to the attainment of knowledge of other religions, as a general misunderstanding of children and adolescents:

> Children are not so easily wounded or led astray. They are resilient, purposeful, and intellectually capable—no doubt far more so than most adults give them credit for being. Children are not so brittle as to be shattered by exposure to beliefs that are different from their own or so plastic as to be immediately remolded by such exposure. To the contrary, a sincere display of another's beliefs can hearten and inspire a young person. Such a display can result in an affirmation of the child's own spiritual inclinations, instead of— as in the danger of religious censorship—an implicit denial of the validity of faith. As in so many other ways, misguided attempts to shelter children do nothing more than interfere with their own natural needs and inclinations.[16]

Thus, according to Damon, students might, as a result of learning about other religions, deepen their commitment to their tradition.

Because youths can handle exposure to new religious ideas and beliefs does not mean that educators should critically deconstruct students' faith traditions by suggesting that one reading, including the academic reading, is more "logical" or accurate than another. Rather, educators need to recognize that students bring to school a set of inherited beliefs—beliefs they use to navigate through difficult times known as childhood and adolescence.

In *The Spiritual Life of Children*, Pulitzer Prize winning author and renowned psychiatrist, Robert Coles, gives readers a unique glimpse inside the religious world of children. In the third chapter titled "The Face of God," Coles describes several of the images and accompanying conversations that resulted from a request he made to several hundred children to "draw a picture of God."[17] The artwork produced is fascinating; the conversations, I think, are equally as telling. As Coles recounts some of the dialogue that he had with the children, a common theme appears: Most of the children qualify their comments based on an authority figure from their family or faith tradition. In other words, they express their understanding of God (and related existential matters) in terms and philosophies consistent with family members and/or faith leaders. Regardless of children's religious, or non-religious, background they tend to ground their images and remarks in a tradition transported from home and community to other realms, including the classroom. Educators, therefore, encounter students with preformed ideas and commitments primarily based on their parents' allegiances.

While this observation should inform how educators think about teaching religious studies to young students, some teachers do not make the connection. At a conference I attended in Denver, Colorado, I explained to a secondary religious studies teacher that part of my presentation would deal with the relational question of child and adolescent faith development and educational courses about religion. This well-educated teacher remarked, and I am paraphrasing, "Why does that question matter? Religious Studies is an academic discipline with historical and factual data and kids must learn the material, regardless of where they reside on the continuum of faith development." My response then and now is based on the discussion above and observations of how students use their faith systems.

Children and adolescents use a received faith system as a kind of map to guide them through the often trying and confusing times of childhood and adolescence. Because parents hold the primary responsibility for indoctrinating their children into a faith system, educators must not steer students away from the traditions that they import to the classroom. Moreover, because children use their faith as a framework for making sense of a complex world, educators must be cautious not to take apart students' faith traditions. As James Fowler notes in his seminal work, *Stages of Faith*: "...the adolescent's religious hunger is for a God who knows, accepts and confirms the self deeply, and who serves as an infinite guarantor of the self with its forming myth of personal identity and faith."[18] Children and adolescents invoke religious authority in the most confusing times to recenter themselves in a world that can easily appear overwhelming. For these reasons, educators need to consider the relationship between child and adolescent faith development and course content and methods.

If religious studies teachers are to accept the religious convictions of their students, then what, exactly, does the teacher do in the classroom? And, how should teachers respond to those extreme students whom we often label "fundamentalist?" First, religious studies teachers model for students how one is to debate both robustly and respectfully. This task alone can be extraordinarily challenging, particularly when dogmatism rules the worldview of one or two students. Second, teachers provide a safe environment for students of all faiths or of no faith to express their views openly and honestly. Third, religious studies teachers expose students to a variety of worldviews and accompanying beliefs. Finally, all educators should guide students toward becoming principled individuals living in a democratic society. Narcissus and Goldmund (to return to the Hesseian analogy) love one another deeply, even though both recognize that Goldmund could not live the life of Narcissus and vice versa. Focusing on these four goals alone will eliminate many potential controversies tied to fundamentalist views, whether these views are voiced from the ardent atheist or the combative Christian.

As the field of religious studies gains a more secure position in an already overcrowded curriculum, educators must not replace traditional interpretations with academic perspectives. Of course, include academic readings, but do not do so at the expense of traditional interpretations. Teachers should be careful about evaluating one interpretation vis-à-vis the other, acknowledging the classroom as an educational (i.e., not devotional or academic) setting. Lastly, and most importantly, educators should remember that they are instructing other people's children about their ultimate concerns.

At the writing of the first draft of this essay, a federal appeals court panel from the 9th Circuit and the Supreme Court issued two rulings directly tied to religion and education. Two of the three judges on the 9th Circuit panel ruled unconstitutional the recitation of the Pledge of

Allegiance in public schools, due to the phrase "Under God." The Supreme Court upheld a Cleveland, Ohio, voucher plan that gives parents a choice in where their children matriculate. (Having witnessed oral arguments of *Zelman vs. Simmons-Harris*, I am not surprised by the 5–4 decision). The panel from the 9th Circuit delivered its opinion on Wednesday, June 26, 2002; the Supreme Court's majority opinion was issued on Thursday, June 27, 2002. In the first case, a court found a pithy reference to God to be an entanglement between government and religion. In the second case, five of the Court's nine justices agreed that tax dollars could be appropriated to parents for religious schooling, as long as parents have a choice on whether their children attend parochial, private, public, or charter schools. Taken together, these rulings send convoluted messages to educators on the appropriate relationship between religion/religious viewpoints and education.

Both cases remind us, however, that living in a political democracy where religious freedom is a fundamental tenet of public and private life is necessarily messy. They also suggest that religious voices and religious ideas must be accommodated in the educational arena lest balkanization occur. How we accommodate religious viewpoints in education hinges on the premise that we allow individuals to be themselves in all spheres of private and public life. How do we accomplish this goal in education?

According to Br. David Steindl-Rast and Sharon Lebell,

> Personal uniqueness thrives in an atmosphere of feeling at home and safe in the world. Most of us fear we won't be accepted as who we are. One of Thomas Merton's continuous and stunning admonitions to monastic communities was, "Make room for idiosyncrasies." We should not accept people only on condition that they conform. That isn't a creative way to build community; not one that promises success. Merton knew that there could be no creativity in any community if one made conformity the criterion for belonging. The criterion for belonging must be commitment to a shared ideal, a common goal. In order to achieve that goal, we need to help one another be our best selves.[19]

Admittedly, I have given only cursory attention to very large and complicated subjects as they are connected to religion and education. The relationship between K–12 religious education and First Amendment concerns, civic education, developmental psychology, the history of American education, and pedagogical strategies deserve far more attention and study than can be offered in a single essay. Nevertheless, my hope has been to emphasize that, in fact, these relationships do exist and to note that they all impact why and how we educate children.

Lastly, there are two interwoven themes running through this essay. The first carries the idea that religious studies and religious voices in K–12 education should exist because their presence simply allows students to be themselves, to be human. The second suggests that the methods we adopt should reflect the commitment to allow students to be who they are philosophically, intellectually, and developmentally. This idea, the why and the related approaches, the how, are consistent with our nature, our civic principles, and our educational mission. Both themes are bound together by the premise that "The spiritual life is first of all a *life*." (original emphasis)[20]

Notes

[1] See Susan Douglass, *Teaching about Religion in National and State Social Studies Standards* (Fountain Valley, CA: Council on Islamic Education and First Amendment Center, 2000).

[2] Many of the consensus documents appear in Charles C. Haynes and Oliver Thomas, *Finding Common Ground: A First Amendment Guide to Religion and Public Education* (Nashville: First Amendment Center, 2002).

[3] Quoted in Edwin S. Gaustad, *Liberty of Conscience: Roger Williams in America* (Valley Forge: Judson Press, 1999), 209.

[4] See Warren A. Nord, *Religion and American Education: Rethinking a National Dilemma* (Chapel Hill: University of North Carolina Press, 1995), 138–59.

[5] From a speech delivered by Reverend Charles P. Price at the National Association of Independent Schools annual conference held March 4, 1972, recorded in, "Religion

and Education: A Discussion" (Boston: National Association of Independent Schools, 1972), 9–10.

6 Unfortunately, many scholars and religious leaders have tried to avoid the complex of issues associated with religion and public life by replacing the term *religious* with the term *spiritual*. Educational settings must allow individual students to express their transcendent, ultimate concerns (their spirituality), even if they do so based on the teachings of an organized religion. The term *existential* should not be confused with the philosophy of Existentialism. See Charles C. Haynes, "Averting Culture Wars over Religion," *Educational Leadership* 56.4 (Dec. 1998/Jan. 1999): 24–27.

7 Some of my best students have been like Goldmund. The point is not one of value, but of fairness to all students.

8 See James W. Fraser, *Between Church and State: Religion and Education in a Multicultural America* (New York: St. Martin's Griffin, 1999), 102.

9 John Dewey, *A Common Faith* (New Haven: Yale University Press, 1934), 32.

10 Pluralism, Exclusivism, and Inclusivism are technical terms used to identify how individuals or religious traditions relate to and understand the existence of other traditions. Pluralism is "the theory that the great world religions constitute variant conceptions and perceptions of, and responses to, the one ultimate, mysterious divine reality." [John Hick, "Religious Pluralism," in *The Encyclopedia of Religion, Volume 12,* Mircea Eliade, ed. (New York: Macmillan Publishing Company, 1987), 331–33.] It differs, by definition, from these other two major theories. Therefore, it is a single perspective or philosophy that competes with other philosophies or perspectives. My argument is simply that none of these positions should be adopted as a solution for how to teach religion in classes pre–K through 12 because different students ally themselves with different positions based on their inherited tradition.

11 Parker J. Palmer, *To Know as We Are Known: Education as a Spiritual Journey* (San Francisco, CA: HarperSan Francisco, 1993), 67.

12 John Dewey, "Democracy and Educational Administration," in J. A. Boydston, ed., *John Dewey: The Later Works 1925–1953,* vol. 2 (Carbondale: Southern Illinois University Press, 1981), 217–25.

13 *Religious Liberty, Public Education, and the Future of American Democracy: A Statement of Principles*, endorsed by twenty-four diverse organizations. The pamphlet is available by calling 1–800–830–3733 and requesting publication no. 95–F07.

14 Sharon Tubbs, "The Bible—Without Religion," *St. Petersburg Times,* July 5, 2001: *Floridian* 1D.

15 Charles Lussier, "Alternative Course being Developed for Memphis Schools," April 14, 2002. http://www.theadvocate.com/news/story.asp?storyid=29243.

16 William Damon, *Greater Expectations: Overcoming the Culture of Indulgence in Our Homes and Schools* (New York: Free Press Paperbacks, 1995), 92–93.

17 Robert Coles, *The Spiritual Life of Children* (Boston: Houghton Mifflin Company, 1990), 40–68.

[18] James W. Fowler, *Stages of Faith: The Psychology of Human Development and the Quest for Meaning* (New York: HarperCollins, 1981), 153.

[19] David Steindl-Rast and Sharon Lebell, *Music of Silence: A Sacred Journey through the Hours of the Day* (Berkeley: Seastone, 2002), 111–12.

[20] Thomas Merton, *Thoughts in Solitude* (New York: Farrar, Straus and Giroux, 1999), 37. Original emphasis.

Works Consulted

Abington Township v. Schempp, 374 U.S. 203 (1963).

Boydston, J. A., ed. *John Dewey: The Later Works 1925–1953.* Vol. 2. Carbondale: Southern Illinois University Press, 1981.

Coles, Robert. *The Spiritual Life of Children.* Boston: Houghton Mifflin, 1990.

Damon, William. *Greater Expectations: Overcoming the Culture of Indulgence in Our Homes and Schools.* New York: Free Press, 1995.

Dewey, John. *A Common Faith.* New Haven, CT: Yale University Press, 1934.

Douglass, Susan. *Teaching about Religion in National and State Social Studies Standards.* Fountain Valley, CA: Council on Islamic Education and First Amendment Center, 2000.

Eliade, Mircea, ed. *The Encyclopedia of Religion.* Vol. 12. New York: Macmillan, 1987.

Fowler, James W. *Stages of Faith: The Psychology of Human Development and the Quest for Meaning.* New York: HarperCollins, 1981.

Fraser, James W. *Between Church and State: Religion and Education in a Multicultural America.* New York: St. Martin's Griffin, 1999.

Gaustad, Edwin S. *Liberty of Conscience: Roger Williams in America.* Valley Forge, PA: Judson Press, 1999.

Haynes, Charles C. "Averting Culture Wars." *Educational Leadership* 56.4 (1998/1999): 24–27.

Haynes, Charles C., and Oliver Thomas. *Finding Common Ground: A First Amendment Guide to Religion and Public Education.* Nashville, TN: First Amendment Center, 2002.

Hesse, Hermann. *Narcissus and Goldmund.* Trans. U. Moinaro. 1930. New York: Farrar, Straus and Giroux, 2003.

Lussier, C. *Alternative Course Being Developed for Memphis Schools,* April 2002. Online http://www.theadvocate.com/news/story.asp?storyid=29243.

Merton, Thomas. *Thoughts in Solitude.* New York: Farrar, Straus and Giroux, 1999.

Nord, Warren A. *Religion and American Education: Rethinking a National Dilemma.* Chapel Hill, NC: University of North Carolina Press, 1995.

Palmer, Parker. *To Know as We Are Known: Education as a Spiritual Journey.* San Francisco, CA: HarperSanFrancisco, 1993.

Steindl-Rast, David, and Sharon Lebell. *Music of Silence: A Sacred Journey Through the Hours of the Day:* Berkeley, CA: Seastone, 2002.

Tubbs, Sharon. "The Bible—Without Religion." St. Petersburg, FL: *St. Petersburg Times*, 2001.

Chapter 13

Religion in the Public Schools: Released Time Reconsidered

Jonathan Vinson

Out of fear of entangling church and state, public-school teachers rarely introduce religion into their classrooms.[1] When religion is discussed, it is often presented in a way that creates little more than a caricature of the various faiths being considered. This is unfortunate. Unless religion is incorporated within the public school curricula, religious misunderstandings among students, as well as the negative feelings and consequences associated with them, are likely to occur.[2] In addition, without a proper introduction to religion and religious thought, many subjects (e.g., art, literature, and history) taken up in the standard curricula run the risk of not being fully appreciated or meaningfully understood. Students are in need of comprehending the role that religion has historically played—and continues to play—in the formation of our country, its majority values, and its social conscience. One viable avenue in this venture is through released-time education.[3]

The History of Released Time

The origin of released time is generally traced back to a proposal made by Dr. George U. Wenner, at a New York meeting of the Inter-Church Conference in November 1905.[4] At the meeting, Wenner suggested and outlined a plan that would allow students, with parental consent and carrying a certificate of attendance, to be excused from public school one day each week for the purpose of religious education. To insure that students not suffer academically, it was hoped that public schools would adopt a more accommodating curriculum.[5] Though Wenner's proposal was warmly received by the Conference (which quickly adopted a resolution based upon it), outside opposition to it proved strong. Nearly ten years would pass before a similar plan/program would be broadly and successfully established within the public-school system.

In 1914, a plan for released-time education was designed and implemented, in Gary, Indiana, by school superintendent Dr. William Wirt. "Wirt's plan sought to rotate the schedules of the children during the school-day so that some were in class, others were in the library, still others in the playground. And some, he suggested to the leading ministers of the City, might be released to attend religious classes if the churches of the City cooperated and provided them."[6] Seven churches and two synagogues took advantage of his offer.[7] In its first year (1914–15) the plan permitted students, at parental request, to be released during the auditorium periods of the public school, in order to receive religious instruction. A record of attendance was kept, insuring that students were either present or at church/synagogue. The following year, the plan was altered so that students went "from home to church and then to public school, or...from public school to church school and then home, so that attendance at church school [was] entirely a matter of co-operation between the latter and home."[8] In this way, the public school avoided the appearance and/or reality of compelling students to attend church/synagogue. It simply offered "parents the opportunity to take advantage of its schedule and send their children to...church for instruction regularly if they wish[ed]."[9] By its second year, the Gary program, represented in eight church schools, enrolled approximately 561 students.[10] Its success was visibly apparent, which prompted its adoption and modification by other communities.

Within a few years, the number of released-time programs, modeled on the Gary plan, increased significantly. By 1922, released-time programs claimed an estimated 40,000 students, covering 200 school districts in 23 states.[11] By 1947, the number of students rose to nearly 2,000,000.[12] As programs multiplied, so did the number of legal challenges brought against them. Litigation culminated the following year in the U.S. Supreme Court case of *McCollum v. Board of Education* (1948).

The origin of the case dates back to 1940. In that year, a voluntary association of Jews, Roman Catholics, and Protestants obtained permission from the Champaign, Illinois, Board of Education to offer released-time classes to students, grades 4–9. Classes were held weekly and conducted within the public-school buildings by instructors employed directly by the association.[13] In order to participate in the program, students were required to have written parental permission; attendance was mandated. Students who chose not to participate were required to exit the classroom in which released-time instruction would be given, and to pursue secular studies at other locations within the building.

In 1945, a petition for mandamus against the Champaign Board of Education was brought before the Circuit Court of Champaign County. The appellant, Mrs. Vashti McCollum, a parent whose son had attended public school in Champaign, alleged that the program violated the First and Fourteenth Amendments to the U.S. Constitution.[14] The Circuit Court denied her petition, prompting an appeal to the Illinois Supreme Court, which affirmed the decision of the lower court. A second appeal was made to the U.S. Supreme Court, which, on March 8, 1948, reversed the State Court in favor of Mrs. McCollum, by a vote of 8 to 1.[15]

The opinion of the High Court, delivered by Justice Hugo L. Black, stated that "the use of tax-supported property for religious instruction," as well as "the close cooperation between the school authorities and the religious council in promoting religious education," amounted to "a utilization of the tax-established and tax-supported public school system to aid religious groups to spread their faith."[16] As such, it was in violation of the First Amendment as the Court interpreted it in *Everson v. Board of Education.*[17]

In a concurring opinion, Justice Felix Frankfurter, joined by Justices Harold H. Burton, Robert H. Jackson, and Wiley B. Rutledge, underscored the Court's decision but was unwilling "to sweepingly declare illegal all forms and varieties of religious programs similar in any way to the Champaign plan."[18]

> We do not consider, as indeed we could not, school programs not before us which, though colloquially characterized as "released time," present situations differing in aspects that may well be constitutionally crucial.... We do not now attempt to weigh in the Constitutional scale every separate detail or various combination of factors which may establish a valid "released time" program.[19]

Justice Jackson, though having joined in the above opinion and concurring with the Court in its decision, expressed reservations. He was unsure whether or not the Court could claim jurisdiction in the present case and questioned whether it was desirable, or even possible, to purge all religious elements from secular education.

> The fact is that, for good or for ill, nearly everything in our culture worth transmitting, everything which gives meaning to life, is saturated with religious influences, derived from paganism, Judaism, Christianity—both Catholic and Protestant—and other faiths accepted by a large part of the world's peoples. One can hardly respect a system of education that would leave the student wholly ignorant of the currents of religious thought that move the world society for a part in which he is being prepared.[20]

Justice Stanley F. Reed, alone, dissented. Reed criticized the Court's interpretation of the Establishment Clause, and stated that he found "it difficult to extract from [their] opinions any conclusion as to what it [was] in the Champaign plan that [was] unconstitutional."[21] He pointed to the many places in American history where both church and state have been found in cooperation and thought it difficult to believe that the Constitution prohibited religious instruction in this instance.

The Court's decision in the *McCollum* case generated much criticism.[22] Within four years, it was called upon to consider the constitutionality of another released-time program.

On July 28, 1948, a petition was filed in the Supreme Court of New York, Kings County, which challenged the legality of a local New York City released-time program.[23] After a number of appeals, the *Zorach-Gluck* case, as it was called, came before the U.S. Supreme Court (henceforth, *Zorach v. Clauson*). The Court, on April 28, 1952, in keeping with the prior decision of the New York Court of Appeals, affirmed the constitutionality of the program by a vote of 7 to 3.[24]

Justice William O. Douglas, delivering the opinion of the Court, stated that, unlike the program described in the *McCollum* case, the New York program "involve[d] neither religious instruction in public school classrooms nor the expenditure of public funds."[25] It was felt that, in affirming the program, the state of New York had made no law respecting an establishment of religion nor prohibited its free exercise, as outlined in the First Amendment. The Court pointed to the voluntary nature of the program and stated that "[i]t [took] obtuse reasoning to inject any issue of the 'free exercise' of religion into the...case. No one [was] forced to go to the religious classroom and no religious exercise or instruction [was] brought to the classrooms of the public schools."[26] Without denying the underlying philosophy of the First Amendment, the Court also claimed that separation of church and state did not necessarily apply "in every and all respects."[27] Noting that Americans "are a religious people whose institutions presuppose a Supreme Being," it advanced an "accommodationist" approach toward the Establishment Clause.[28] The belief was that "[w]hen the state encourages religious instruction or cooperates with religious authorities by adjusting the schedule of public events to sectarian needs, it follows the best of our traditions. For it then respects the religious nature of our people and accommodates the public service to their spiritual needs."[29] In the New York program, the public schools accommodated their schedules for the purpose of outside religious instruction.

In a dissenting opinion, Justice Black confessed an inability to discern any significant difference between the Champaign program and that of New York City. In *McCollum*, the Court had clearly stated that Illinois "could not constitutionally manipulate the compelled classroom hours of its compulsory school machinery so as to channel children into sectarian classes."[30] However, this was something of which New York was guilty and of which the present Court approved. Black agreed with the Court that Americans are "a religious people whose institutions presuppose a Supreme Being," but pointed out that such was true not only when the First Amendment was adopted but when the Court issued its decision in the *McCollum* case. In his view, the consequences of mixing church and state—however limited—presented an unacceptable risk.

Issuing a separate opinion, Justice Jackson tersely stated that the New York program was based upon the "State's power of coercion" and that alone, for him, determined the program's unconstitutionality.[31] Justice Frankfurter, in addition to agreeing with Jackson, was critical of the majority's denial of coercion when, in fact, the appellants had been denied a trial on this issue by the New York Court of Appeals. "When constitutional issues turn on facts," stated Frankfurter, "it is a strange procedure indeed not to permit the facts to be established."[32]

"The Court's understanding of the Establishment Clause...has evolved since [its] decision in *Zorach v. Clauson*; nevertheless, *Zorach* is still a valid statement of current law" and important for understanding and defending the constitutionality of released time.[33] Since *Zorach*, the number of cases filed against released-time programs has drastically declined, as has the number of programs. Cases on record have generally been concerned with the level of state aid given to individuals implementing programs or to the level of accommodation provided by the state in their maintenance.[34] Currently, it is estimated that approximately 600,000 students, in 32 states, are enrolled in released-time programs nationwide.[35]

The Constitutionality of Released Time

Though released time, in principle, has been judged constitutional by the U.S. Supreme Court, the same does not hold true for every program instituted by a state or local school district. In order for a program to be constitutional, certain general requirements must be met. First, a program must avoid the use of public funds. This applies both to its implementation and to its maintenance. For example, public funds may not be used to advertise or promote the program, or to provide teachers with attendance blanks or parents with consent forms. Second, it must exist and operate outside of the public school facilities. Local churches are often used for this purpose, as are privately owned buildings standing in close proximity to the school. Finally, programs should avoid being promoted, endorsed, or otherwise favored (e.g., through recruitment, registration, and so on) by the public school and its faculty.[36]

Students are not invested with the right, under the Constitution, to participate in released time; it is state policy and, at times, the policy of the local school board, that determines whether or not a program can be established within a given school.[37] According to a brief made available to the public by the Rutherford Institute, revised September 13, 2002, at least nineteen state legislatures—Arizona, California, Florida, Hawaii, Idaho, Indiana, Iowa, Maine, Michigan, Minnesota, Montana, New Mexico, New York, North Dakota, Oregon, Pennsylvania, South Dakota, Vermont, and Wisconsin—have passed statutes setting up a state policy regarding released-time programs.[38] The statutes vary in detail and in the guidance that they supply. In large part, it is the local school board that determines the particulars of the program.[39]

Advantages and Disadvantages of Released Time

As noted above, religion has served, and continues to serve, an important role in the formation of culture, aiding in the creation of values and social mores. Because of this, religion should not be ignored or sidelined, but discussed and appreciated. Regrettably—but understandably—public education has taken a "hands-off" approach to religion, citing both *legal* and *private concerns*. Released time, being *constitutional* and a *matter of choice*, addresses these concerns. Even so, like any plan or program, it is not above criticism. It has advantages and disadvantages, many of which are debated, disputed, and dependent upon the perspective of the person issuing judgment. Before one can come away with a proper understanding of released time, such perspectives need to be taken into account.

As a generalized system, released time has several advantages. It is inclusive, meaning that it is accessible to any religious group that can demonstrate its need to the local school board. Because the number of religious groups able to organize released-time programs is potentially diverse, released-time policies also function to "provide an opportunity for communities to work together."[40] Other advantages relate to its use as an alternative outlet for the public schools. With released time, public schools are given the opportunity to respect the religious liberty of parents in supplementing their child's education during the normative school day, as well as that of acknowledging and respecting the role of religious faith in the lives of its students.[41] Released time may also "function as a service to students who might not otherwise receive religious instruction," but desire it.[42]

One of the major disadvantages of released time is that it is at high risk for abuse. As was noted above, it is illegal for a school and/or its faculty to promote, endorse, or favor released-time programs. However, such actions appear to occur frequently. Examples exist of teachers with vested interests, administrators hoping to reform the moral character of delinquent students, and counselors who are hard-pressed to find an open course in which to place them.[43] A solution to the problem proves difficult, as no remedy seems to exist short of sending out privately funded, third-party "watchdogs" to insure a program's legality.[44] Because released-time programs are community sponsored and driven, they invariably differ in detail, from community to community. Though, in one sense, this offers the obvious advantage of each program being tailored to the needs of a particular people, each program also has its own distinct flaws, and thus the potential for providing points of attack that may then be popularly—and mistakenly—applied to the system (i.e., "released time"). For the system to achieve broad acceptance, a certain level of uniformity must exist among programs, so that when two or more individuals speak of "released time," they are commenting with respect to the same concern. Abuse must be eliminated, to the extent that it can.

Having reviewed the advantages and disadvantages of released time as a system, I propose now to briefly discuss the defining characteristics of specific programs. Programs generally fall into two categories, representing two approaches to religious instruction: devotional and academic.

The majority of released-time programs in the United States are devotional in nature.[45] Such programs are dogmatic and faith-driven. The most obvious advantage to this approach is that it addresses students on a personal level, and is able to offer guidance and edification in areas of need. In addition, it is able to speak comfortably to the numerous ethical issues that students regularly confront (yet, even here, there is controversy—see below). Its primary disadvantage, however, seems to center in the certainty with which it speaks. Because released-time courses that employ this approach are taught from the perspective of a particular religious faith and are unable to be monitored by the state (at least with respect to religious content), the potential for teachers to express dogmatic and unaccommodating positions toward delicate and debatable issues (e.g., divorce, homosexuality, abortion, etc.), when such issues arise, is great. Certain sectarian teachings are at natural odds with the attitudes, sensitivities, and convictions of the larger (public school) student body; it is feared by some that if such teachings are allowed to systematically enter the public school through the released-time students who embrace them, harmful and unnecessary divisions may result among students.

An academic approach to released time has the advantage of being open to all people and religious groups, since its emphasis rests in neutrality and teaching *about* religion, rather than teaching religion.[46] In addition, because it is inclusive and noncommittal, its potential for introducing division among students is weak. In fact, it could be argued that such an approach could advance unity among students as, for instance, in a course covering world religions, it may lead to a greater appreciation of, and understanding between, the faiths.[47] It is also advantageous in that it is unlikely to meet the kind of community protest that a devotional approach would incur from those wary of accommodating religious instruction into the sphere of public education. Its major disadvantage rests in its inability to speak as personally as a devotional approach.

Concluding Thoughts

It is imperative that students recognize and appreciate the role of religion in life and current affairs.[48] Released-time education provides a valuable and constitutional step in fostering this appreciation and recognition. In my own experience as a teacher, it has successfully functioned to enlighten students, from various ideological persuasions, to those aspects of religion and spirituality that permeate, sustain, and form our society. Though not perfect, it offers to educators, as John C. Bennett has noted, "an area of experiment and maneuver."[49] Because of this, it has often succeeded where other attempts at integrating religion into the sphere of public education have failed. If only for these reasons, released time is worthy of our time and consideration.

Notes

Mr. Vinson wishes to dedicate this chapter to his wife, Jenny, and to thank his friend, Carl E. Miller III, Ph.D., J.D., for his valuable insights and aid in certain unfamiliar matters of law and sources.

[1] For a general discussion of religion in the public schools, and its relation to religious liberty, see Jesse H. Choper, *Securing Religious Liberty: Principles for Judicial Interpretation of the Religion Clauses* (Chicago: University of Chicago Press, 1995), 140–52.

[2] "Muslims are terrorists! Their religion makes no sense!"—Such was the exclamation of one of my students, following the terrorist attacks of September 11, 2001. To those knowledgeable of Islam, it is clear that his comment, among other things, was insensitive and false. It is less clear how one could expect him to react in an appropriate and measured manner given the state and context of his education within the public school system.

[3] In this paper, "released time" will refer to programs whereby students, with parental consent, are excused from the public schools for a specified period of time each week, in order to receive religious instruction. Some scholars refer to these programs as "dismissed time" (reserving the term "released time" for sectarian religious classes conducted on school property). Other scholars use the term "dismissed time" to refer to a system under which the public schools cut short the regular school day for the dismissal of all students, allowing those who wish to seek religious instruction.

[4] In actuality, a proposal, similar to the program described in the *McCollum* case (see below), was made two years previous by Jacob G. Schurman. For more, see Joseph H. Crooker, *Religious Freedom in American Education* (Boston: American Unitarian Association, 1903), 39–40.

[5] George U. Wenner, *Religious Education and the Public School: An American Problem* (New York: Bonnell, Silver, and Co., 1907), 44–45.

[6] *McCollum v. Board of Education*, 333 U.S. 203 (1948), at 224.

[7] Arlo A. Brown, "The Week-Day Church Schools of Gary, Indiana: A Report of an Investigation," *Religious Education* 11 (February 1916): 5.

[8] Ibid., 6.

[9] Ibid., 6.

[10] Ibid., 16. There is an apparent discrepancy in the total number of students taught by the Disciples of Christ, as listed by Brown. In one place, he cites the number at 111 (p. 6), which would raise the total number of students in the Gary program to 619, while at another place he cites the number at 93. In the above reference, I have followed the latter citation.

[11] Eric Cochling, Jamie Lathan, and Brandie Oschner, "Time for God: Accommodating Religious Free Exercise through Released-Time Education,"

Pocket Policy #7, ed. Carli Conklin, Jennifer Marshall, and Crystal Roberts (Washington, DC: Family Research Council, 2000): 5. Cited May 24, 2003. Online: http://secure.frc.org/download.cfm.

[12] *New York Times*, September 21, 1947: 22, col. 1.

[13] Though instructors were not employed by the state, they were subject to the approval and supervision of the school superintendent.

[14] The First Amendment, in pertinent part, prohibits congress from making a law respecting an establishment of religion or prohibiting its free exercise. The Fourteenth Amendment provides equal protection under the law, something Mrs. McCollum believed the program denied.

[15] 333 U.S., at 203. Three years after the *McCollum* case, Mrs. McCollum's book, *One Woman's Fight*, was published. The book recounts the circumstances of the case from a familial perspective. See Vashti McCollum, *One Woman's Fight* (Garden City: Doubleday, 1951).

[16] Ibid., 209.

[17] *Everson v. Board of Education*, 330 U.S. 1 (1947). The Court's exegesis of the Establishment Clause in this case has been severely criticized. See, for example, William H. Rehnquist, "The True Meaning of the Establishment Clause: A Dissent," in *How Does the Constitution Protect Freedom?*, ed. Robert A. Goldwin and Art Kaufman (Washington, DC: American Enterprise Institute for Public Policy Research, 1987), 99–113.

[18] Donald E. Boles, *The Bible, Religion, and the Public Schools*, 3d ed. (Ames: Iowa State University Press, 1965), 156.

[19] 333 U.S., at 231.

[20] Ibid., 236.

[21] Ibid., 246.

[22] For a review of the relevant legal and educational criticism of the *McCollum* case, see Donald E. Boles, *The Two Swords: Commentaries and Cases in Religion and Education* (Ames: Iowa State University Press, 1967), 44–47.

[23] For a list of the allegations made in the petition, see "Constitutionality of the New York Released Time Program," *Colum. L. Rev.* 49 (1949): 842, note 32.

[24] *Zorach v. Clauson*, 343 U.S. 306 (1952).

[25] Ibid., 308–9.

[26] Ibid., 311. Like the Illinois program, to attend, written parental consent was required.

[27] Ibid., 312. The Court continued: "Otherwise, the state and religion would be aliens to each other.... Churches could not be required to pay even property taxes. Municipalities would not be permitted to render police or fire protection to religious groups. Policeman who helped parishioners into their places of worship would violate the Constitution.... We would have to press the concept of separation of Church and State to these extremes to condemn the present law on constitutional grounds."

28 Ibid., 313.

29 Ibid.

30 Ibid., 317.

31 Ibid., at 323–24. He continued: "The greater effectiveness of this system over voluntary attendance after school hours is due to the truant officer who, if the youngster fails to go to the Church school, dogs him back to the public schoolroom.... It takes more subtlety of mind than I possess to deny that this is governmental constraint in support of religion. It is as unconstitutional, in my view, when exerted by indirection as when exercised forthrightly."

32 Ibid., 322.

33 The Rutherford Institute, "Released Time Programs," (Ref. No.: B-26. September 2002): 1. Cited 4 May 2003. Online: http://www.rutherford.org/documents/pdf/brief_bank/B26-ReleaseTime.pdf.

34 E.g., *Smith v. Smith*, 523 F.2d 121 (1975); *Lanner v. Wimmer*, 662 F.2d 1349 (1981); *Doe v. Shenandoah County School Board*, 737 F. Supp. 913 (1990).

35 "Religious Released Time," n.p. Online: http://www.acfnewsource.org/religion/religious_released.html. [Accessed October 6, 2003]. I was unable to obtain independent verification of this number.

36 Rutherford Institute, "Released Time Programs," 1–2.

37 In states where no official released-time statute is in place, "a state education department may have promulgated a released time policy." Ibid., 2–3.

38 Ibid., 2.

39 Ibid.

40 Cochling, Lathan, and Oschner, "Time for God," 13.

41 John C. Bennett, *Christians and the State* (New York: Charles Scribner's Sons, 1958), 243.

42 Cochling, Lathan, and Oschner, "Time for God," 3.

43 Further examples may include released-time teachers who enter the school facility to recruit students or coerce former students to aid in this effort.

44 Even here, there is the question of authority (i.e., who would be responsible for such policing?) and the fear of bias reporting on the part of those investigating.

45 The provision of sectarian, devotional teaching is, of course, the traditional point of released time.

46 Legally, academic courses in religion can be taught within the classrooms of the public school. Unfortunately, whether unaware or indifferent to the fact, most public schools fail to offer such courses. For this reason, it is important to emphasize an academic approach to released-time education.

47 This is not to say that an appreciation and understanding of the world's religions cannot occur in a devotional setting, for example, where the various faiths are taught and devotion is given to one in particular. It is only more difficult to foster.

[48] This is especially true in light of the distorted view of religion often fostered by popular culture. For an excellent critique of popular culture and the effect it has on society (with special attention given to how it shapes morality, religion, and education), see Vincent Ryan Ruggiero, *The Moral Imperative* (Nashville: Thomas Nelson, 1994).

[49] Bennett, *Christians and the State*, 243.

Works Consulted

Bennett, John C. *Christians and the State*. New York: Charles Scribner's Sons, 1958.

Boles, Donald E. *The Bible, Religion, and the Public Schools*. 3d ed. Ames: Iowa State University Press, 1965.

———. *The Two Swords: Commentaries and Cases in Religion and Education*. Ames: Iowa State University Press, 1967.

Brown, Arlo A. The Week-Day Church Schools of Gary, Indiana: A Report of An Investigation. *Religious Education* 11, 5 (February 1916).

Choper, Jesse H. *Securing Religious Liberty: Principles for Judicial Interpretation of the Religion Clauses*. Chicago, IL: University of Chicago Press, 1995.

Cochling, Eric, Jamie Lathan, and Brandie Oscher. Time for God: Accommodating Religious Free Exercise Through Time-Release Programs. *Pocket Policy #7*. Washington, D.C.: Family Research Council, 2003.

Crooker, Joseph H. *Religious Freedom in American Education*. Boston: American Unitarian Association, 1903.

Doe v. Shenandoah County School Board, 737 F. Supp. 913 (1990).

Goldwin, Robert, and Art Kaufman, eds. *How Does the Constitution Protect Freedom?* Washington, D. C.: American Enterprise Institute for Public Policy Research, 1987.

Everson v. Board of Education, 330 U.S. 1 (1947).

Lanner v. Wimmer, 662 F.2d 1349 (1981).

McCollum, Vashti. *One Woman's Fight*. Garden City, NY: Doubleday, 1951.

McCollum v. Board of Education, 333 U.S. 203 (1948).

Ruggiero, Vincent R. *The Moral Imperative*. Nashville, TN: Thomas Nelson, 1994.

Rutherford Institute. Released Time Programs. Online document: Ref. No.: B-26, http://www.rutherford.org/documents/pdf/brief_bank/B26-ReleaseTime.pdf, September 2002, accessed by chapter author, May 2003.

Smith v. Smith, 523 F.2d 121 (1975).

Zorach v. Clauson, 343 U.S. 306 (1952).

Chapter 14

Interfaith Service-Learning

Eboo Patel

In the Interfaith Youth Core's Spring 2003 Sacred Stories Performance, Muslim, Christian, and Jewish high school students theatrically
interpreted how their different religious traditions each spoke to the
shared value of hospitality. After the event, a parent of a Jewish participant approached me with tears in her eyes. She praised how the
performance highlighted the commonality between religious traditions while affirming each tradition's particularity. She told me that
the day was especially emotional for her because it stood in sharp contrast to an experience she had had with Jen, her daughter, when Jen
was a little girl.

In an attempt to provide Jen with a strong Jewish upbringing, her
mother had surrounded her exclusively with Jewish influences when
she was growing up. Jen attended a Jewish school, lived in a Jewish
neighborhood and attended Jewish summer camps.

One day, at a fast food restaurant, Jen made a racist comment
about a dark-skinned employee. Her mother was shocked and sad-
dened, but realized that Jen's statement was based on her limited contact with non-Jews. She then decided to encourage Jen to experience
the broadness of American society while remaining committed to her
Jewish tradition. Privately, she harbored a concern that Jen's Jewish
identity would become diluted as she spent less time in direct contact
with the Jewish community and tradition.

Watching Jen tell Jewish stories, explain Jewish holidays, and
quote from Jewish scripture alongside Muslims and Christians,

showed her that her daughter had achieved a difficult but crucial balance: She was comfortable with America's diversity and yet had maintained her strong Jewish identity.

This article explores the approach that nurtured this balance. I call the process interfaith service-learning, and it involves bringing religious diversity together around the common table of social action projects. My laboratory for the interfaith service-learning approach is the Interfaith Youth Core. This organization works with youth groups in different faith communities. These include faith-based schools, religious organizations and houses of worship. This chapter will be particularly relevant for individuals working in K–12 schools.

Service-Learning

The Joint Education Project at the University of Southern California defines service-learning as follows: "At the core of service-learning is the principle that community service can be connected to classroom learning in such a way that service is more informed by the theoretical and conceptual understanding and learning is more informed by the realities of the world."[1]

There exists a range of service-learning methodologies, with varying degrees of emphasis on service and learning. At one end of the spectrum, programs emphasize theoretical learning with small but strategic service opportunities. A good example is a course on housing and homelessness that includes a class service trip to a homeless shelter. At the other end of the spectrum, programs focus largely on the service experience and contain a small but significant reflection component. A typical internship, for example, might have students spending most of their time at a service site and augmenting their real-world experiences with reading, discussion, and journal writing.

A service-learning approach can advance understanding in a traditional subject area. Consider these examples: Working on a campaign gives students in a political science class an understanding of American politics far beyond the textbook. Organizing block clubs helps Urban Studies students appreciate the fabric of city neighborhoods. Advanced physics students can design fun activities that help younger students learn the laws of physics. In each of these cases, students increase their learning in a subject by involving themselves in its applied dimension. Moreover, they learn that one purpose of their education is to help others.

Service-learning is especially beneficial when done as a community. The community provides opportunities for collective reflection on the service experience itself and the insight gained into the subject matter. Group discussions surrounding service projects are often richer than typical classroom discussions because the students' concrete experiences endow them with the ability to speak from a place of deeper insight and connection.

Service-learning is also an excellent way to bring a diverse group into community with one another. Well-established service-learning programs like Public Allies intentionally recruit individuals that come from diverse racial, geographic, educational, and class backgrounds. Doing service is a common table at which these diverse people can meet and come to know one another. Moreover, their diverse backgrounds provide different insights for approaching group service projects, benefiting not only the people being served, but also the team members themselves.

Service-Learning and the Study of World Religions

Huston Smith, whose book *The World's Religions* (first published as *The Religions of Man*) has served as America's primary text on different religions for half a century, reminds us that to truly understand our world we must undertake an appreciative study of what he calls "religion alive." This approach requires learning about how different people view, experience, and understand the world. In Smith's words:

> To glimpse what belonging means to the Japanese; to sense with a Burmese grandmother what passes in life and what endures; to understand how Hindus can regard their personalities as masks that overlay the Infinite within;

to crack the paradox of a Zen monk who assures you that everything is holy
but scrupulously refrains from certain acts—to swing such things into view is
to add dimensions to the glance of spirit. [2]

In Smith's view, to narrow ourselves to understanding only our own
culture's approach to the world is like possessing only one eye, and
thus seeing the world as if it were flat like a postcard. Smith goes on to
describe the central feature of our historical moment:

> We live in a fantastic century... Lands across the planet have become our
> neighbors, China across the street, the Middle East at our back door...We
> hear that East and West are meeting, but it is an understatement. They are
> being flung at one another... When historians look back on our century, they
> may remember it most ... as the time when the peoples of the world came to
> take one another seriously. [3]

Because of the high-velocity interaction between diverse cultures,
the importance of an appreciative understanding of a central source of
our worldviews—religion—is increasingly apparent. Unfortunately,
until quite recently, America's K–12 educational institutions have not
given the study of the world's religions the serious attention they deserve. At the 1993 Parliament of the World's Religions, Harvard professor Diana Eck remarked that most high school students have to
dissect a frog to graduate, but very few are required to know anything
about Islam, the religious tradition of one-fifth of humankind.

Currently, if students are taught at all, world religions are approached in a sterile way. At the high school I attended in the suburbs
of Chicago, world religions were considered part of the world history
curriculum. Islam was presented as an ancient desert phenomenon,
and Christianity was a set of arguments, some of which turned into
wars that took place mostly in the Middle Ages.

This approach not only fails to engage most teenagers, but it also
does not give them an insight into Huston Smith's "religion alive."
However, religion alive is very much around us—in the architecture of
the synagogues, mosques, and churches in our neighborhoods; in the

use of religious symbols from the cross to the Star of David to the bindi; in comments made by politicians to justify everything from starting wars to committing more resources to AIDS prevention efforts; and in the hearts of most human beings who walk the Earth.

As I stated earlier, service-learning, by definition, emphasizes the applied dimension of the particular subject area it is advancing. All of the world's major religions teach the imperative of social justice work. These mandates come in a variety of forms, and include everything from a basic "feed the poor" command to a broader vision of ensuring the dignity of all God's creation. Faith-based social justice work successfully exposes students to a diversity of religions in an engaged, interesting way. Furthermore, it introduces students to the social justice teachings of different religions, and allows them to participate in the social justice projects of different religious communities.

Students can, for example, learn about the Hadith of the Prophet Muhammad, which says, "No one of you truly believes until he wants for his brother what he wants for himself," and then help prepare an *iftar* dinner at a mosque that feeds not only Muslims breaking their Ramadan fast, but also poor people in the neighborhood. This form of involvement provides an opportunity to see a Muslim teaching in practice, to ask the community about its understanding of the connection between the teaching and the preparation of the meal, and to experience some of the energy of a religious community in the act of living one of its core teachings.

There are, of course, parallel concepts in all the world's religions. And in our increasingly religiously diverse America, there are many religious communities putting these teachings into practice. A careful study of the American religious landscape will reveal numerous initiatives that seek to apply the Jewish concept of *tikkun olam* (repair of the world), projects that practice the social justice teachings of Hindu sages such as Vivekananda and Gandhi, and efforts that give concrete shape to the Buddhist notion of compassion.

One excellent illustration of how a service-learning approach can give insight into a religious social justice teaching is provided in Harvard professor Robert Coles's book *The Call of Service*. He writes about taking Harvard students to work with Dorothy Day at the St. Joseph's Catholic Worker soup kitchen on New York City's lower east side in the 1970s. The students were already familiar with the basic Christian concepts that inspired Dorothy Day's life of commitment to serving—and living in solidarity with—the poor. Still, they were struck when they walked into St. Joseph's and saw this frail but strong eighty-year-old woman cutting celery and carrots for that evening's soup kitchen. Dorothy told the Harvard students: "If I pray by making soup and serving soup, I feel I'm praying by doing. If I pray by saying words, I can sometimes feel frustrated. Where's the action that follows the words or precedes them?"[4]

Dorothy went on to talk about feeling the spirit of Christ in the work of the soup kitchen, and saying she felt God calling her to serve in this way. A skeptical student asked, "How do you know [God calls you to do this]?"[5]

Dorothy replied, "He has told us—in His way." Dorothy then proceeded to tell several stories about life at St. Joseph's. How a well-to-do elderly couple had baked cakes for the community, and how they held a birthday party for all the members. Dorothy mentioned that many of these people, who would be living on the streets if not for St. Joseph's, cried openly because they could not remember the last time they had had a birthday celebration. She talked about the bread maker who always saved his first few loaves to give to St. Joseph's for use in the soup kitchen, calling them "Catholic Worker ryes." Coles described how the students were taken with these stories, and how they began to feel comfortable in the world of the soup kitchen.[6]

The opportunity to see Dorothy Day in action taught the students about the texture of Dorothy's Christian inspiration. They had the opportunity to hear stories about life at St. Joseph's and to inhabit that world. Moreover, they had a chance to serve in the soup kitchen, and get a visceral sense of the energy that Dorothy and her colleagues brought to their service.

A service-learning approach to social justice teachings in world religions provides a platform for a more sophisticated exploration of theology and its applications. Through this approach, students will clearly see the similarities between different traditions, but a careful study will also reveal important distinctions between religious traditions in this area. For example, unlike Christianity, there is no strong tradition of voluntary poverty within either Judaism or Islam. A movement such as the Catholic Worker, where people are asked to give up their possessions and live in solidarity with the poor, is uniquely aligned with Christian social justice teachings.

There are many advantages to combining service-learning programs with teaching the social justice aspects of the world's religions. Among them is a glimpse into an important way that religion is alive for people and an opportunity to see how different traditions speak in particular ways to the shared value of helping others. There is the additional benefit of portraying a positive aspect of religion. There is a great deal of public attention focused on the role that religion plays in bigotry and war. By involving students in the social justice work of religious communities, they become aware of the ways in which religion makes important contributions to the health of our society.

Interfaith Service-Learning

I will refer to service-learning programs that intentionally engage the religious diversity of a group as "interfaith service-learning." The difference between what I call interfaith service-learning and the topic I discussed in the last section, service-learning, as a method for teaching the world's religions, is the nature of the group itself, namely, whether it is religiously diverse and whether that religious diversity is actively engaged through the program. While valuable, having a group of exclusively Christian youths do a service-learning project that explores the ethics of Islam and Judaism does not qualify as "interfaith service-learning."

In her book entitled *A New Religious America*, Diana Eck describes how she went from being a scholar of comparative religion in India to realizing that her Harvard classroom was becoming increasingly religiously diverse:

> When I began teaching comparative religion at Harvard in the mid-1970s, the challenge was to get my students to take seriously what the world might look like from the perspective of a Hindu, Muslim, or Sikh, those people whose lives and families I had come to know on the other side of the world ... But never did I imagine as I started teaching at Harvard in the 1970s that by the 1990s there would be scores of Hindu, Muslim, and Sikh students in my classes—not just international students from India, but second-generation Americans.[7]

This is another example of religious diversity being not an "out there" phenomenon, but a "right here" dynamic. The dangers of ignoring religious identity are alarmingly clear—misunderstandings that can lead to harassment and marginalization, even to violence and murder. A service-learning approach provides a crucial antidote to these tragedies. I will now explain the necessary steps for implementing the service-learning approach.

The first step is to gather a religiously diverse group of kids. In many cases, the religious diversity is right in front of us—in our schools, neighborhoods, YMCAs, and beyond.

The second step is to give the religiously diverse group a common service experience. Unless the group is exploring a particular theme, the type of project is not as important as the opportunity it provides to create strong relationships within the group, helping them form a sense of "us."

The third step is to create an opportunity for group reflection. This should take place in a comfortable and safe space that encourages people to both share and listen. An experienced facilitator should run the group. Topics can range from personal reflections on people's feelings to thoughts on becoming more effective agents of social change.

Group reflection is the time to deeply engage matters of religious diversity. Group members should be asked to share how their religious traditions inspire service. There are many ways members can do this. They can speak about heroes in their faith traditions that provide examples of service, scripture that commands service, prayers, or rituals that speak to the importance of service, holidays, and family practice where service is provided. Group facilitators may start the process by telling their own story.

There exists a variety of ways to make interfaith service-learning more sophisticated. One way is to combine interfaith service-learning with teaching world religions, the difference being that the teaching world religions program emphasizes studying comparative religious ethics, and interfaith service-learning emphasizes the religious identities of members of the group. Clearly, one complements the other, and I suggest combining the two whenever possible. One way to do this is to study comparative religious ethics with a religiously diverse group of young people, and to follow up with a service project and a reflection session in which the participants can share how they relate to the teachings of their traditions when putting them into practice.

Interfaith service-learning can also be done in a range of formats. These include: one-time events for a religiously diverse class; bringing Christian, Muslim, Jewish, and other youth groups or schools together to explore comparative religious ethics through interfaith service-learning; organizing a city-wide Day of Interfaith Youth Service with a broad range of kids from public, private, and parochial schools.

The Interfaith Youth Core (IFYC)

The Interfaith Youth Core is a Chicago-based international organization whose mission is to bring youths (loosely defined as 13–25) from different religious communities together to deepen their religious identities, expand their understanding of other religions, build positive relations between religious communities, develop leadership skills, and work for social justice. The Interfaith Youth Core organizes interfaith service-learning programs, develops educational resources for these programs, and organizes conferences to train others to run these types of programs.

At the heart of the Interfaith Youth Core's service-learning programs is what we call the "shared values" approach. All religious traditions share values such as hospitality, justice, service, compassion, peace, and pluralism. Each tradition speaks to these values in distinct ways, through its own particular texts and stories. The idea is to show the distinctiveness of each tradition's approach to the value, while highlighting the value's commonality. Finally, the Interfaith Youth Core pushes young people to create concrete projects that apply this value.

The first step the Interfaith Youth Core takes is to gather a religiously diverse group of young people and asks them to commit to a regular schedule of meetings. Students are recruited from faith-based schools, houses of worship, and religious organizations. The Interfaith Youth Core takes special care to develop a trusting relationship with the students' youth advisors, parents, and religious leaders.

Story-telling is an important part of our meetings. Interfaith Youth Core staff members tell the participants that we are here to discuss how our different religions speak to a particular shared value, such as hospitality. The students are then challenged to share what they do with their faith communities in the spirit of hospitality and are encouraged to talk about aspects of their traditions such as religious holidays and religious stories. Once one participant tells his or her story, the others invariably remember their own. The Interfaith Youth Core staff encourages a discussion emphasizing similarities between faith traditions as well as things that are unique to each community.

At the end of the meeting, the Interfaith Youth Core staff gives the students some homework—to find stories of hospitality in their sacred texts, for example, or talk to their older relatives about how the faith community they attended generations ago practiced hospitality. This process keeps the young people engaged in the topic between meetings, and further immerses them in their own religious tradition.

An important goal of these discussions is to have the youths tell two types of stories of hospitality: first, the activities they do with their family and faith community which show hospitality; and second, the teachings and stories on hospitality within their religious traditions. Ideally, the youths connect these two, thus becoming more aware that they are interpreting and applying age-old stories and teachings. For example, Christian youths will often tell stories of giving gifts to needy families on Christmas. Helping them to articulate how this activity is connected to the story of Christ's birth helps them see their action in a broader religious context.

After several meetings in which participants discuss hospitality, we pose the following question to our youths: How are we going to live up to the ethics of our traditions and provide hospitality? During the 2003 Interfaith Youth Core program session, our youths decided to apply the value of hospitality to the issue of challenges faced by recent immigrants in the United States. Almost immediately they recognized how big the issue was and chose to address it through a variety of projects. One project was participating in a "cultural night" with refugee children. A second project was advocating for legislative changes regarding undocumented immigrant students and access to higher education. A third project was recording a CD of faith stories from their different traditions that speak to welcoming the stranger. This turned into a fourth project when they wove their stories from the CD together into the theater performance discussed at the beginning of this chapter.

After completing a project, the Interfaith Youth Core organizes evaluations that involve as many stakeholders as possible. These include: youth advisors, parents and leaders from the religious communities involved; Interfaith Youth Core Board members and staff;

leadership from the other organizations we worked with; and, of course, the youths themselves. We bring these different constituencies together in discussion sessions that focus on how well we met larger IFYC objectives through this specific project. Two examples include: How deep was the connection between shared faith values and the social action project? Did the social action project create lasting relationships between diverse religious communities, and lasting relationships between those religious communities and the issue or organizations highlighted by the project? We also develop a written evaluation for our youth participants. Finally, we make sure to solicit specific suggestions for future projects.

The Interfaith Youth Core not only runs interfaith service-learning programs, it also seeks to nurture a movement that will allow religious youths all over America to have the experience that Jen and the other IFYC youths had, that is, the opportunity to affirm their own particular religious identity while learning to understand and appreciate the religious diversity around them, and to understand that religiously diverse people share important values and should work cooperatively to implement those values in ways that benefit others.

Notes

The author gratefully acknowledges the contributions of Jeffrey Clinger, Seminarian, Garrett Evangelical Seminary and Intern, Interfaith Youth Core, and Alex Frell-Levy, undergraduate student and Project Assistant, Interfaith Youth Core, in the preparation of this article.

[1] *Service-Learning: A Working Definition.* University of Southern California. September 30, 2003. http://www.usc.edu/dept/LAS/JEPj_sl/def.htm

[2] Huston Smith, *The World's Religions: Our Great Wisdom Traditions* (New York: HarperCollins Publishers, 1958), 8.

[3] Ibid., 6–7.

[4] Robert Coles, *The Call of Service: A Witness to Idealism* (New York: Houghton Mifflin Company, 1993), 209–10.

[5] Ibid., 210.

[6] Ibid., 210–14.

[7] Diana Eck, *A New Religious America: How a "Christian Country" Has Become the World's Most Religiously Diverse Nation* (New York: HarperCollins Publishers, Inc., 2001), 12.

Works Consulted

Coles, Robert. *The Call of Service: A Witness to Idealism.* New York: Houghton Mifflin Company, 1993.

Eck, Diana. *A New Religious America: How a "Christian Country" Has Become the World's Most Religiously Diverse Nation.* New York: HarperCollins, 2001.

Smith, Huston. *The World's Religions: Our Great Wisdom Traditions.* 1958. Reprint. New York: HarperCollins, 1999.

Chapter 15

God's Autograph:
Taking the Soul Seriously
in the Classroom

Patricia M. Lyons

In February of 2002, a small news story floated below the fold in many newspapers across the country. The printing of the story was an emblem of our Internet age. The elements of the story were simple. Using the world's largest online auction website E-Bay, a young man at the University of Washington tried to auction off his soul. The self-described atheist advertised his commodity on the Web site by saying, "Please realize, I make no warranties as to the condition of the soul. As of now, it is in near mint condition, with only minor scratches." The bidding began at 5 cents, and apparently his former girlfriend bid $6.66 before a more serious buyer from Des Moines offered $400. At that point, site managers at E-Bay removed the listing. As a teacher, I saw the story as a blunt manifestation of a question central to adolescent self-understanding: Is my soul worth anything to anyone?

We should not be surprised that any member of this generation of young people would enter the worldwide marketplace of E-Bay to see if or what anyone would bid for his or her individuality. The evidence that our culture is making a commodity of human life is everywhere. Just look at university newspapers carrying solicitations to buy eggs and sperm from undergraduates, or "reality" television shows showcasing every kind of plastic surgery as the newest fad for teens to design and buy the body they want—often by means of monetary birthday or graduation gifts from parents. Despite the admitted hu-

morous intention of the young soul-seller, I saw this particular event
as a cry for help from a perhaps socially marginalized or disaffected
young person. However, when I read the story to my high school ethics classes, my students did not see it that way at first. The soul-
seller's attempted sale played well with his peers with whom I spoke,
and he emerged in their view as a savvy opportunist in the Internet
marketplace. In fact, most described the failed sale as "creative," "en-
trepreneurial," or even "smart." It was as if he was selling a pair of his
shoes. But somewhere in their "so what" or "more power to him" tone
there was the whisper of mourning. I could hear it, though faintly. In
time, I saw that I was not the only one.

Despite the fact that the vast majority of students appeared tacitly
entertained or even reservedly impressed by the resourcefulness of
the soul seller, I did sense subtle gestures of unease among a small
number of silent students. It took a moment or two, but slowly a few
students in every class broke the mob's ice of disingenuous pleasure
from the story with words of shy but certain lament. "How sad" was
the most common response among those few who were haunted by
even the possibility of selling a soul. Asked why the sale struck them
as morose, most could only say things like "I don't know—it just
makes me sad." Others diagnosed the seller as "lonely," "depressed,"
or "socially isolated." In time, most students came to agree that there
was something haunting about the act of disowning one's soul, even in
jest. In fact, with Socratic patience, the concerned few were able to get
the initial majority to admit that their laughing and congratulating
was only from thinking the seller's intentions to be humorous. I was
amazed to watch that, without adult guidance, each class came to the
same conclusion: In their words, if "he *really* meant" to disown his
soul, then there would be little a person could do that was more re-
grettable or more tragic. Time and time again, I watched deep convictions about the soul come, however shyly and however diverse, into
full view and enjoy nearly universal recognition.

In an attempt to find out how young people define the soul itself, I asked my students why selling a soul was different from selling one's time, one's ideas, or one's art. The conversations confirmed what I have observed since first becoming a teacher: that there is among our youths both a vitality of the concept of the soul, as well as a myriad of understandings for what a soul might be.

Countless interactions I have with my students remind me that there is a soul in every human being and that teenagers know it. This is my only explanation as to why life is so painful for so many young people. Their pain is the proof that there is something in them—of which they are vaguely aware—that speaks at every moment a sense of sacredness and meaning. This voice calls the adolescent to know its reality and results in the young person never feeling quite at home in environments or relationships that deny the holiness of humanity. As a result, much of the materialistic meritocracies of our culture and certainly our first-world classrooms become a source of pain for teenagers. Often we force them to choose between developing two sets of skills: the skills in listening to their interior experience and the skills for performing in our pedagogies of perfection. When we ignore or sideline the spiritual projects of their maturation, we lead adolescents in distant exile from the moral and spiritual compass of their own soul. We thereby wound their sense of direction and make our vocation as parents and teachers more difficult by disabling the spiritual organ of the soul—the very part of a person that responds to moral and spiritual inspiration in the first place. When we do not acknowledge the soul of the adolescent, we remove the spool of the music box. Veteran star of stage and screen Lily Thomlin offered priceless wisdom to those of us involved in secondary education when she once referred to the problem of running in a rat race, possibly winning, and still being a rat.

Every interaction I have with young people convinces me beyond any doubt that they are struggling to understand the experience they have with their own spiritual selves in an age where little or no consistent and constructive help is offered to them in this endeavor. The notion that there is something sacred at the core of every human being is obviously under attack in our world. The adolescents in our schools experience so many assaults on their sacredness in any given day that often they arrive in the classroom with minds and faces that are dizzy, disconnected and deflated in confidence, hope, and sense of purpose in life. To speak of the possibility of the soul is to carry the soul of a teenager out of a burning building. It is to whisper to teens that the cry of their own soul is not fiction or wishful thinking; but rather, that it is the truth about them and the source of dignity and direction in life. So much of adolescent behavior can be better understood when the adults involved consider seriously the reality and impact of the soul on a young person's emotional, social, and intellectual response to the world. We can either help these students hear the homing device of their soul, or we can distract that life-saving voice of peace and purpose by poor pedagogies caught up in the rat races of academic punishment and reward.

At some point teachers and adults need to come to terms with the fact that the rich learning environments we create for our children often do more harm to the maturing many than they do good for the fittest few. I see a disturbing pain in the faces of young people trapped in our performance-based communities of reward and punishment. In the meritocracy of schooling—where adults have created largely arbitrary and impersonal standards of success and failure—our students receive two clear and equally depressing messages. The first is that winning in the meritocracy of schools only unfolds an uninspiring and stressful future of maintaining greatness. The second is that losing at any point paints a future of masking one's mediocrity. When there is no overt presentation and defense of the spiritual dimension of every person nurtured in the classroom against the unchecked materialistic messages that life is a commodity, the worth and beauty of any one life is lost and the ultimate purpose for both the winner and the loser is unclear. No teacher can deny that despite the innate goodness of all the priceless opportunities we offer our students, these gifts can feed into a larger social reality of crushing pressure on our teens. How can our young people not withdraw emotionally and wilt spiritually when the media showcase material rewards for the winners that grow ever more absurd by the moment, while the shame of possessing unmarketable skills and gifts is ever paraded as the punch line of our culture's comedy. After the family, the classroom is the next society that a teenager meets and herein rests both the daunting challenge and the inestimable gift of teaching. By creating classrooms that acknowledge and profess in daily practice the spiritual character and permanent dignity of every person, we make the learning process a lever against the spiritual reductionism of our culture, rather than letting our pedagogy become its instrument.

To work in a high school is to share time with teens in the dark shadows of insecurity cast by the staggering stature of our cultural "Superpower." We are all afraid of failure. We are all trying to market our gifts and mask our liabilities. So I am always personally uplifted when I hear young people speak of the soul in the school setting. To converse about a part of the human person that is potentially transcendent, utterly unique and permanently beautiful is to perform a subversive act in a culture that tends to reduce the human being to consumer and competitor. Students come alive in the classroom when space is created to consider the human being as something spiritual and not merely material. When students are encouraged to offer their creative definitions of the soul, they find voices within themselves and among their peers of unique empowerment against the levers of stress in their lives from the media, educational and parental expectations, advertising, and the social forces of economic competition or social discrimination. Conversations about any topic in history, science, philosophy, language, medicine, or social development are transformed when the question is raised: What is a human person beyond his or her material existence? Not all students agree on the existence of some kind of spiritual dimension of the person, but to listen to young people talk with one another about the possibility of meaning beyond materiality is to hear them examine the possibility of begotten dignity and then play out its implications in their conception of self. Our first-world students are saturated with the philosophy and reality of mainstream materialism, whether they enjoy material stability or not. It is stunning to see them revived from this destructive flood of mixed messages when the classroom conversation includes both spiritual and material analysis of human life.

To speak of spirituality in schools is to raise eyebrows. I do not here mean to open schools up to a rigid religious endeavor. Rather than impose particular religious projects, I mean to state my deepest conviction that to teach is to perform a spiritual labor in the lives of young people. Moreover, to administrate in a school is to either support this spiritual journey of teachers as they awaken young people or to leave teachers unsupported as they try to create a community that honors the soul of its members. This spiritual climate of the school is why some children run into a school every day with a smile because they feel fantastic and why some kids would rather cut classes or never darken the doors of certain rooms because they feel uniquely worthless inside the school building.

When a learning community is shy or silent about spiritual ideas, it is most natural for adolescents to assume that the academy has done so intentionally and in defense of the intellectual growth of its members. Schools are like teenagers. They tend to talk about what matters to them. So to avoid talk of spiritual ideas is to communicate to young people that these ideas do not matter to us. As adults, we often defend this neglect with self-serving reasons for avoiding the socially contentious terms and ideas of the spiritual life. Too often in efforts to avoid verbal offenses, we participate in the denial of the reality and potential of human spirituality, and our young people do not miss the message. Many topics are difficult to talk about in schools; sex, economic disparity or race relations. However, students watch us go to blows if necessary to have these hard conversations anyway in our curriculum, school assemblies and parents' meetings because we know the damage of not having them. Therefore the argument for avoiding spiritual talk because of potential controversy is a hallow one. The strong schools and the courageous educators are not daunted by uproar surrounding difficult topics. Such courage is needed for creating space for spiritual language. Schools, public and private, will feel and will teach and will be soulless so long as spiritual ideas are not safe to live and to inspire the community. The soul of a community is similar to the soul of a person. It is a place generating peace, a source of security, a voice celebrating individuality and, if needed, a lever defending dignity. I have never been in a school, for either part of a day or for part of a career, in which I did not develop a sense of whether or not the place had a soul. Nor have I ever heard other educators cease from making similar diagnoses with soul language, whether they had a personal religion or not. Even among the most diverse groups of adults, I have seen universal recognition of the power of the simple words "the place has no soul."

Listen to people of all ages talk and one can hear the word "soul" make its way through daily conversation, obeying few rules on usage. It is a rebellious word that wanders like an alley cat through our culture's public squares. It is a puzzling word because it describes everything from food to music, perhaps causing listeners to assume that it is a homeless word in search of permanence and stability. However, listen more carefully to those who use it for anything, and one will sense that the speakers do not see this word as empty and vague. Rather, they are often reaching for a way to talk about the essence of a person, or a way to describe some kind of essential power of a thing that enables it to touch a person deeply, to bring satisfaction and to sustain joy.

Although this word *soul* enjoys widespread use in the language of many generations and genres, it is certainly not an orphan. Many traditional religious communities have long histories building to a passionate present defense of this word as the private property of their most central doctrines about humanity. It is a word foundational to monotheistic understanding of God, the person, and eternal life. Nevertheless we hear this word daily as the star of many a stanza of popular music or marketing campaigns for any number of products from blue jeans to diamonds. Just listen in coffee houses, shopping malls or schools. Soul is a word used by anyone, but owned by no one. Thank goodness. If there were even the faintest sense that a single generation or subculture could successfully set the rules for this term, young people would only touch it to challenge it. It would never have become what my work has witnessed it to be: a word that can express a young person's most uplifting and life-changing hopes for their life and all human life.

For a decade, I have been listening to the many ways in which young people express their thoughts. This listening has led me to the belief that a teenager's use of the word *soul* is perhaps the most essential expression to focus on in analyzing an adolescent's emotional and spiritual health. It is an important word not because of what we as adults think it means, but because of what teenagers say it means to them. Just ask a teenager or two about how they would define this word. Whether religious in any way or not at all, young people I have worked with have some notion of soul meaning. When they begin their descriptions, a window opens that helps us see their deepest assumptions and questions about life, hope, and purpose.

I have discovered three things that are true about young people and their use of the word soul. First, every student has some notion of the soul. I have simply never had a student answer back, "I have never heard of the soul before." It is hard for students—for anyone—to define the soul because there is no discernable image of it and no consensus about its essence. This ambiguity has not silenced students, but instead allowed for definitions that are as varied as the people who offer them. Second, universally positive definitions of the soul are offered regardless of race, gender, or socioeconomic background. Third, even among students who question its existence, I have heard no condemnation of the idea. Teens discuss it as a "place" or "space" in people where there might be peace, purpose, and rest; acceptance, communion with God or even eternal life; identity, uniqueness, and personality. Not once in a decade of teaching has any one of my students spoken in a derogatory way about the soul. While their descriptions of most other things—family, friends, music, politics, academics—seem a constant mix of those uniquely adolescent words of rebellion, personalization or lack of interest, "the soul" emerges as a thing of goodness, and even beauty and promise.

However, before any adult gets excited about this confidence in the inherent goodness of this thing called "the soul," I need to share another finding. Rarely, if ever, do students talk about the soul by using one of the most common words of their adolescent years: "mine." Formal and informal interviews with students over the last few years bring out endless statements about *"my* music," *"my* stuff," *"my* friends," *"my* ideas," or *"my* life." Rarely though, if ever, have I come across adolescents who define the soul using the words of possession. Instead, they speak of *"a* soul" or *"the* soul," as if the whole idea were a rumor that they cannot substantiate or are somehow afraid to claim as their own. The business of adolescence is to reject or to possess things and ideas in a relentless pursuit of identity creation. Even so, the word *soul* is left unclaimed as a tool in this personal process. It is spared the bipolar energies of rebellion and the personalization of other social, academic, or cultural ideas that surround our teens. To put it another way, while students see no threat in the idea of a soul to their total idea system, many see no real potency for working with it either. This skill set for knowing one's soul is what I believe we must teach students in our care.

Let's admit that this polite sidelining of "soul" is at the very least odd among teenagers who are ever quick to strike down as an act of self-determination and freedom many of the inherited ideas of adults. One would think that "soul" would be a prize target of criticism and rejection as a word that carries for grown-ups such religious overtones. Nevertheless, for young people in our day, the word is given immunity where so little traditional language is given the same permission to exist in youth culture. Adult ears should perk up and discern an interesting sign of spiritual significance whenever teenagers speak positively of an idea not of their generation without hint of rejection or suspicion.

So if young people do not reject or claim the soul, why should we care what they say about it at all? We should care because their words about the soul are incredibly hopeful and uplifting. Even so, the beauty and power of the ideas do not seem to create a confidence in teenagers that the soul is a truth in their lives. They have so much hope in the existence of something like a soul that animates and dignifies human life, yet they show little personal witness that they know the soul within themselves.

What matters is that young people locate such resources as peace, meaning, joy, and purpose in the soul. They ask the soul to hold all these assets. I am convinced that using this word in conversation creates a safe space for teenagers to dream out loud and to hope for the wholeness, and perhaps even the holiness of humanity. Because the word belongs to no one, there is no sense of trespassing on a certain traditional meaning. Young people hear the word in their favorite music and movies, and they feel inspired to express their own narratives of meaning and love with it. They feel free with the word because who can tell them that they are wrong? The word is free for use for those who are religious and not religious, those who are open to faith and those who feel burned by it, those who hate God and those who report that they speak to God every day.

For any age, to speak the word "soul" is to open a window to one's view of humanity. The word invites teenagers to express majestic truths about humanity's meaning and purpose; to carve out in conversation a sanctuary of safe expression for loving and defending life. My most self-deprecating students simply do not soul-deprecate. It is stunning and inspiring to hear. I want more adults to ask young people about the soul, because it invites teens to express their hope in beauty and human connection against a culture of materialism and lonely individualism. Asking teenagers to speak of the soul invites them to dream in a spiritual way. Their answers are an exhibit of deepest hopes for the global family; visions that the adults who love them the most have perhaps never seen or heard from their lips.

As a committed believer in the soul, I have searched for where and how teens express themselves in a way that older folks have traditionally called "religion." I have found that their most hopeful and faithful thoughts are not found in religious frameworks or even in the rejection of religious forms of expression such as for Generation X. Contrary to much commentary on current adolescents, I do not see young people expressing or finding confidence in meaning and purpose in drugs or sex—both of which get mixed reviews with young people, even among those who engage in both frequently. No, it is not even in money and power; both of which are feared as much as revered among young people. However, a safe haven that their imaginations construct as a reliable resource of sacredness and purpose seems to be this thing called "the soul." At times, words about the soul are the only uncritical and wholesome things I have heard them say about humanity.

So if creating a safe space to speak spiritually is how they use the word, the question still remains as to why young people use this word at all—without any real clarity for its meaning or reality. I believe it is because they are like every generation before them. They use the word soul because they cannot stop doing so. Humans pass on this word from age to age because it is the truth about the human person. I believe that every person, to differing degrees depending on their experience of the world, holds out some possibility for the existence of the soul because so many human interactions whisper to each person that some kind of soul exists.

The word *soul* is around us because its voice is in us. We cannot let go of it because it is holding us. Whether we feel deep pain or intense joy, there is something within every person that operates like a warning light for truth and meaning. Our frustration over racism, our anger when we are misunderstood, our fear of violence, our desire to be loved without condition or compromise, and our hope that suffering will give way to relief and even to meaning are all cries of the human soul. Centuries of evidence to the contrary of these hopes have proved unable to hush these spiritual dreams because they are the agenda of the soul and they are eternal. I am convinced that it is not genetic material that looks and longs for meaning and justice. It is the presence of the soul in every person that insists on the ultimate reality of these things despite evidence to the contrary. We feel the soul grieve within us when our experiences do not demonstrate the soul's real dreams of dignity and direction. Our pain is the proof that we are meant for more than lives of social striving and self-preservation.

The soul is like the black box of an airplane, at times buried beneath daily consciousness by life's tragedies, though still sending that faint signal to those who are listening and trying to get closer to the living sound. Our culture, and so often the culture of our schools, has so sadly separated young people from this inner voice; a voice implanted to lead them to peace and hope and faith. Miraculously, they still believe the soul is out there, somewhere. If we neglect them in this search and rescue mission for the God-given resources of the soul, we should not be surprised to see them searching for truth, meaning, and love in every shallow hole of our culture. Adolescents cannot help searching because they hear *something*. Adolescents cannot help following because they feel drawn to follow *something*. Those of us who know the meaning and beauty in that voice of the soul need to help teenagers discover it and experience the wholeness that comes with living in the logic of their being.

The good news is that the soul of any person is not actually lost; it is deep within every person where it was created to be. What is often lost is the adolescent's confidence that the resources they describe as being of the soul are actually within their reach. Mentors of teenagers do not have to create souls. Through intentional love and radical hospitality becoming a habit in the classroom, teenagers will see that there is something in them worthy of our loving and honoring. Teens will respond to the passion that adults demonstrate for their spiritual selves. They will seek to understand what it is that we see in them. A young person begins to develop the skills of spirituality when they become curious enough to check out the adult-planted affirming messages about their spiritual identity. The moment a young person looks in the mirror to see what the adult who loves and names their soul has pointed to—this is a moment of spiritual homecoming. This is the moment when the teenager begins to feel that his or her life might indeed be sacred and priceless, not for what it does, but because that is how it was created to be.

It stands to reason then that our response as teachers to this lack of spiritual skills among our youth must be to set out and find ways to lead young people to locate the soul within their own lives. The only thing they need from us initially is the idea that these resources are in fact a spiritual part of their being at every moment. We do not have to create a belief in these realities for the young person. Teenagers are innately spiritual, though their developmental stage leads them to focus much energy on the external. What we must do is listen to where they locate their spiritual experiences—in their music, art, social life and media interests—and then be a witness to the teenager that there is a direct spiritual experience of the soul awaiting in them. The meritocracies of our nation's classrooms are doing their work of creating pain and a sense of isolation and despair. The wounds are bleeding. The students and the teachers can feel the inner cries for spiritual skills that are more than those aimed merely at preparing for participation in the material world. The demand for the supply of spiritual language in a school is obvious.

The spiritual directing of adolescents might seem to adults to be a simple process of just looking at the young person and saying, "This soul that you describe is your own," as if that settled the matter. However, the bottom line for which adults must take responsibility is that we send students confusing messages every day that this beautiful and spiritual aspect of their being does not matter or does not exist. As a result of the daily assault on the notion of the soul that is inescapable in cultures of materialism, it should not surprise anyone that it will take equally constant and intentional conversations about spiritual realities to get teenagers to believe us. It is not impossible to get young people to embrace their spiritual lives and believe that their own visions of the soul are truths about them at every moment. But this notion must be loved into them. There is no other way.

There are loving ways that we can mentor, teach, and parent that awaken young people to the reality of the soul as their own source of dignity and freedom. We often want the quick fix—as if we could just click on the notion of soul and drag it with a mouse onto the self-perception of our teenager and leave it there. We must be constant and creative if our young people are to believe that this apparently distant but safe space holding their hopes is a reality in which they can trust and live because it is a reality that lives in them.

When young people come to call the soul "mine," it gives them a place to stand in a fractured world and feel a sense of belonging to God and belonging to one another. Having a soul is something that they share with every other person, challenging and healing their worst fears that they are alone in life. A firm embrace of the soul as a fact of their being becomes a rock stronger than the eroding cultural forces that undermine the essential self. A belief in one's soul nurtures an ontology of natural and unbreakable connection to others and to the creator of one's being. It is in the bonds of relationship that people of all ages experience a sense of peace. The soul is the seat of our relatedness.

Ultimately, awareness of the soul is an experience of belonging and love. To believe that one has been created by God and given a soul as a connection to God and to everyone else created by God is to have peace. Believing in the beauty and the belonging to God and others that the soul accomplishes does not save anyone from life's trials, but such faith does make a bridge through the struggle. This step in belief is so enormous for young people—for all people. Meaningful religion and particular faith convictions come after the foundational confidence that one's creation came through love and that the connection to both creator and creation is made permanent by the soul. Religion of any stripe without this confidence is hollow and hard to relate to daily experience. If the great identity search of adolescence does not include a notion that the soul grounds dignity and meaning in the person, then there is a question mark at the center of the teenager about their ultimate purpose and goodness. Any religious endeavor for this kind of student will become just one more painful and futile game to earn dignity through external accomplishments.

One way I engage my students to think about the soul is to ask, "Are you an onion made only of the layers of needs and labels, beneath which there is nothing but more layers? Or are you an artichoke, covered, yes, with many layers and labels of family and culture, but beneath those externals created with a soul designed by God to sit at the heart of your life?" To stand idly by and watch our teenagers move out of adolescence without a belief in a sacred soul in each one of their precious lives is to leave a hole at the center of their life, and to invite endless years of adulthood spent on seeking to fill the void.

An 18-year-old teenager of Liberian refugees, living a high school life of economic and social instability, gave me the most potent and inspiring definition of the soul of any student with whom I have worked. Known by both peers and adults as a young man of incredible strength and resilience and joy, I asked him to share with me his definition of the soul. His answer demonstrates the inseparable connection between healthy thinking about the soul and healthy living through adolescence. "It is God's autograph in me...the real thing...not a fake...and I have it to keep forever."

I want, and the world desperately needs, all teenagers to feel such confidence in the presence of God—the real presence, not a fake—at the core of their being. Where I have found this confidence in students and where I have tried to nurture its growth, I have found adolescent lives that can not only endure unspeakable hardships, but also sing with joy.

Michelangelo wrote in his diary that he looked at slabs of stone and saw majestic figures trapped within the rock, crying out to be freed by his hands. For this unparalleled artist, to begin any work was simply to commit himself not to create the beauty, but to free the beauty. I believe that the soul is the beauty within each adolescent, and I want to hear a stronger cry from young people that they feel the beauty within themselves. To abandon the cry is to leave grace imprisoned. When we endeavor to hear the words of young people as they try to express the experience of their soul, we free them to find the truths of their creation. Theirs is a language that is not easily understood. However, there is an opportunity for those who love young people to be sculptors who seek the spiritual liberation of adolescents. As teachers and parents, adolescent slabs of sacred stone surround us. Often the world sees and fears the fortified edges of teenagers. But for those of us who live and serve in the quarries of young people, the cry of the soul is everywhere and longing to be free.

Conclusion

Ann M. Thurber

This book is a gate through which we walk to explore the field of education and spirituality. While the past few years have witnessed significant research devoted to brain-based learning, multiple intelligence theories, multiculturalism, and spiritual awareness, we continue to search for the nexus that will best nourish the spiritual formation of young people from pre-school through twelfth grade. The point in time at which we pause to reflect on our search influences our view of the landscape. What conclusions can be harvested now about the field?

Education and spirituality are interconnected as matters of historical convergence and the human condition. The relationship is apparent in classroom conversations about current events. Interest in the arts, environmental and socioeconomic issues, culture wars, scientific advances, and technological complexities is accompanied by an awareness of power that can be both creative and destructive. References to the inner journey and the outer pilgrimage speak to our existential yearning for self-immanent and self-transcendent meaning.

Religious beliefs and controversies that have existed for millennia continue to shape the human condition. We perennially espouse the validity of our own truths over others, but emerging global concerns suggest that certain divisions no longer serve the human family. Whether due to divine presence or evolutionary process, we search for different ways of sharing common ground. How can we better befriend the fear that still constrains acknowledgment of the wisdom found in diverse religious traditions? Imaginative visions that transcend particular religious doctrines, structures, or traditions need to be discovered and integrated in the pre-collegiate curriculum.

Sources of innovative visions abound if we can be alert to their presence. They are embedded in intra-faith and inter-religious webs as well as in the work of myriad community groups and school classrooms. Children and young adults who show signs of spiritual giftedness have as much to teach us about authentic living as do our elders and ancestors. We have only to stop, look, and listen to the wisdom spoken from our own and others' hearts, minds, and souls to be inspired.

Religious and spiritual illiteracies are untenable in the twenty-first century. More than fifty years have passed since court rulings overturned Protestant hegemony. Sweeping cultural changes, many of which are related to religion, have significant consequences for young people living in an increasingly interconnected world. Caring for the livelihood of our multicultural society involves finding academically appropriate and constitutionally permissible ways to include religious studies and contemporary spirituality in independent and public schools. As asserted by several of our authors, the geography and history of religion are relevant to virtually every academic discipline. While religious literacy—that learning of the doctrine, ethos, and history of faith traditions—is assuming greater importance, a stronger case must continue to be made for an infused, interdisciplinary approach to the study of global religions and spiritual understanding in pre-school through twelfth grade. Failure to do so ignores the existence of students' spiritual viewpoints and of the significance of religion and spirituality in our world.

Spiritual literacy, based on what now seems to be a universal human capacity or intelligence that informs other capacities or learning styles, needs to be nourished by using language that develops hopefulness, honor, integrity, intuitive awareness, and symbolic imagination; fosters compassionate service; and aids the wise discernment of the sacred from the profane. This wisdom language is often found in the verbal and nonverbal narratives of the world's many faith traditions, material that marks the intersection of religion, spirituality, and education. Substantially more and better resources are becoming available to remedy the lack of basic knowledge about world religions, sacred texts, and practices.

Education must attend to formation of the whole person. Such attention includes spiritual formation. How it occurs is significant, for among the many contradictory images and options available in our culture are those that foster exile, isolation, and wrath, or abuse, addiction, and violence. Connecting young people to those who can live spiritually with the paradoxes of the human condition generates talk about life's legacies and truths so worthy of being shared and discussed.

Encouraging respectful acceptance of individual learning styles, academic proclivities and differing abilities, as well as of ethnicity, gender, spiritual persuasion, and religious background, enhances human dignity and contributes to healthy development of the whole child. Awakening curiosity and wonder facilitates analogical thinking, open-ended questioning, and receptive awareness of spirit. Mentoring students' capacities for concentration and contemplative listening gives them keys to success in virtually all endeavors. Modeling and valuing attributes such as kindness help to form spiritual character. Recognizing reverential behavior in caring for self, others, and the environment supports a positive habit of the soul. Honoring the ethical process for spiritual companionship in administration and teaching means that religion and spirituality may be harbored safely together in the classroom.

By the ages of two through five, many children are in day care, nursery, pre-school, entering kindergarten, or being home-schooled. These are threshold years for spiritual formation. In many societies, formation relies upon a "Community of Elders." Buddhism, Christianity, Hinduism, Islam, Judaism, and Afro-Caribbean and Native American Indian belief systems, for example, draw on clerical, monastic, rabbinical, and tribal leaders for spiritual guidance. Older generations today observe that children often appear radically disconnected from their families, communities, and faith traditions. Identifying elders or those people who embody spiritual discernment and wisdom is one way to create intergenerational connections, to allow opportunities for sacred listening, and to be true to our responsibility as adults. Diane Moore, Director of the Harvard Divinity School's Program in Religion and Secondary Education, advises a balancing of perspectives because meeting one person is "but one expression of a particular tradition."[1] Gathering together a group of elders enables young people to appreciate the benefits of learning about different traditions and to see that the whole tapestry is beautifully woven.

There is a growing body of research about the nature of childhood and adolescent spiritual formation that has implications for all schools. Recent studies in the newly emerging field of neuro-theology suggest connections between our brain hemispheres and faith development. We appear to grow spirits together with our cells, muscles, organs, and neuro-electrical synaptic transmitters through the sensory-motor, pre-conventional, pre-operational periods of childhood to conventional and post-conventional levels of adolescence, adulthood, and aging. We therefore need to take seriously spiritual growth as it occurs in our nation's classrooms so that students can link their own theological beliefs to personal journeys.

Pedagogical models and instructional methodologies related to current research studies are just beginning to emerge. Each of our authors contributes a unique perspective on the process of incorporating religion and spirituality in education. Every school offers courses and co-curricular activities that yield teachable moments to inspire ethical, existential, and spiritual awareness in students whose profiles span the academic spectrum. Given increasingly diverse student enrollments, establishing a hospitable, communal context for relational learning is crucial to affective and effective spiritual formation at all grade levels.

Discussions that focus on finding God within various religious traditions and sustaining the relationship through spiritual practices are very important. Students must be able to grapple with ethical, moral, and spiritual issues to make informed, empathetic decisions. Such grappling requires patience so that faculty and students can listen and respond to each other's thoughts about specific allegiances, absolute or relative truth, agnosticism, atheism, creationism, earth-centered and cyber-spaced spiritualities, feminine images of the Divine, fundamentalism, neo-paganism, oppression, pseudo-religions, religious doubt, celebrations and rituals, spiritual intelligence, sacred envy, sufficiency, and yearning, and whether spirituality is lived through religious traditions or outside of them.

Abstract religious and spiritual concepts such as charity, compassion, unconditional loving-kindness or mercy connect with concrete needs through service-learning projects. Such projects are often structured around the themes of caring for animals, people, place, and peace. Depending upon the grade level, projects occur on campus or offer students the opportunity to serve on local, regional, national, and international levels, thus exemplifying the Golden Rule:

> Desire not for anyone the things that ye would not desire for yourselves.
> *Tablets of Baha'u'llah, Baha'I*
> Hurt not others in ways that you yourself would find hurtful.
> *Udana-Varga, 5:18, Buddhism*
> In everything do to others as you would have them do to you; for this is the law and the prophets.
> *Gospel According to Matthew 7:12, Christianity*
> Do not unto others what you would not have them do unto you.
> *Analects 15:23, Confucianism*
> Never do to others what would pain thyself.
> *Panchatantra III.104, Hinduism*
> Do unto all as you would they should do unto you.
> *Mishkat-el-Masabih, Islam*
> In happiness and suffering, in joy and grief, we should regard all creatures as we regard our own self.
> *Lord Mahavira, 24th Tirthankara, Jainism*
> What is hateful to you, do not to your fellow... That is the law; all the rest is commentary.

> *Talmud, Shabbat 31a, Judaism*

Respect for all life is the foundation.
> *Native American Indian Great Law of Peace*

Treat others as thou wouldst be treated thyself.
> *Sikhism*

Regard your neighbor's gain as your own gain and your neighbor's loss as your own loss.
> *Taoism*

We covenant to affirm and promote the inherent worth and dignity of every person.
> *First Unitarian Universalist Principle*

That nature alone is good which refrains from doing unto another whatsoever is not good for itself.
> *Zoroastrianism*[2]

Speaking openly about our human right to freedom of belief, conscience and faith, companioned by our responsibility to protect that right and to serve the needs of others, brings all truths to the table and assists young people in the making of meaning. Students learn how to internalize their experiences as well as how to articulate their perceptions in readily appreciable ways. When allowed to do so, they affirm their pre-existing spirituality as well as nurture the spirit with which they will confront future realities.

The field of spirituality as it relates to education is fluid and multifaceted. Given the range of articles, books, chat-rooms, seminars and symposia, which are now appearing both nationally and internationally, educators seem more willing to include religious and spiritual frameworks to explore deeply essential questions about the concept and nature of truth. Such exploration requires a climate of trust and an intentional, institutional acknowledgment of the spiritual enterprise.

Acknowledgment calls for broad, deep articulation of curricular goals and objectives about religious studies and spiritual awareness on and across grade levels. Pedagogies and methodologies are rightfully discussed within departmental circles, yet the questions "Where are our students in terms of their spirituality?" and "Where ought they to be when they leave us?" involve dimensions of institutional mission that can be only fully answered by the whole school or school system. The challenge is to find comfort zones and time enough to converse about, and to reflect upon, the connections between spirituality and learning that transcend cultural, ethnic, and religious affiliations. Recognizing the visible diversity in our world can stimulate awareness of the invisible diversity within our selves, aiding in our becoming more fully creative, complex, and multifaceted human beings. Consultations and retreats are strongly encouraged for renewal of the vocational call to nurture character and full personhood in all school settings.

"What We Are to Be, We Are Now Becoming" is the motto of New Canaan High School, New Canaan, Connecticut, my own *alma mater*. Assessing students' growth in the spiritual attributes of being hopeful, peaceful, creative, trusting, open to mystery, compassionate, loving, willing to serve, self-immanent, or self-transcendent is a subjective process. Spiritual seeds present at birth or planted in early childhood grow at different rates. They may sprout, leaf, or flower during the pre-collegiate or collegiate years, within the family or work environments, or later in life. Perhaps what can be best ascertained now is the degree to which students are educated to have an informed understanding of religion and spirituality and can use related constructs to probe and to ponder questions of ultimate meaning. It is our students' intelligent use of innate spiritual capacities today that will lead them through life's gates in ways that offer promise of personal and social transformation for tomorrow's world.

Notes

[1] Diane Moore as cited in Tom Levinson, "Holy, Holey," *Independent School* (Washington, D.C.: National Association of Independent Schools, Spring 2004), 83.
[2] These expressions of The Golden Rule are often used in the public domain and are available online from sites such as www.templeofunderstanding.org.

Contributors

Sister Ramona Bascom, O.P., member of the Dominican Sisters of Mission San Jose, California, Congregation, holds an M.A. in English from Holy Names College and an M.Ed. in Counseling and Guidance from Loyola University, Los Angeles. With more than four decades of combined administrative and teaching experience, Sr. Ramona has authored numerous articles at Congregational and school levels.

Peter W. Cobb, editor, is President of Cobb & Associates, an Atlanta-based international consultancy. With an extensive background in independent education, he is a highly regarded facilitator on topics pertaining to the moral leadership and spiritual climate of schools. Former Executive Director and Trustee of the Council for Spiritual and Ethical Education, Cobb holds an M.A. in International Relations from American University and an M.Div. from Union Theological Seminary. He authored Teaching in an Age of Religious Pluralism, Skepticism, Resurgence, and Ambivalence, 2002 Winter Issue, *Independent School*, which won a Gold Award for Outstanding Feature Story, Society of National Association Publishers.

Matthew Hicks, Associate Director, Council for Spiritual and Ethical Education, holds a master's degree in Theological Studies from Emory University and an M.A. in Religious Studies from the University of Georgia. Author of a state-approved curriculum entitled *An Introduction to the Hebrew Scriptures: A Curriculum for Secondary Schools*, Hicks has taught in secondary and postsecondary settings.

Amanda Millay Hughes, M.F.A., Goddard College, is Director of Special Projects at the Ackland Art Museum, Chapel Hill, North Carolina. She is a nationally recognized speaker on issues of faith formation, spirituality, and sacred art. Hughes is author of *Lost and Found: Adolescence, Parenting, and Formation of Faith*, principal author of *Journey to Adulthood, The Five Faiths Curricular Resource*, and *Five Voices Five Faiths: An Interfaith Primer*.

Rachael Kessler is the Executive Director of The PassageWays Institute, Boulder, Colorado. She holds an M.A. in American Studies from Yale University. Kessler is the author of *The Soul of Education: Helping Students Find Connection, Compassion, and Character at School*, co-author *of Promoting Social and Emotional Learning: Guidelines for Educators,* and contributing author to *Schools with Spirit: Nurturing the Inner Lives of Children and Teachers; Nurturing Our Wholeness: Perspectives on Spirituality in Education; Stories of the Courage to Teach: Honoring the Teacher's Heart;* and *Teaching, Loving and Learning.*

Patricia M. Lyons received an M.Div. from Harvard Divinity School and is currently teaching Religion and Ethics at St. Stephen's and St. Agnes' School, Alexandria, Virginia. She has written numerous articles on adolescent faith development and consults for independent and parochial schools on developing spiritual and ethical education initiatives. Lyons is the founder and editor of *Chapel Talk*, an ecumenical journal for mentors of adolescents.

Manish K. Mishra is a seminarian at Harvard Divinity School, preparing for ordination as a Unitarian Universalist minister in 2005. He holds a B.Sc. in Foreign Service from Georgetown University, graduating Phi Beta Kappa, magna cum laude, Omicron Delta Epsilon, and is the recipient of the Hudson Medal in Arab/Islamic Studies. Mishra served as a diplomat during the Clinton Administration, receiving the U.S. Department of State's Superior and Meritorious Honor Awards for his role as a member of the U.S. Delegation to the U.N. Human Rights Commission in Geneva. He has taught World Religions and Ethics at Milton Academy and Introduction to Religious Studies and Ethics at Northfield Mount Herman School.

Timothy L. Morehouse, recently ordained an Episcopal priest, holds an M.Div. from Princeton Theological Seminary, an M.A. in the Study of Religion from Harvard University, and an M.A. in Sacred

Theology from The General Theological Seminary. Morehouse currently serves as Chaplain at Trinity School, New York, and serves as Priest Associate at The Church of the Holy Apostles, New York. His research interests include religion and the environment, religious poetry, the literature of pilgrimage, and the history of Asian religions in the United States.

Warren A. Nord received his Ph.D. in Philosophy from the University of North Carolina at Chapel Hill, where he served as Director of the University's Program in the Humanities and Human Values from 1979 to 2004. He continues to teach Philosophy of Religion and Philosophy of Education at UNC–Chapel Hill. Nord is author of thirty articles and book chapters, and two books: *Religion and American Education: Rethinking a National Dilemma* (1995), and, with Charles C. Haynes, *Taking Religion Seriously Across the Curriculum* (1998).

Eboo Patel, Rhodes Scholar, completed the Ph.D. in the Sociology of Religion at Oxford University. Founder and Executive Director of Interfaith Youth Core, Patel was named one of "thirty social visionaries" by *Utne Magazine* in 2002, and awarded the honor of Fellow, 2004–2007, by Ashoka: Innovators for the Public in 2004. He serves on the Boards of the International Interfaith Centre, the North American Interfaith Network, the Interfaith Initiative of the Points of Light Foundation, and the Global Action Network, and is currently President of the Board of *CrossCurrents Magazine*. Patel's essays have appeared in *God Within, Global Uprising, Initiative, Interreligious Insight*, and *Spiritual Perspectives on America's Role as a SuperPower*.

Catherine Powell, M.Div., Union Theological Seminary, is Chaplain for grades 4–8, National Cathedral School, Washington, D.C. She has served in parishes and on the Education Committees in the Dioceses of Washington, North Carolina, and Massachusetts. Author of *Let the Children Come*, a pre-school curriculum currently distributed by Living the Good News, Rev. Powell continues her ministry with pre-school children at St. David's Episcopal Church, Washington, D.C.

Mark Rigg received his M.A. in religion from Yale Divinity School. He began his career as a lay chaplain and an instructor of English and Theology at The Hotchkiss School. Rigg is now Chair of the English Department, Director of Community Service, and a member of the Theology Department, The Hill School, Pottstown, Pennsylvania.

John J. Roberts holds the Ph.D. in English from Tulane University and has taught in four universities as well as in grades 6–12 at The Westminster Schools in Atlanta, Georgia. The author of two textbooks and some thirty professional articles and reviews, Roberts has served as a consultant with the National Endowment for the Humanities, the College Board, Educational Testing Service, Council for Spiritual and Ethical Education, and several publishing houses.

Arthur J. Schwartz, Ed.D. in Moral Education, Harvard University, is Vice President for Programs and Research in the Human Sciences at the John Templeton Foundation. He received special recognition by President George Bush in 1990 for his accomplishments as director of dropout prevention programs for the School District of Philadelphia. Schwartz has authored articles in publications such as the *Harvard Educational Review, Journal of Moral Education,* and *Educational Record.*

Ann M. Thurber, Associate, Cobb & Associates, earned an A.B. *cum laude* from Mount Holyoke College with a major in English Composition and a minor in Philosophy of Religion. She completed the General Theological Seminary *Amicitia* Program through the Center for Spirituality–West. Thurber has held numerous administrative and faculty positions since 1970, serving all grade levels from nursery through graduate school in both the independent and public sectors.

Jonathan Vinson, who holds an M.A. degree in Biblical Studies from the University of Georgia, has taught university courses in Western religious traditions. He now teaches released time religion courses to public school students at Centerpoint, a local nonprofit organization in Hall County, Georgia, dedicated to the education, counseling, and mentoring of today's youth.

Meera S. Viswanathan completed her Ph.D. at Stanford University. Her areas of specialization include medieval literature, both Japanese and English; Japanese poetics and aesthetics; women's studies; and travel literature. She is presently an Associate Professor of Comparative Literature and East Asian Studies at Brown University, residing and teaching as well at Deerfield Academy, Deerfield, Massachusetts. Viswanathan is KCJS Visiting Professor, the Stanford Japan Center in Kyoto, from 2003 to 2005.

Index

Peter L. Laurence &
Victor H. Kazanjian, Jr.
General Editors

Studies in Education and Spirituality presents the reader with the most recent thinking about the role of religion and spirituality in higher education.
It includes a wide variety of perspectives, including students, faculty, administrators, religious life and student life professionals, and representatives of related educational and religious institutions. These are people who
have thought deeply about the topic and share their insights and experiences through this series. These works address the questions: What is the
impact of religious diversity on higher education? What is the potential of
religious pluralism as a strategy to address the dramatic growth of religious
diversity in American colleges and universities? To what extent do institutions of higher learning desire to prepare their students for life and work in
a religiously pluralistic world? What is the role of spirituality at colleges
and   universities,
particularly in relationship to teaching and learning pedagogy, the
cultivation of values, moral and ethical development, and the fostering of
global learning communities and responsible global citizens?

For additional information about this series or for the submission of manu-
scripts, please contact:

> Peter L. Laurence
> 5 Trading Post Lane
> Putnam Valley, NY 10579

To order other books in this series, please contact our Customer Service
Department:

> (800) 770-LANG (within the U.S.)
> (212) 647-7706 (outside the U.S.)
> (212) 647-7707 FAX

Or browse online by series:

> www.peterlangusa.com